MW00583570

Madness, Power and the Media

Madness, Power and the Media

Class, Gender and Race in Popular Representations of Mental Distress

Stephen Harper

Senior Lecturer in Media Studies, University of Portsmouth, UK

First published 2009 by
PALGRAVE MACMILLAN

Palgrave Macmillan in the UK is an imprint of Macmillan Publishers Limited,
registered in England, company number 785998, of Houndmills, Basingstoke,
Hampshire RG21 6XS.

Palgrave Macmillan in the US is a division of St Martin's Press LLC,
175 Fifth Avenue, New York, NY 10010.

Palgrave Macmillan is the global academic imprint of the above companies
and has companies and representatives throughout the world.

Palgrave® and Macmillan® are registered trademarks in the United States,
the United Kingdom, Europe and other countries.

ISBN-13: 978–0–230–21880–2 hardback

This book is printed on paper suitable for recycling and made from fully
managed and sustained forest sources. Logging, pulping and manufacturing
processes are expected to conform to the environmental regulations of the
country of origin.

A catalogue record for this book is available from the British Library.

A catalog record for this book is available from the Library of Congress.

10   9   8   7   6   5   4   3   2   1
18 17 16 15 14 13 12 11 10 09

Printed and bound in Great Britain by
CPI Antony Rowe, Chippenham and Eastbourne

Contents

Acknowledgements

So many individuals made the writing of this book easier and more bearable that it is impossible to mention them all here. I would particularly like to thank, however, the following academics who contributed advice and encouragement during the period in which this book was conceived and written: Emma Bell, Simon Cross, Ben Franks, Angie McClanahan and Sophia Wood; regrettably, none of them can be blamed in any way for the book's deficiencies. Several other friends and students pointed me towards media texts that eventually made it into the book; I thank them all.

Finally, I am grateful to the students at the University of Glasgow and the University of Portsmouth for their ideas and inspiration over several years.

This book is dedicated to my mother, Sandra, and to the memory of my father, Tony.

1
Framing Madness: Historical and Cultural Debates

This book is about the representation of mental distress in the media today. Any critical analysis of public images of madness must first engage, however, with some controversial and long-standing epistemological, terminological and methodological questions. What is madness or 'mental illness'? Is it a biological fact or a cultural construction? How, historically, has madness been regarded by its sufferers and its observers? What terminology ought to be used in critical discussions of madness? These are large questions and it is beyond the scope of this chapter to provide an exhaustive response of any one of them. In order to set the scene for my subsequent theoretical discussions and textual analyses, however, I shall briefly outline my perspective on the issues they raise.

The aim of this chapter is to address the questions raised above with a view to establishing some of the key propositions underpinning this book. They are as follows:

- that mental distress has always – and continues to be – constructed both 'negatively' and 'positively' in Western culture and that media critics ought to analyse the supposedly 'positive', as well as the overtly 'negative' constructions;
- that public and institutional discourses around psychological distress have proliferated in advanced capitalist societies, in response to shifting economic interests and subjective investments;
- that madness is best understood in relation to its social, political and economic contexts rather than the medical model of 'mental illness'.

While none of these propositions is wholly original, each is controversial. In arguing in support of them, I hope to create a conceptual framework that will inform my later analyses of media texts.

From stigmatisation to glorification: Changing Western perceptions of madness

If historians of madness – and most media critics – agree on one point, it is that madness has been systematically stigmatised in Western culture. The cultural suspicion of madness has its origin in the ancient association between mental distress and spiritual turpitude. Greek and Roman medicine developed rational explanations and cures for madness, ranging from physical remedies to music therapy, which persisted into the Middle Ages and beyond (Graham, 1967). From the beginning of the medieval period, however, the rationalist approach was supplemented – although never completely ousted – by irrational and superstitious explanations and cures for madness. The religious and didactic writers of the Middle Ages tended to regard illness, whether physical or 'mental' (although madness was seen in somatic terms), as a divine punishment for sin and as a dire warning to others to avoid temptation (Doob, 1974). The medieval chronicler Bede (1968: 108–9), for instance, relates how the seventh-century Anglo-Saxon king Eadbald was stricken with madness after an incestuous marriage. The Old Testament books of the Bible also frequently connect sin with madness. Zechariah, for instance, prophesises that those who attack Jerusalem will be punished with insanity: 'On that day, says the Lord, I will strike every horse with panic and its rider with madness' (Zechariah 12: 4). In Deuteronomy, which rests on ancient tradition, Moses warns his people that if they 'will not obey the voice of the Lord your God or be careful to do all his commandments and his statutes [...] the Lord will smite [them] with madness and blindness and confusion of mind' (Deuteronomy 28: 15, 28). Designating madness as a punishable abdication of God-given reason, the Christian Bible can be seen as the earliest 'media text' to stigmatise mental distress. The medieval religious perspective on madness was applied not only to individuals, but also to groups and was adopted by secular as well as church authorities. The Peasants' Revolt of 1381, for example, was described within official discourse as an outbreak of diabolical madness which threatened to overturn the supposedly natural and divinely ordained feudal hierarchy (Patterson, 1990).

Medieval attitudes towards madness have proved to be remarkably enduring. While post-Enlightenment, psychiatric practices towards mental distress – such as 'moral therapy' – were ostensibly less brutal than earlier ones, they nonetheless involved subjecting the mad to constant scrutiny and punishment, instilling in patients a sense of guilt which would eventually be internalised by them (Foucault, 2005a).

Today, religious ideologies powerfully shape constructions of mental distress, both explicitly – demonic possession remains a common 'schizophrenic' fantasy, for example – and implicitly, as manifested in the pervasive stigmatisation of madness as shameful.

Yet to focus on the stigmatisation of madness is to consider only one half of the history of madness. From the Middle Ages onwards, madness has been revered as much as feared. David Cooper (1978: 155), in his introduction to Foucault's *Madness and Civilisation*, goes so far as to claim that madness in medieval Europe 'was respected as a different way of being and knowing, perhaps a privileged way with a more direct access to heaven' and that it was only in the seventeenth and eighteenth centuries that madness began to be excluded. In itself, this seems a partial account of early conceptions and experiences of madness; after all, medieval and early modern experiences of madness were often as distressing as they are today and violent individuals were commonly confined in secure buildings long before the seventeenth century (Midelfort, 1980: 253). Yet it is true that medieval accounts of madness often conceive of madness as a blessed state, paving the way for the secular re-evaluation of madness as heroic and progressive.

The growing influence of medical education in European universities in the later Middle Ages contributed to a massive preoccupation with the theme of madness and may have enabled a certain separation of religious and secular perspectives on madness (Clarke, 1975). In Europe from the twelfth century onwards, fictional narratives containing spectacular tales about mad heroes proliferated. Alongside religious denunciations of madness as the manifestation of spiritual taint, Europe developed a tradition of poetry, prose fiction and autobiography dealing with the tribulations of disturbed characters, from the Celtic hero Suibhne to the ranting King Herod of the Mystery Plays (Doob, 1974). While many of these stories attest to the Christian abhorrence of madness, many also prefigure a new, humanistic understanding of madness as a condition that involves suffering and demands sympathy and even admiration rather than condemnation. The Arthurian romances plainly describe the wilful, intemperate heroes Lancelot and Tristan, for example, as mad; but these heroes are also rebels who contest and confound an oppressive social order (Merrill, 1987). It is perhaps not too fanciful to suggest that the immoderate behaviour of the Arthurian heroes foreshadows that of Hollywood's troubled musclemen, such as the Vietnam veterans Travis Bickle and John Rambo, who – like Arthur's best knights – serve as champions of the very society from which they are later outcast. At all events, from the later Middle

Ages onwards, madness and heroic, alienated individualism became inextricably intertwined.

In contrast with the raving King Herod, the mad knights of medieval romance are introspective, troubled subjects. Indeed, in the later Middle Ages, madness, which had previously been understood in somatic terms, was increasingly articulated in terms of 'inner', subjective, mental experience. Madness came to be used as a narrative device enabling the exploration of issues of personal identity. Indeed, the first auto-biographers in English language – the late medieval writers Thomas Hoccleve and Margery Kempe – wrote extensively and in Hoccleve's case highly self-consciously about their experiences of madness (Doob, 1974; Neaman, 1975). Kempe and Hoccleve recount their travails as, respectively, an aspiring saint and an impecunious civil servant; for both, mental distress is inextricably linked with anxiety about social status (Harper, 2003). Already in this early period, then, madness was linked with experiences of interiority and questions of social identity and presented in terms that could elicit sympathy rather than condemnation. No longer merely a sign of moral taint, madness now betokened personal, perhaps even existential crisis.

Madness also functions in medieval narratives as a vehicle through which spiritual truth might be revealed, or as a turning point in the life of an individual. In an increasingly individualistic culture, the mental 'breakdown' became a cardinal point in the moral transformation of the heroic subject. A central theme in the literary genre of the saint's life, madness became the mark of the exceptional human being, who through faith transcended her tribulations to emerge as a spiritually transformed being. Divested of its religious import, the transformational theme of these ancient narratives persists in contemporary media texts. As I shall suggest later, the conception of madness as heroic transcendence holds an enormous appeal in contemporary Western culture, in which ideologies of individualism and self-fashioning are regnant.

An increasingly compassionate conception of madness is discernible in Early Modern literature: the distracted Hamlet and the other-worldly Ophelia, for example, attract sympathy rather than condemnation and prefigure the gendered constructions of mental distress in contemporary film and media fictions. Later, of course, the exceptionality of the medieval and Renaissance madman became the 'genius' of the Byronic Romantic iconoclast, whose legacy, I shall argue later, is evident in contemporary cinematic constructions of madness.

The nineteenth century remains a key period in the reconfiguration of Western practices of exclusion and dissent. In the Victorian period, those deemed mad were increasingly incarcerated – the 'Great

Confinement' which Foucault (2005a) locates in the seventeenth century did not, according to Roy Porter (1990), begin until the introduction of the asylum system in Britain and America from the later
eighteenth century. While Western culture has always understood 'mad
behaviour', it has not always maintained a concept of 'mad people';
these were 'created', according to Foucault, through the practice of confinement. In late eighteenth-century Britain and America, the 'dividing
practices' (Foucault, 1983) of psychiatry started to 'produce' the mad
as subjects to be regulated and controlled; Yannick Ripa's (1990) classic
multi-disciplinary study of female incarceration in nineteenth-century
France shows how bourgeois psychiatry constituted a powerful means of
ideological and physical containment which was often wielded against
'unruly' women, in particular. As Foucault (2005a) argues, in confinement, madness, silenced by Reason, lost its erstwhile power to point to
the truth. For Foucault, the rise of scientific, 'humanitarian' and 'moral'
treatments of the insane pioneered by alienists such as Philippe Pinel
and Samuel Tuke were in fact no less controlling than previous, usually
physical treatments and therapies. Partly in response to increasing psychiatric coercion, cultural texts such as Emily Dickinson's poem 'Much
madness is divinest sense' (1890) attest to an ongoing cultural revaluation of madness. Echoes of Dickinson's contestatory perspective on
what had become known as 'the female malady' (Showalter, 1987a) can
be found, as I shall argue later, in contemporary narratives of female
madness. Indeed, since at least Charlotte Perkins Gilman's *The Yellow
Wallpaper* (1998 [1899]), madness has been reinterpreted by feminist
critics as symbolic of female subjugation (Ehrenreich and English, 1978).
As Elaine Showalter (1987a: 204–5) points out, the equation of madness
with oppression featured prominently in women-oriented or overtly
feminist cultural texts throughout the twentieth century:

> In surrealist texts, such as Andre Breton's *Nadja* (1928), in Yeats's
> Crazy Jane poems of the 1930s and in Jean Giraudoux's *The Mad-
> woman of the Chaillot* (1945), psychotic women become the artist's
> muse, and speak for a revolutionary potential repressed in the soci-
> ety at large. Films such as Ingmar Bergman's *Persona* and *Through a
> Glass Darkly*, Robert Altman's *Images*, Richard Benner's *Outrageous*,
> and John Cassavetes' *A Woman Under the Influence* also use the female
> schizophrenic as symbol.

The form, as well as the content, of much twentieth-century art can
also be understood through the metaphor of madness. Many of the key
formal characteristics of Modernist art – fragmentation, multiple views,

etc. – are also characteristic of supposedly mad thought and behaviour, as are as some of Modernism's thematic concerns, such as the challenge to authority (Sass, 1992). However, as Stallybrass and White (1986: 200) warn in relation to Foucault's celebration of Romantic images of madness, the transgressive and oppositional interpretation of madness is not necessarily the preserve of the Modernist avant garde; postmodern popular culture is equally capable of registering the critical and liberatory dimensions of mental distress.

For example, madness in the contemporary popular media frequently serves to illustrate the craziness of capitalist normality. Bret Easton Ellis's novel *American Psycho* and its cinematic adaptation, for example, and David Greenwalt and John McNamara's satirical television serial *Profit* (Fox, 1996), feature conscience-free anti-heroes who epitomise the values of corporate capitalism and who are nonetheless – or perhaps therefore – merciless killers. Such representations are problematic. On the one hand, they may, as Otto Wahl (1995) worries, risk misrepresenting all mentally distressed people as violent. On the other hand, the 'madness' that such dramatic portrayals announce is not only that of the individual characters, but also that of the capitalist system which they embody; this satirical use of madness parallels the finding of psychologists that some 'personality disorders' are more prevalent among managers than criminals (Board and Fritzon, 2005). In many media texts, meanwhile, madness appears as a perfectly understandable response to oppression or persecution. The paranoia of the mathematical genius Max Cohen in Darren Aronofsky's dark thriller *Pi* (1998), for instance, seems a natural enough response to the fear instilled in him by the stock market analysts and religious fundamentalists who pursue him to exploit his knowledge. Fundamental to all of these texts is a view of madness as a form of alienation, the existential and psychological corollary of unequal social relations.

We ought not to lose sight, then, of the satirical, disruptive and sometimes oppositional significance of madness in contemporary film and media texts. Indeed, this book is not primarily concerned with judging the 'accuracy' of media representations of mental distress according to their conformity or otherwise to psychiatric definitions of 'mental illness'. It also explores the politically subversive potential of narratives of madness, their capacity to articulate counter-hegemonic discourses and to illuminate and interrogate what Erich Fromm (1963) called 'the pathology of normalcy'. The book attempts not simply to applaud or condemn media and film images of madness as 'positive' or 'negative' from the inevitably narrow perspective of medical discourse, but also to understand how these images can underline or reinforce the unequal relations of class, race and gender which characterise contemporary capitalist societies.

An inherent danger of any such attempt, of course, is that of romanticising mental distress. The anti-psychiatry movement retrospectively attributed to R. D. Laing and others in the 1960s was certainly fruitful in re-evaluating and reframing debates about madness. Often this re-evaluation involved looking to other cultures in which 'mental illness' is valorised rather than marginalised (as in shamanism), or to other historical epochs in which the mad were supposedly treated more liberally. Yet the premises and conclusions of the anti-psychiatric paradigm have been justly criticised, especially since the 1980s. Most notably, perhaps, Peter Sedgwick (1982) sharply critiqued the practical futility of romanticising madness and demonising psychiatry. This trend is apparent in more recent, post-structuralist writing. Deleuze and Guattari's *Anti-Oedipus: Capitalism and Schizophrenia* (1983), for example, can be seen to valorise schizophrenia while downplaying the seriousness of psychological suffering. Even critics sympathetic to Deleuze and Guattari's project have taken issue with what seems to be their romanticisation of serious psychological disturbance (Glass, 1993).

Indeed, for several cultural critics, the pendulum has swung rather too far in the latter direction. In his broadside *Arrested Development: Popular Culture and the Erosion of Adulthood* (1998), for example, Andrew Calcutt laments the elevation of madness into a key cultural trope since the 1950s. The beats and dropouts of the 1950s and 1960s had an obvious appeal in the post-austerity period following the Second World War, argues Calcutt; but by embracing a sense of victimhood and vulnerability, Western culture has succumbed to an infantilising celebration of mental fragility, a development which undermines the capacity of human subjects to take control of their lives or to engage in political activity. Calcutt's is a provocative argument, not least because it contrasts so sharply with the arguments of the liberal anti-stigma critics: while academics and pressure groups often condemn popular culture for *vilifying* madness, Calcutt attacks popular culture for *glorifying* it.

Calcutt's arguments are supported by the invectives of his ideological stablemate Frank Furedi (2004) against 'therapy culture'. Furedi deplores the depoliticising fatalism of the belief that we are all 'at risk' of mental ill-health. In the same vein, Michael Fitzpatrick (2006a) notes with dismay that many types of illness now attract social approval in popular culture, creating a society of 'victims', 'survivors' and 'sufferers'. Following Calcutt and Furedi, Fitzpatrick (2006b) concludes elsewhere that the rise of therapy culture serves to erode confidence in the effectiveness of human agents to change the social world. The subdivision of humanity into a variety of suffering groups might be seen to dovetail neatly with the postmodern emphasis on difference, which fractures working-class coherency into a variety of 'special interest' groups, reducing its capacity for collective action. Although the cultural drift towards identity politics is sometimes critiqued from a politically liberal perspective (e.g. Gitlin, 1995), the critique is also common among radical critics such as Wendy Brown (1995, 2006) and it is one to which I am also sympathetic.

The critique of 'schizophilia' constitutes a salient objection, then, to naïvely celebratory evaluations of mental distress. Nonetheless, as well as attracting some dubious bedfellows – such as the splenetic conservative pundits Norman Podhoretz and Paul Johnston – Calcutt's attack on a popular culture that supposedly 'celebrates' madness probably bends the stick too far in the opposite direction. For one thing, Calcutt's diatribe against the fetishisation of madness overlooks the ways in which diagnoses of mental illness have been (and continue to be) used as the pretext for a variety of social oppressions in the past century. In twentieth century, the diagnosis of 'mental illness' served not only as an excuse for eugenicist programmes from the US and UK to Nazi Germany (Wahl, 1995: 96; Read and Masson, 2004), but also as a pretext for the incarceration and torture of political dissidents, as in the brutal repression of anarchists, communists and social democrats following the Spanish Civil War and of dissidents in the Soviet Union. Of course, in contemporary Western liberal polities, allegations of political and social 'deviance' are seldom used to justify detention on psychiatric grounds (e.g. McCallum, 1997: 56). But lest it be imagined that ideological manipulation of psychiatry for oppressive ends belongs to bygone ages or exotic locations, we need only recall that homosexuality was removed from the Diagnostic and Statistical Manual (DSM)'s list of mental disorders only in 1974, while other groups, such as transgendered people, are still listed in the manual. Soviet-style incarceration, meanwhile, along with drug treatment and other forms of torture, are still being used to silence political dissidents in psychiatric institutions across the globe, from Uzbekistan (Parfitt, 2005) to China (Harding, 2005) and the practice has reappeared in the Russian Federation under President Vladimir Putin (Politkovskaya, 2004; Gee, 2007). While Calcutt and Furedi complain that madness has become a lifestyle choice for feckless nihilists in Western cultures, we should remember that in many parts of the world, being labelled 'mad' can be tantamount to receiving a death sentence.

Secondly, while madness does indeed function as a trope of liberation, redemption or salvation within contemporary Western culture, madness is also (often simultaneously) presented in ways that may be damaging to those suffering mental distress and those who care for them, as I shall argue later. Even when contemporary cultural representations of madness are 'positive', they are never simply or uniformly 'glorifying'; on the contrary, they also reinforce discriminations of social class, race and gender. As I argue later in this book, whatever lustre does attach to madness is mainly reserved for white middle-class males, while women and visible minorities are often presented as tragic victims of mental distress or are simply ignored. As a result, Calcutt's critique of a madness-loving culture seems over-generalised.

Public understanding of madness in Western culture, then, is variable and context-dependent. The othering of unreason has historically resulted in its being treated in two quite divergent ways: either persecuted or lionised. To make sense of contemporary media representations of madness, then, we must understand that madness has always been a complex and ambiguous formation towards which many contradictory responses are possible, ranging from stigmatisation and horror to admiration and awe.

Personal malady or social sickness? The medical model and the social model

Many critics of media and film representations of madness profess allegiance to the medical model of madness (Wahl, 1995; Philo, 1996). In the introduction to her book on madness in film, Jacqueline Noll Zimmerman (2003: xvi), for example, flatly asserts that 'mental illness is, first, exactly that – illness'. From the beginning of the twentieth century, however, psychiatrists have struggled unsuccessfully and sometimes desperately to prove the somatic origins of mental distress. Andrew Scull's book *Madhouse* (2007) shows that the early twentieth-century American psychiatrist Henry Cotton was acting entirely within the scientific mainstream when he advocated major surgeries – including the removal of stomachs, spleens and colons – to treat mental disturbance in the belief that mental distress was caused by chronic infections.

In some ways, the biomedical science of mental disorder has advanced little in the century since Cotton. While biological phenomena inevitably accompany 'mental illness', most theories of biological causation remain unproven and quickly fall out of fashion, as in the case of 'chemical imbalance', a psychiatric cliché that is no longer in clinical use, although it still enjoys wide currency in pharmaceutical advertising (Moore, 2007: 23). It is certainly possible that certain psychiatric conditions may have physical origins; depression, for example, may be associated with magnesium deficiency (Rasmussen, Mortensen and Jensen, 1989; Kirov et al., 1994); yet in such a case the psychiatric symptom can hardly be regarded as an illness.

Most psychiatric diagnoses, meanwhile, are not scientifically defensible. Patients identified as 'schizophrenic', for example, share neither common symptoms nor prognoses (Read, 2004) and the scientific validity of 'schizophrenia' has been comprehensively demolished (Boyle, 2002). As the clinical psychologist Elie Godsi (2004: 47) writes of psychiatric diagnoses:

> Countless attempts to define particular illnesses through obsessively detailed descriptions have failed to achieve anything like acceptable levels of consistency. In any other branch of science this level of unreliability would have led by now to the abandonment of the original concept and a search for another.

It is hardly surprising, then, that criminologist Herschel Prins (2005: 340) sounds hopeful rather than convinced when he writes that 'there are certainly likely to be neuro-biochemical factors which may determine the onset and course of [schizophrenia] in the first instance.' The validity of the medical model seems to be rooted in discourses of power rather than empirical reality.

Since the end of the period of post-war reconstruction and social reformism in the 1970s, the medical model of madness has enjoyed a resurgence, switching the focus of research from social to biological contexts. As a result, the parameters for the public discussion of the causes of mental distress have narrowed. As Bradley Lewis (2006: 47) writes in his discussion of contemporary ideas about depression, 'this is an era that seems naïve and unsophisticated about the multiple dimensions of depression. The vast majority of clinical discourse embraces a biological model that describes depression as a medical disease involving neurological pathology.' Lewis goes on to argue that the biological model of madness needs to be supplemented by other perspectives and refers approvingly to Chekhov's play *Ivanov*, in which various characters offer conflicting interpretations of the young hero's existential malaise. Within the play's pluralistic perspective on madness, the medical model becomes just one account among many.

It seems wise to follow Lewis in stepping back from the medical model. After all, mental distress is diagnosed on the basis of behaviour that violates social norms or which is harmful to the sufferer or others, not on the basis of any physical lesion. Even the psychiatric community itself is deeply divided over the validity of many psychiatric diagnoses and high-profile legal cases involving insanity pleas reveal the lack of professional consensus around the identification of mental illness. In 2003, for example, Allan Menzies was tried at the High Court in Edinburgh for the brutal murder of his friend after watching a horror film (King, 2003: 1). Admitting that he had battered his best friend and drunk his blood, Menzies had claimed he was suffering from paranoid schizophrenia; a psychiatric consultant's report supported this defence. Menzies was eventually convicted, however, on the basis of testimony from three other experts, who rejected the insanity plea, telling the court that Menzies was merely a 'vivid fantasist' suffering from an anti-social personality disorder.

Given the lack of biological evidence for, and diagnostic consensus over, mental illness, it is unsurprising that many psychiatrists have abandoned biological explanations and treatments for distress. An army of dissenters including Breggin (1994), Levine (2003), Healy (2004), Leventhal and Martell (2005), Double (2006) and Warmé (2006) have criticised the psychiatric definition of various forms of mental distress as illness and the drift from psychotherapeutic to pharmacological therapies. Their scepticism about the value of psychiatric medication is well founded: some research shows that antidepressant drugs in general are significantly effective only in the treatment of severe depression and in conjunction with psychotherapy (Elkin et al., 1989; Gardner, 2003). Moncrieff and Kirsh's (2005) meta-analysis review of the efficacy of Selective Serotonin Reuptake Inhibitors (SSRIs), meanwhile, suggests that SSRIs do not offer clinically meaningful advantages over placebo in the treatment of mild or severe depression and expresses concerns over the side effects of the drugs. In place of drug therapy, critics of biopsychiatry advocate behavioural or talking therapies to treat symptoms, a preference also expressed by many users' groups (Rogers and Pilgrim, 2001: 180). Many of these critics are also generally critical of psychiatry's narrow focus on individual sufferers and propose reframing the understanding of personal experiences of distress within social and political contexts (Rogers and Pilgrim, 2003; Godsi, 2004; Smail, 2005).

Indeed, the arguments presented in the book presuppose the legitimacy of the 'social model' of distress, according to which psychological disorders are conditioned by social pressures. At the micro level, the term 'social' might designate the individual's relationship with her family. Relationship breakdowns and bereavement, for example, are common causes of mental distress. In cases of long-term distress, childhood experiences of neglect or abuse, whether physical, verbal or sexual, are also very important. Godsi (2004: 65) states of those who experience chronic mental distress that 'invariably their distress or violence essentially originates from tragic or traumatic childhood experiences'. As Rogers and Pilgrim (2001: 67) summarise, 'reviews of the literature on the immediate and long-term effects of sexual abuse on child victims come to the conclusion that there is strong evidence that they are significantly more prone to mental distress than non-abused children.' Such domestic experiences of powerlessness and victimisation are surely related to the dynamics of capitalist society, which increasingly pits individuals against each other in a battle for employment and resources (Godsi, 2004: 198–9).

Indeed, at a macro level, the overlap between mental distress and social inequality is not difficult to demonstrate. Studies have long shown links between serious mental distress and social isolation (Faris and Dunham, 1939), unemployment (Brenner, 1973; Clark and Oswald, 1994; Biddle et al., 2008) and poverty or low pay (Brown and Harris, 1978; Campbell, Cope and Teasdale, 1983; Theodossiou, 1998; Werner, Malaspina and Rabinowitz, 2007). A study conducted by the Greater Glasgow Health Board in 1999, meanwhile, showed very strong correlations between poor mental well-being, poverty and alcohol and drug abuse (McKeown, 1999: 14). Social class plays a key role here: Brown and Harris (1978), for example, found that working-class women were four times more likely to experience depression than middle-class women. Indeed, 'the finding that higher prevalence rates for a range of mental health problems are to be found amongst those in the lowest social classes is firmly established' (Rogers and Pilgrim, 2003: 18).

Of course, the nature and causative direction of this correlation is contentious: the debate between social causation theory and 'social drift' theory – according to which social deprivation is a consequence rather than a cause of diagnosis – has proved difficult to resolve (Pilgrim and Rogers, 1993: 13–16). But Christopher Hudson's (2005) large-scale, seven-year study of the correlation between mental distress and unemployment, poverty and housing unaffordability in the US strongly supports the theory of the social causation as opposed to drift theory, as well as showing large gaps in mental illness rates between people from rich and poor areas. At the very least, we can say that the research mentioned above, combined with the paucity of evidence for biological causation, warrants the assumption that 'a large proportion of behaviors that are currently regarded as mental illnesses are normal consequences of stressful social arrangements' (Horwitz, 2002: 37).

To the injuries of poverty and class we must add the psychological effects of the insecurity, both objective and subjective, that now pervade Western societies. In addition to job insecurity (Salamon, 2000: 150), Western workers must now contend with the erosion of the welfare state, a rise in low-paid, part-time work, increases in levels of personal debt, massive reductions in real-terms salaries, the removal of pension schemes and the deferment of retirement age. There have also been enormous increases in working hours in recent years for all categories of workers (Bunting, 2004). We should also consider the role of compulsory or 'voluntary' overtime necessitated by falling real-terms wages. Zygmunt Bauman (2000: 161), following Pierre Bourdieu, hints at the psychological impact of the new uncertainty, arguing that 'precariousness, instability, vulnerability is the most widespread (as well as the most painfully felt) feature of contemporary life conditions.' This precariousness 'is the combined experience of *insecurity* (of possession, entitlements and livelihood), of *uncertainty* (as to their continuation and future stability) and of *unsafety* (of one's body, one's self and their extensions: possessions, neighbourhood, community)'. Under such conditions, psycho-pharmaceuticals are widely used as coping strategies (Foti, 2004). While the new insecurity is felt most keenly by low-income, working-class individuals, it is not restricted to them. Even many relatively affluent professional workers in the West are subject to increasing working pressures that threaten psychological well-being (Godsi, 2004: 191–2; Elliot and Lemert, 2005). As these pressures intensify, it is not surprising that rates of mental distress seem to be particularly high in those states following the aggressively neoliberal, Anglo-Saxon model of capitalism as opposed to the arguably more stable social-democratic European states (James, 2008).

Liberal capitalist writers such as John Schumaker (2001), Tim Kasser (2003), John de Graaf, Naylor and Wann (2005) and the British government adviser and academic Professor Richard Layard (2005) argue that mental distress is rising in Western societies despite – or even in consequence of – supposedly increasing levels of affluence, a process de Graaf et al. call 'affluenza'. The solution they offer is individualistic: people must guard against mental distress, they argue, by curtailing their consumption and being satisfied with what they already have. Another affluenza theorist, Oliver James (1995, 1998, 2007, 2008), does much better, recognising the socio-political determinants of personal distress.

The solutions James suggests are broader but nonetheless problematic; to achieve psychic well-being, individuals, James argues, must be less acquisitive and governments must allocate more money to social provision – a perspective recalling the welfarist arguments of Galbraith's post-war classic *The Affluent Society* (1958). For James, mental distress is generated by the oppressive social relations of neoliberal, laissez-faire or what James (2008) calls 'selfish' capitalism; yet this overlooks the drive of a crisis-ridden capitalism *as a whole* towards intensifying exploitation. Social insecurity is growing even in the 'social democratic' nations of Europe, such as France, where the worst excesses of capitalist exploitation have hitherto been mitigated by relatively high levels of working-class militancy.

Mental distress is not solely a matter of poverty and insecurity, however; it is also arguably the result of workers' alienation from the products of their labour within the production process (Marx, 1978). Following Marx's early writings (whose arguments Marx later developed, but never abandoned), alienation inheres not just in the worker's separation from her products through her reduction to an economic unit, but in her estrangement from others through the divisive practices of capitalist competition and control. Although differing markedly in their proposed solutions, both Marx and Durkheim's classic theoretical explanations of alienation and anomie described and condemned the psychological effects of capitalism. Marx (1999) discusses the links between suicide and the alienating social relations of capitalism and the family in an early and little-known work on suicide, while Durkheim's *Suicide* (1897) focused on an expression of severe self-alienation, 'anomic suicide'. The theme of alienation from both self and others is taken up in Erich Fromm's book *The Sane Society* (1963), which argues that capitalist competition results in an 'insane' society that not only fails to meet humanity's material requirements, but also thwarts its need for a sense of belonging and interconnectedness.

Under capitalism – and particularly, it might be suggested, in the neoliberal moment – the notion that there exists a collective responsibility for the psychological well-being of individuals is unpopular, both in the media and among many psychiatrists. When media texts *do* discuss social determinants of mental distress, they often do so in support of conservative ideologies. The political manipulation of mental distress is particularly evident in the news media. In recent years, for example, the UK's Conservative Party-supporting newspaper the *Daily Mail* has reported that children from homes with two parents of opposite sexes are happier than others (ignoring the possibility that the 'unhappiness' of children of broken homes may result from social stigmatisation) and that the Labour government's 'obsession' with testing is damaging the mental health of schoolchildren. While such stories certainly gesture towards some possible social determinants of mental distress, they do so primarily in pursuit of factional agendas and do not address the psychological impact of capitalism as a whole.

Psychiatric discourse also tends to elide the social factors surrounding the onset of distress. As psychologist Paula J. Caplan (2001: 16) writes in relation to Post-Menstrual Dysphoric Disorder (PMDD):

> The problem with PMDD is not the women who report premenstrual mood problems but the diagnosis of PMDD itself. Excellent research shows that these women are significantly more likely than other women to be in upsetting life situations, such as being battered or being mistreated at work. To label them mentally disordered – to send the message that their problems are individual, psychological ones – hides the real, external sources of their trouble.

A key argument of this book is that mental distress is often framed by the contemporary media in reductively medical terms, obscuring both its social origins in class, gender or racial oppression and the possibility of preventing or mitigating it through radical social transformation. As Errol Francis (1993: 204) puts it, 'psychiatry is a class problem because it has always transposed social, economic and political reality as disease and illness.' Francis also notes that madness among black people is often deferred to a problem of 'culture' through the apparently enlightened argument of transcultural psychiatry that 'normal' black behaviours are 'easily mistakable' for mental distress. Yet this, as Francis notes, is simply a liberal version of the blame-the-victim strategy that overlooks the hugely problematic nature of psychiatric diagnoses as applied to *any* social group. It is the presupposition of this book that the origins of psychological affliction are usually to be found neither in brain chemistry nor in a set of 'cultural' dispositions, but in the spectrum of social violence, ranging from child abuse and other abuses of domestic power to the structural violence of unemployment and wage labour. Yet as the example of PMDD indicates, mental distress is caused not only by poverty and alienation, but also by the sexual and racial oppressions of capitalism. Dominant discourses about madness have always expressed sexist and racist elements (Gilman, 1985; Showalter, 1987a); I shall argue in this book that these largely persist in the contemporary media, despite the ostensible rise of anti-stigma discourse.

Darkness visible: Proliferating discourses of madness in late modernity

As I have already noted, madness has been a popular Western cultural trope as well as a medical concern since the twelfth century. Yet as the current outpouring of autobiographical books detailing personal experiences depression or therapy (Brampton, 2008; Martin, 2008; Merritt, 2008) suggests, ours is an era of intensifying preoccupation with mental distress and its treatment.

Longitudinal changes in the incidence of mental distress in Western cultures are difficult to determine for objective and subjective reasons. First, there is the vexed question of definition. Different forms of mental disturbance vary significantly from one another in severity and there is not always much agreement among professionals about what 'counts' as mental distress. There are insufficient epidemiological studies to draw firm conclusions about incidence, while sufferers are often reluctant to disclose their problems for fear of financial or social discrimination. However, mental distress can be argued to have risen dramatically in the Western countries in the past 100 years. In Britain, for example, there seems to have been a startling rise in depression, suicide and substance abuse in the post-war period (James, 1998). Violent 'crimes against the person' have also risen enormously in the same period (James, 1995; Godsi, 2004: 172–4). The Royal College of Psychiatrists and mental health charities such as Mind and the Mental Health Foundation state that one in four adults in Britain will suffer from a mental illness at some stage in their lives. Depression, in particular, is estimated by the World Health Organisation (2007) to affect 121 million people globally – the fourth most significant contributor to worldwide disease and predicted, by 2020, to be the second.

Whatever the incidence of mental distress, Western social institutions, in a process that has been ongoing since the nineteenth century, have become increasingly involved in the management of public mental health. The psychiatric profession, together with numerous mental health awareness organisations, has expanded enormously within the private and public sectors in Western countries in the past 30 years, creating a huge demand for counsellors, in particular. In Britain, for example, the Conservative government's 1990 decision to allow general practitioners to recoup 70% of the costs of hiring counsellors 'paved the way', according to Elliot and Atkinson (1998: 213), for the ' "emotional control" culture of the late 1990s'. Moreover, the preoccupation with mental distress and therapy is no longer solely the concern of the psychiatric profession, but has become hegemonic. A recent British health and social care White Paper (Department of Health, 2006), for example, noted that the second most important service people wanted from the British National Health Service, after free care for the elderly, was access to more counselling and therapy.

Several factors contribute to this state of affairs. First, the boundaries of psychiatric disorder are drawn with ever-increasing liberality. Thomas Szasz (1970: 3) noted 40 years ago that since the nineteenth century 'psychiatry (together with its sister disciplines, psychoanalysis and psychology) has laid claim to progressively larger areas of personal conduct and social relations.' In the early twentieth century, for example, psychiatry 'was fundamentally transformed from a discipline concerned primarily with insanity to one equally concerned with normality, as focused on normal persons and their problems as on the recognized insane' (Lunbeck, 1994: 3). Today, many psychiatric diagnoses are applied to those who would not be clinically diagnosed as 'mentally ill'. The distinction between psychiatric disorder and what is often labelled 'stress', for example, has become nebulous in both popular and medical discourse, as Angela Patmore (2006) laments, while emotions such as sadness and shyness have been pathologised as depression and 'social phobia' (Horwitz and Wakefield, 2007; Lane, 2007) and diagnoses of new 'disorders' such as Attention Deficit Hyperactivity Disorder (ADHD) have increased colossally in a very short time period (Timimi, 2003). Through the massive expansion of the DSM and the symbiotic growth of pharmaceutical industry, psychiatry labels a growing number of human problems and emotions as mental illnesses, encouraging the public to reify conditions such as low self-esteem as medical entities (Kramer, 1993; Hewitt, Fraser and Berger, 2000).

In popular psychology, meanwhile, numerous new, mild forms of mental distress are constantly being identified. Sometimes such diagnoses are offered in a somewhat ironic mode, as in the currently popular notion of 'affluenza'. However frivolous such neologisms may seem, the medicalising discourses of popular psychiatry and psychology are undoubtedly deeply embedded in Western culture. Burr and Butt (2000: 186), following Szasz and others, argue that the proliferation of named syndromes and pathologies leads to a 'pathologization of everyday life':

> More and more aspects of our lives are becoming problematic. We are now used to feeling and expressing doubt about our performance as parents, as lovers, as workers, and we scrutinise our thoughts and feelings for signs of some developmental flaw, perversion, or personal

inadequacy. In turn, the problems we reveal are viewed as the proper concern of therapists and counselors.

The resulting 'psychologisation' of problems which might otherwise be seen and addressed in relation to social conditions (poverty, capitalism and patriarchy) has undoubtedly boosted the therapeutic and counselling industries (Furedi, 2004).

It is not only therapeutic professionals who benefit from psychiatric expansionism. Employers and the state also have a vested interest in the maintenance of a contented and mentally fit workforce. Since the early twentieth century, industrial psychiatry has attempted to transform sullen and unmotivated workers into efficient drones of industry (Miller, 1986; Lunbeck, 1994: 242). Antonio Gramsci (1971: 279–80) wrote presciently in 1936 about 'psychoanalysis and its enormous diffusion since the war, as the expression of the increased moral coercion exercised by the apparatus of the State and society on single individuals'. The remit of the American National Mental Health Act of 1946 and, in Britain, the National Health Service (NHS), was in part to improve national mental and physical health and to pre-empt social unrest following the Second World War. Indeed, John Huston's 1946 film *Let There Be Light* depicts the cure of psychiatric conditions by various psycho-therapeutic methods – a theme ordained by the US government, which was concerned by the cost to the post-war economy of maintaining the population's mental health.

Recent Western governments have been equally exercised by the economic costs of psychological distress and its impact on 'employability': as a British government White Paper put it: 'mental illness and stress-related conditions are now the most common cause of sickness absence' (Department of Health, 2006: 35). At the time of writing, the British government is eager to reduce the level of Incapacity Benefit paid to one million Britons each year. According to the Depression Report, published by New Labour's mental health adviser Richard Layard and a group from the London School of Economics, mental illness has overtaken unemployment as today's greatest social problem. The report claims that the loss of output because of depression and chronic anxiety costs the government £12 billion each year (Centre for Economic Performance, 2006: 6). Such calculations help to explain why states such as the UK and the US are keen to embrace the 'mental health agenda' in the name of 'social inclusion', emphasising new, cost-effective therapies. On 10 October 2007, indeed, the British government announced a massive investment in the provision of the relatively inexpensive therapy,

Cognitive Behaviour Therapy (CBT), in an attempt to drive down the economic cost of dealing with mental distress.

The interests of the pharmaceutical sector must also be considered. In recent years, biopsychiatry has extended its 'regime of truth' across the world: the initial resistance towards, but eventual acceptance of SSRI drugs in Japan encapsulates the global spread of pharmacological treatments for depression. Pharmaceutical companies, like governments, have a strong interest in widening diagnostic criteria for psychiatric conditions and in promoting the notion that there is widespread 'unmet need' for antidepressants and other drugs (Mosher, Gosden and Beder, 2004; Moynihan and Cassels, 2005: 29–33), especially in the treatment of broad-spectrum conditions, such as anxiety-related disorders. In September 2006, the prescription of antidepressant drugs in the UK was widely reported to have increased by 50% over the preceding decade and between 1993 and 2003 prescriptions of anti-psychotics for children in the US rose fivefold (Martin, 2007: 13). This has in turn generated concerns about the regulation of pharmaceuticals marketing. In the US, direct-to-consumer prescription drug advertising on television is flimsily regulated (Jaramillo, 2006) and pharmaceutical representatives increasingly pressurise medical professionals to purchase their drugs through patenting strategies, pay-offs, lobbying and advertising (Greider, 2003). A study by the Boston School of Public Health (Sagar and Socolar, 2001) reported that, in 2000, American drug makers employed 39% of their staff in marketing and 22% in research and development, and the gap between expenditure in research and development versus marketing has been steadily widening. For example, manufacturers employed 48,527 people in research and development in 2000, down from 49,409 in 1995, while employment in marketing increased from 55,348 to 87,810 during the same period. A similar situation obtains in the UK, where direct-to-consumer pharmaceutical marketing is illegal. Pharmaceutical companies have considerable influence over psychiatric publications. Thus Arthur Crisp (2001: 485), in his review of the anti-stigma book *The Image of Madness: The Public Facing Mental Illness and Psychiatric Treatment*, notes ominously that 'the hand of the pharmaceutical industry is obvious' in the text. More broadly, as Moncrieff and Kirsh (2005: 84) warn, pharmaceutical companies are increasingly involved in paying for 'consulting fees, research grants, educational sponsorship and all forms of hospitality'.

Pharmaceutical companies also maintain strong links with mental health pressure groups. In the US, for example, the National Alliance on Mental Illness (NAMI), which presents itself as a 'grassroots' organisation and is often seen as the 'voice' of the mad community, receives significant funding from several pharmaceutical companies. Eli Lilly, manufacturers of Prozac, have been the organisation's major funder (Silverstein, 1999). Sometimes the links between the pharmaceuticals and the pressure groups are more personal. For example, the husband of the British group SANE's Chief Executive, Marjorie Wallace, was a board member of Glaxo Wellcome before its merger with SmithKline Beecham, a fact that raises questions about the integrity of Wallace's statements about Glaxo ('Glaxo settles New York drug suit', 2004) and about the independence of mental health pressure groups in general. This is not, of course, to question every aspect of the work of all mental health charities. In Britain, Mind, for example, has led campaigns against electroconvulsive therapy (ECT) and media stigmatisation in the 1990s and users/survivors of the mental health system play a significant role in the organisation; Mind has also maintained a healthy scepticism about the role of medicine in psychiatry and their publications stress the links between poverty and mental distress.

So far, I have written as though discourses of mental health and illness are produced and regulated solely by the forces of capital and the state. Increasingly, however, the hegemony of mental health discourse is also sustained by individuals and groups in civil society. In particular, the intensifying interest in therapy and the care of the self in capitalist societies coincides with the rise of Bourdieu's (1984) 'new petite bourgeoisie'. Mike Featherstone (1991: 171) points to the calculatedly hedonistic habitus of this post-war middle-class faction. Yet while it rejects traditional petit bourgeois moral restraints, this class does not succumb to wild abandon, but tries to regulate the body and mind through disciplinary programmes and practices. This new petite bourgeoisie is directly related to the rise of the therapeutic society with its corps of professionals, ready to offer advice on issues of physical and mental health. As I shall show later, advertising, talk shows and documentaries as well as 'human interest' and celebrity journalism have hegemonised this 'will to health'. As Featherstone's phrase 'calculated hedonism' suggests, the theory of the 'risk society' (Beck, 1992) is another useful context in which to understand this cultural preoccupation with mental distress. Drawing on the work of Foucault, Robert Castel (1991: 281) notes a shift in the past few hundred years from the confinement and control of dangerous individuals to the social administration of abstract risks. Individuals, as well as governments and companies, are increasingly preoccupied with explaining or managing the risk of mental distress. The widespread concern with mental health among Western populations can be seen as a personalised form of psychological risk management, as individuals increasingly 'monitor and evaluate mood, emotion and cognition according to a finer and more continuous process of self-scrutiny' (Rose, 2007: 223).

Given the explosion of state, corporate and consumer discourse around issues of mental health and the imperative to create consumers for new pharmaceutical products, it is perhaps unsurprising that contemporary media and film representations of mental distress are often very far from stigmatising or hostile towards people suffering mental distress and are in fact often sympathetic and 'positive' (my quotation marks indicate a certain scepticism towards the semantic haziness and simplistic binarism inherent in talk about 'positive' and 'negative' images of madness). Yet this new 'positivity' about mental distress needs to be regarded with at least as much scepticism as Foucault (2005a) reserves for the 'humane' 'moral treatment' of the nineteenth-century alienists. In addition to familiar psychiatric concerns about 'stigmatisation' and 'inaccuracy', any contemporary evaluation of media images of madness must also remain alert to the ideological nature of the state and corporate interests which inform and regulate discourses of mental distress.

Madness, illness or distress?

From a psychiatric standpoint, critical discussions of mental distress abound in terminological confusions and misunderstandings. These often involve misuses of diagnostic categories. To take a well-worn example, media texts often conflate 'psychosis' and 'psychopathy', for instance, while 'schizophrenia' is often assumed to imply a 'split personality' or identity disorder – even if psychiatrists' continued use of a term with such a misleading etymology is partly to blame for the latter confusion (Crichton, 2000). In the Glasgow Media Group's research into the audience reception of a British soap opera, for example, one female focus group member commented that: 'In *Brookside*, that man who is the child-abuser and the wife-beater, he looks like a schizophrenic – he's like a split personality, like two different people' (quoted in Philo, 1997: 55). As we shall see later, such misprisions are also apparent within film and media texts themselves. For anti-stigma critics, these are not simply unfortunate lapses into psychiatric inaccuracy; they may also have implications for the ways in which mental disturbance is regarded by sufferers, those who care for them, and society at large. Certainly, it is important to consider carefully the terminology used to denote and describe mental distress, since this is a crucial part of the cultural representation of madness.

One immediate problem here is that not all commentators agree on the need for such caution. Some might argue, for instance, that it is the *intention* to stigmatise, rather than the vocabulary used, that matters. Yet this argument assumes that the meaning of an utterance is governed by its speaker's intentions rather than determined by the recipient of the utterance. Cultural critics from a variety of political positions and disciplinary perspectives have advanced powerful arguments contradicting such 'intentionalist' assumptions (e.g. Wimsatt and Beardsley, 1954; Barthes, 1977). Another, slightly more sophisticated argument is that the terms we use to replace problematic or stigmatising terms can themselves be co-opted for stigmatising purposes. As Slavoj Žižek (1999: 254) suggests:

> The catch is [...] that this censoring activity itself, by a kind of devilish dialectical reversal, starts to participate in what it purports to censor and fight – is it not immediately evident how, in designating somebody as 'mentally challenged' instead of 'stupid', an ironic distance can always creep in and give rise to an excess of humiliating aggressivity – one adds insult to injury, as it were, by the supplementary polite patronising dimension (it is well-known that aggressivity coated in politeness can be much more painful than directly abusive words, since violence is heightened by the additional contrast between the aggressive content and the polite surface form).

Žižek's point is nicely illustrated in Mark Haddon's (2004: 56) novel *The Curious Incident of the Dog in the Night-time*, whose hero, Christopher, is a 15 year-old with Asperger's Syndrome and an obsession with prime numbers.

> All the other children at my school are stupid. Except I'm not meant to call them stupid, even though this is what they are. I'm meant to say that they have learning difficulties or that they have special needs ... Siobhan said we have to use those words because people used to call children like the children at school *spaz* and *crip* and *mong* which were nasty words. But that is stupid too because sometimes the children from the school down the road see us in the street when we're getting off the bus and they shout, 'Special Needs! Special Needs!'

This danger of 'correct' language being turned to ill purposes is ever-present. Žižek's point about the limits of linguistic prescriptivism, how-ever, only reminds us that language is a site of continual cultural struggle and does not in itself constitute an argument for clinging to language that is widely felt to be abusive or dehumanising.

Others attack the so-called political correctness of anti-stigma crit-ics by asserting that language ought to be 'purely descriptive', robustly unconcerned with the modish preoccupations of liberal critics and minority sensitivities. The call to keep language 'objective' comes not only from the right-wing tabloid press, but from liberal critics of politi-cal correctness, such as Robert Hughes (1993). For such critics, 'cripple' is the 'real' or 'objective' word to describe somebody who cannot walk; minority sensibilities should simply fall into line with this semantic hegemony. Thus a mentally distressed person can be called a 'loony' on the grounds that this, as Haddon's Christopher puts it, 'is what they are'; in Christopher's socially unadapted mind, meaning is fixed and unchanging, like his beloved prime numbers. This view is even found among left-wing polemicists. Terry Eagleton (2003: 187), for example, laconically asserts that 'if the disabled do not walk, at least they can redesignate themselves as challenged', dismissing the last term as a 'voluntaristic cliché'. Yet while linguistic choices will not change the reality of being unable to walk, they may nonetheless impact upon the experience of disabled people. To those on the receiving end of abu-sive language, terms such as 'cripple' – or indeed 'nuts', 'psycho' and 'mental' – are anything but objective.

What the crusaders against political correctness refuse to accept is that language can never be pure, neutral, objective and denotative. All language contains associative connotations as well as literal deno-tations (Cameron, 1995; see also Spender, 1998). For this reason, George Orwell's celebrated advocacy of a purely denotative language that would be as transparent as a pane of glass, is merely fanciful. In the light of the Sapir–Whorf hypothesis, most linguists now broadly accept some version of linguistic relativism – the hypothesis that language at least partly constructs, rather than simply reflects reality (Montgomery, 1986). Moreover, as critical discourse analysts argue, language shapes the world, often in the interests of powerful groups (Fairclough, 1995; 2001). The conservative argument that there is some objective, neutral and descriptive terminology to describe those suffering with mental distress is therefore deeply flawed. Incidentally, this argument often involves a moral double standard: those who level accusations of political correct-ness typically present themselves as stolid guardians of objectivity and common sense in the face of woolly liberal relativism; yet conservative critics of political correctness in the linguistic domain often call for censorship in other spheres, such as television and film representations of sexuality, in the name of moral standards or decency.

The arguments presented above suggest two things: first, that liberal and radical critics are right, or at least not wrong, to consider carefully the language they use, as well as the language used to describe mental distress within media texts. Second, and perhaps more controversially, they suggest that since language is not fixed, it is foolhardy to prescribe any terms once and for all as the 'correct' ones, a move that simply replicates the linguistic essentialism of those context-blind conservative critics who wish to 'fix' language once and for all.

Having accepted the need for linguistic sensitivity in the discussion of mental distress, we must ask what terminology is appropriate for the discussion of mental distress. I have avoided certain phrases in this book. For example, I generally avoid narrowly legalistic terms, such as 'insanity', for the reason that these do not encompass the wider social understandings of mental distress which circulate in the media and popular culture. I also eschew the nominalised phrase 'the mentally ill', which could be argued to reify or objectivise people suffering from mental distress and the problems they face, as though sufferers have foregone their personhood, their identities entirely subsumed by their experiences of distress. This book also avoids the term 'mental illness', except when paraphrasing the arguments of others. The validity and utility of this phrase have been attacked from many angles. Most famously, perhaps, Szasz (1970) pointed out that 'mental illness' is a contradiction in terms, since illnesses are by definition physical. I am sympathetic to this argument against the psychiatric appropriation of the term 'illness' to describe mental or emotional distress. Since Szasz launched his first salvos against psychiatric imperialism, psychiatry has insisted ever more strongly on a biological aetiology for madness – although evidence for a biological 'smoking gun' for any so-called mental illness remains in desperately short supply. Nor is it clear how, if a somatic cause for a particular form of distress *were* identified, the 'illness' could thereafter be described as 'mental' (Valenstein, 1998).

The movement against psychiatric diagnostic labels is now well established and Richard Bentall (2003) is just one of a number of well-qualified psychiatric heretics who propose forgoing them altogether. As Szasz noted, psychiatric terminology is pseudo-scientific, unhelpful and potentially stigmatising, failing to illuminate or explain any more than non-specialist terms. The label 'depression', for example, adds little to the meaning of 'unhappiness', while the schizophrenia symptom 'agonomia' seems positively obscure compared to its plain English paraphrase, 'inability to adapt to social norms'. As Godsi (2004: 38) puts it:

> the language of medicine, and psychiatry in particular, is so wedded to pathologising views of distress as 'disorders' or 'dysfunctions' and so embedded within a particular biologised world view, that these explanations merely mystify and obscure our common understanding further.

Furthermore, clinical diagnoses can themselves be stigmatising; the rather alarming term 'aural hallucination', for example, might better be described as 'voice'.

If the concept of 'mental illness' is problematic, even unintelligible, what language can we use to describe our subject? Near-synonyms for 'mental illness', including 'mental health problems' and 'mental distress', are preferred by some. I regard 'mental health problems' as potentially stigmatising, as the phrase again tends to reify individuals as 'problems', while 'health' invokes its obverse of disease, implying that madness is a dangerous contagion. 'Mental distress' – the term preferred by the Glasgow Media Group (1996) – is, however, a useful umbrella term which is especially valuable in discussions of conditions which are nebulous or which lack a clear definition (such as many of those featured in media and film texts). The phrase 'mental distress' quite properly acknowledges the suffering that people diagnosed as 'bipolar' or 'schizophrenic' often endure, even if there is no biological cause of their condition.

Even here, however, some caution is required. While most forms of 'madness' involve distress to the sufferer, others – such as personality disorders – are characterised by verbal or sometimes physical violence towards others. Moreover, anthropological research into experiences of madness in certain cultural milieux suggests that the concept of 'mental distress' is not universally intelligible. Experiences of mental distress are inflected strongly by cultural context (Gu, 2006) and different cultures produce their distinctive forms or modes of mental distress (such as, famously within cultural psychiatry, running *amuk* in Malaysia). Often phenomenological accounts of non-Western experiences of madness contain elements familiar to Western psychiatry, together with culturally specific elements of religious doctrine, magical thinking and folk belief (Good, Subandi and DelVecchio Good, 2007). In many countries, psychiatric labels are regarded with suspicion (Jorm et al., 2005) and not all cultures and languages even have a conception of the 'mental'. The adjective 'mental' presupposes certain distinctions, including the Cartesian bifurcation of mind and body, which are specific to post-Enlightenment Western culture. For example, Fenton and Sadiq-Sangster's (1996) research on the expression of mental distress among South Asian women in Britain indicates that while a range of terms is used to describe psychiatrically recognisable experiences ('thinking illness', 'falling heart'), the terms 'mind' and 'mental' are never used, suggesting a somatic, rather than a mentalistic, conception of madness. The concept of 'myself' is seldom used in these contexts, either, suggesting perhaps that South Asian women in Britain have a less individualistic perspective on their distress than White ethnic groups.

Partly in view of the need for a culturally and historically inclusive terminology, I use the term 'madness' throughout the book. 'Madness' often seems *le mot juste* in discussions of historical cases or representations, since pre-modern conceptions of what is now called mental illness were generally somatic rather than mentalistic (Clarke, 1975). While psychiatrists often call for more 'accurate' representations of mental distress in the contemporary media, non-Cartesian conceptions of madness cannot necessarily be grasped using psychiatric terminology. The term 'madness' also problematises and challenges the pathologising implications of the phrase 'mental illness': hence its use by radical pressure groups such as Mad Pride concerned not only to improve perceptions and conditions of people diagnosed with mental illnesses, but also to challenge psychiatric hegemony. While the term arguably carries more stigmatising connotations than 'mental illness' in certain contexts, it also eludes psychiatric reification.

'Madness' also seems an appropriately comprehensive term to use where the focus is upon cultural contexts – as in Fleming and Manvell's historical survey, *Images of Madness* (1985). In many cases, talk of 'madness' rather than 'mental illness' also permits a shift in critical focus from marginalised individuals to questions of institutional and social disorder. Simon Cross (2004: 203) shows how the discourse of 'madness' functions in this way in his discussion of Fred Wiseman's controversial 1967 documentary about a psychiatric prison, *Titicut Follies*:

> A sequence in which the 'mad' screw sings a duet with an inmate he had previously castigated for being black appears to trade on the popular aphorism 'you don't have to be mad to work here but it helps!' Wiseman's open-ended style refuses to close down options

for identifying the mad within the prison; inmates, guards, and psychiatrists all appear mad.

The term 'madness' is also used by Wahl in a way that keeps its subversive connotations in play: the nicely ambiguous title of his 1995 book – *Media Madness* – adverts to the 'craziness' of the media as well as those represented (or misrepresented) by it.

Coverage and approach of this book

This book covers a large number of texts and three media forms: film, television and print media (newspapers and magazines). Although radio and the Internet are much understudied media in terms of the mental health-related content, I have excluded these from consideration, partly for reasons of space and partly out of a desire to focus on media forms already examined by previous critics, such as Wahl (1995) and Philo (1996), in the hope of comparing some of my conclusions with theirs. I hope, however, that my own analysis might be tested against other media forms in future studies.

Some previous studies have sought to list all media texts dealing with mental distress: Wahl (1995), for example, appends to his book a list of relevant films and television programmes. Useful as they are, such lists can never be exhaustive; I have therefore attempted no comparable feat and this book has no pretensions to comprehensiveness. With the exponential increase in books, films, magazines, television dramas and documentaries about mental distress within the Anglophone world alone, an attempt to list all treatments touching on the theme of madness would be doomed to fail. To maintain coherence, I concentrate on the British media, although I also touch on US texts (most notably, Hollywood and some other English-language films, but also US soap operas), especially where these are widely known in the UK. Despite this British focus, I hope that my discussion will be relevant to the media cultures of other advanced capitalist countries.

Content analysis, of course, offers one solution to the problems presented by a vast sample. The Glasgow Media Group (Philo, 1996) has used content analysis of media representations over quite specific time periods to provide a representative snapshot of media content. These quantitative studies, I shall argue in Chapter 2, have been extremely useful and influential, although I also suggest that they also suffer from some of the common limitations of content analysis; in particular, a certain tendency towards the decontextualisation of content. My own approach is qualitative, combining textual analysis with historical contextualisation and social theory to produce detailed, if not exhaustive, readings of the texts. Moreover, while repeated, fleeting images of mental distress may cumulatively exercise considerable cultural force, exigencies of space preclude discussion of every text that briefly depicts or mentions mental distress.

For many critics, of course, textual analysis alone is methodologically insufficient. In recent years the importance of audience research has been convincingly argued by many commentators within media studies and ethnographic approaches are now dominant within media and film studies. I would certainly acknowledge that media audiences can construct their own, often contradictory understandings about mental distress from primary media texts. In the case of film and television texts, for example, the briefest glance as Internet discussion boards shows that audiences often are able to negotiate representations of distress with considerable sophistication. For example, a discussion forum of the Digital Spy website devoted to the BBC1 soap opera *EastEnders* contains a lengthy exchange about the bipolar condition of the character Jean Slater, in which participants discuss diagnoses, make comparisons with their personal experiences with sufferers of mental distress and even anticipate how the narrative will progress ('I bet she becomes ill again'). Exchanges such as these illustrate a high level of public interest in, and engagement with, soap opera storylines about mental distress. In another Digital Spy discussion thread on an episode of the US teen television drama *Smallville*, one contributor complains that the episode used horror film clichés in a stereotypical fashion:

> [...] Where it got actively offensive was in its antediluvian prejudice against mental illness, with characters talking about it like some shameful personal failing, and about mental-health treatment as some Bedlamesque horror to be avoided at all costs. That's just shameful.

Another *Smallville* fan, however, adopts a different stance:

> I don't agree. The episode seemed to take the perspective of Chloe, who does have misgivings with mental illness; she's afraid of it. If you ask me, the ending made it very clear that once Chloe was able to face it, she found that she was wrong about her feelings. When faced with her mother, she saw her not as a 'crazy' person, but the mother that's been missing from her life for her entire teenage life, leading into adulthood. So, needless to say, I don't feel they were being offensive.

From this evidence alone it is clear that audiences are often aware of the issues surrounding mental distress and the processes of mediation which complicate discussions about stereotyping. Clearly, too, audiences are not passive receptors of images of mental distress.

Nonetheless, exigencies of space have restricted this study to the analysis of primary texts – in negotiation, of course, with secondary criticism. (I have been rather less concerned with what John Fiske [1987] calls 'tertiary texts' – texts produced by media audiences.) This is, without doubt, a limitation – although I hope not a flaw – of the book. Since audiences do indeed negotiate the meaning of texts, we should be wary of what John Thompson (1990) calls the 'fallacy of internalism', according to which media discourse determines meaning. I have no space to engage deeply with these long-standing debates here. As a minimal defence of my textual analysis approach, however, I would propose that the power of film, television and the print media to create meaning outweighs the potential of audiences to oppose it. Even one of the pioneers of media audience research, David Morley (1995: 308–9), has noted that 'the power of viewers to reinterpret meanings is hardly equivalent to the discursive power of centralised media institutions to construct the texts which the viewer then interprets; to imagine otherwise is simply foolish'. It is often asserted that one cannot 'read off' ideology from media texts. If by 'ideology' here one means the ideological meaning understood by the reader/audience, this is of course true; yet that does not mean that media critics cannot make valid judgements, based on textual and contextual evidence, about a text's preferred reading or its socio-political valence.

It has also been necessary to limit the historical scope of this study. I have restricted my analysis to media texts first issued, broadcast or released since the mid-1990s. By focusing on the period since the publication of the major studies by Wahl (1995) and Greg Philo and the Glasgow Media Group (1996) in the mid-1990s, I hope to discover how media representations of madness have changed in the years since those texts were published. While many of the representational strategies criticised by those researchers remain unaltered, some discernible shifts in the nature of the media representation of madness have occurred in recent years. The emergence of media narratives of 'celebrity distress' since the mid-1990s is perhaps the most striking of these developments.

I have also decided to concentrate on film and media texts intended for teenaged and adult consumption. Children's television contains numerous insidious examples of stigmatising language (Philo, 1999: 59) and Wilson's et al. (2000) study of children's television reveals a tendency to make light of mental distress through derogatory language and 'wacky' imagery. Valuable as these studies are, there is no space to consider them, or the programmes they analyse, here.

While it is impossible to give an absolute definition of mental distress, some boundaries can be drawn nonetheless. In particular, I avoid discussion of congenital mental disorders such as 'mental deficiency' or 'retardation'. Some media and film critics (e.g. Smith, 1999) include media representations of congenital disorders alongside mental distress. Even the anti-stigma critic Wahl, having warned of the importance of distinguishing between 'mental illness' and other kinds of mental disorder, including 'psychopathy' (Wahl, 1995: 16–20), brackets psychopathy with mental distress in his review of stigmatising films (1995: 58) and popular music (1995: 65). However, congenital and non-pathological conditions such as mental retardation or other intellectual impairments are not generally understood, either psychiatrically or popularly, as forms of mental distress. Characters such as Benny in the classic British soap opera *Crossroads* (ITV, 1964–1988), or his namesake in the US drama *L.A. Law* (NBC, 1986–1994), or the protagonists of films such as *Regarding Henry* (Mike Nichols, 1993) and *Slingblade* (Billy Bob Thornton, 1996) are developmentally disabled, but not mentally distressed (although congenitally disabled people may sometimes, of course, experience mental distress). Accordingly, such characters are not discussed in this book.

Finally, it is necessary to comment on the disciplinary approach adopted here. I have approached my subject from a multi-disciplinary perspective, attempting to assess patterns of representation and detect shifts in the cultural politics of madness, paying particular attention to categories of social difference. After all, the media never represent 'madness itself', but always madness as embodied by persons of a particular gender, race and class. Many existing analyses of media misrepresentation have been conducted from the critical vantage point of psychiatric discourse, setting out to measure the accuracy of media representations of madness in relation to the psychiatric paradigm. As I have already argued, however, it cannot be assumed that psychiatry is the only discipline capable of comprehending, or warranted to speak about madness. To understand media representations of distress we must consider their historical, social and political dimensions. Accordingly, my argument draws upon social and political theory as well as gender studies in order to interrogate the relationship between images of mental distress and contemporary culture.

Before examining any media texts, however, it is necessary to channel what has so far been a very general discussion into a rather more focused engagement with some of the critical and theoretical debates about the media representation of distress.

2
Stigmatisation, Violence and Media Criticism

From a long historical perspective, the stigma of mental distress is not what it used to be. The rise of medicine in Europe from the later Middle Ages onwards promoted increasingly rational, rather than supernatural explanations of insanity. In the cultural sphere, the Bible has been replaced as Western society's principle source of ideas and information about madness by secular forms, beginning with literature and eventually the mass media. Freudian psychotherapy has asserted the normalcy of madness and, in the last 40 years, sociology has developed frameworks for analysing the processes that underlie stigmatisation. Since Erving Goffman's writing on the subject, the reduction or eradication of stigma – a mark or token of infamy, disgrace or reproach or 'an attribute that is deeply discrediting' (Goffman, 1963: 3) – has become a major concern in psychiatric and academic discourse. None of these developments, however, has eradicated stigmatising media representations of madness. On the contrary, Western media culture retains traces of the deep-rooted medieval association between madness and sinfulness, as reflected in continuing stereotypes of mental distress as 'frightening, shameful, imaginary, feigned and incurable, while psychiatric patients are characterised as dangerous, unpredictable, untrustworthy, unstable, lazy, weak, worthless and/or helpless' (Lawrie, 1999: 129).

It is sometimes suggested that too much discussion is devoted to the stigmatisation of mental distress today. Recently, for example, contributors to the online magazine *spiked* (a continuation of the now defunct *Living Marxism*) have, reasonably enough perhaps, questioned psychiatric estimates of the incidence of mental distress in the population (widely quoted as '1 in 4') and have criticised what they regard as a liberal obsession with issues of stigmatisation and representation at the expense of practical and medical support (Outen, 2000, 2001; Appleton, 2001). While it is undoubtedly true that representational considerations are not more important than such immediate practical issues, it seems impossible to detach the two areas of concern; as anti-stigma campaigners often point out, stigmatisation may deter sufferers from seeking medical assistance in the first place.

Wahl (1995: 110–31) argues that media stereotypes of madness persist for a number of reasons. First of all, madness is a 'crowd-pleaser', drawing large audiences, especially in the 'slasher' film subgenre. Ignorance also plays a role: many media and film workers are, quite simply, ill-informed about psychiatric diagnoses and prognoses relating to mental distress. Psychological reassurance may also explain stigmatisation. Some people may draw solace from the fact that they do not suffer the mental torments endured by other, 'weaker' individuals. As I argue later, such *Schadenfreude* may underlie many magazine articles about 'mad' celebrities. Finally, a lack of feedback can lead to the continuation of 'negative' images of madness: media personnel, Wahl argues, should solicit audience responses to their productions; if they were to feel that their output was being badly received, they would be less likely to produce offensive materials.

The misrepresentation of madness may have a number of unfortunate effects, as noted by Wahl (1995: 87–109). These include the decreased ability of sufferers and carers to comprehend psychiatric diagnoses. There may also be a tendency to withdraw support for psychiatric patients or community projects which aim to help them; Philo (1999: 56), for example, found that people who perceive a link between madness and violence from Hollywood film and television drama were less likely to respond positively to community care policies. Wahl (1995: 92–3) describes an experiment in which he showed two films to two groups of college students. One group watched a TV movie *Murder: By Reason of Insanity*, which features a violent mentally distressed character, while a control group watched a film involving murder but not mental distress. Both groups were then asked to complete a questionnaire assessing attitudes towards mental health. The responses of the group that had watched *Murder: By Reason of Insanity*, Wahl noted, evidenced 'harsher' attitudes about mental distress than the control group. Even factual accounts of distress, such as the news reports of mentally distressed murderers, could have such effects. There might also be a tendency to self-stigmatisation and a fear of disclosure.

Studies of the effects of film on individuals and groups are fraught with methodological problems, of course, raising, amongst other issues, the difficulty of separating media effects from other environmental factors, and the question of the reliability of 'laboratory' studies of audience responses (Gauntlett, 2002: 28–33). Moreover, studying reactions to a single film, as in the Wahl study mentioned above, is not adequate to determine the influence of films in general. I tend to agree with Karen Boyle (2005) that the scientific search for media effects is over. Nevertheless, since a strong correlation exists between media content and audience beliefs (Philo and Berry, 2004), there can be little doubt that cinematic representations of madness contribute towards reflecting and amplifying dominant cultural attitudes towards people with mental distress, even if it is safer to talk of media 'influence' rather than 'effects' (Corner, 2000).

Understandably, then, the media's role in the stigmatisation of mental distress has become a central concern among media watchdogs and campaigners in Britain and the US. This has not been a sudden development. Controversies over cultural representations of mental distress have often drawn psychiatrists and artists into confrontations that have played out in the media: in 1968, Roy Boulting's dark psychological thriller *The Twisted Nerve*, for instance, was publicly accused by psychiatrists of implying a link between mongolism and psychopathy ('Roy Boulting defends mental illness film', 1968: 4). More recently, there has been a remarkable proliferation of discourse in the UK and the US aimed at reducing the stigmatisation of mental distress. This is largely the result of the campaigning of mental health pressure groups, support groups and coalitions of sufferers/survivors and professional medical organisations such as the Institute of Psychiatry and Royal College of Psychiatrists. Such groups have generated reports, critical studies, Internet sites, Public Service Announcements and information films dedicated to promoting understanding of mental distress and exploding media-created myths. In the creative arts, meanwhile, several events have aimed at increasing awareness and promoting discussion of mental health issues, such as the Reel Madness festival at London's Institute of Contemporary Arts, organised by Mental Health Media in 2003.

Direct anti-stigma campaigning, meanwhile, has been effective, especially in the US. Wahl (1995: 145) describes how the National Stigma Clearinghouse lobbied D.C. Comics, its editors, and its parent company when they planned to kill off their Superman hero in November 1992 through a storyline which involved the superhero's assassination by Doomsday, 'an escapee from an interplanetary insane asylum'. The proposed storyline was dropped. More recently in the US, the ABC drama *Wonderland* (2000), inspired by Milos Forman's film *One Flew Over the*

Cuckoo's Nest (1975) and Frederick Wiseman's *Titicut Follies* (1969), was also cancelled after a public campaign. Writer Peter Berg and his team of writers spent several months researching *Wonderland*, which is shot in a jerky, *verité* style in a seeming bid for 'authenticity'. In the show's pilot, a psychotic man opens fire with a gun on Times Square, while a depressed patient is later revealed to have set his mother alight – both storylines that associate mental distress with unjustified violence towards others. The National Alliance on Mental Illness (NAMI) joined 14 mental health groups in calling for disclaimers to be issued before each broadcast. Mental health professionals called for a boycott of the show and, facing the pressure of heavy competition from the drama *E.R.* in the same timeslot, the programme was deserted by its sponsors and cancelled after just a few episodes. In Britain, the Disability Rights Commission's Shift campaign, supported by all the major mental health charities, began in 2004. It encourages the public to report instances of unacceptable media coverage to the editor or producer responsible or to the broadcast media regulator Ofcom. Other campaigns have involved inviting media workers to attend workshops on stigmatisation and media law is also sometimes mobilised against broadcasters who perpetuate stigmatising images of madness. In October 2004, for example, the South African 'shock jock' DJ Gareth Cliff was found guilty by the South African Broadcasting Complaints Commission of inciting violence against mentally ill people after quipping in his *5fm* drive-time show that people with psychiatric diagnoses should be 'chained in a cell and fed porridge'.

The last few years have seen significant cross-fertilisation between media criticism and psychiatric lobbying. In 1995, 3000 British psychiatrists signed a petition which criticised the media coverage of mental distress, citing research undertaken by the Glasgow Media Group (Philo, 1999: 58). Psychiatric professionals are increasingly concerned about media representation and draw upon media and communication studies research in their discussions of it (Jorm, 2000: 398; Byrne, 2001: 283). Together with these academic and professional interventions, government initiatives such as the Scottish Executive's mental health awareness campaigns now constitute a considerable professional hegemony campaigning against media misrepresentation in the name of mental health awareness.

Anti-stigma discourse tends to adopt the basic tenets of liberal psychiatry as it seeks to expose popular media 'misrepresentations' and 'myths' about 'mental illness', particularly the myth that mentally distressed people are more prone to violence than others. The medical, particularly biopsychiatric, model of mental distress is dominant in anti-stigma discourse:

> A number of organisations campaigning around mental illness, notably the National Alliance on Mental Illness (NAMI) in the United States, and SANE in the United Kingdom, do embrace a conception of mental disorders as diseases with a genetic component and argue that this recognition will reduce stigma associated with such conditions and lead to effective treatment.
>
> (Rose, 2007: 216)

Applying this medical perspective to their meta-analysis of media images of distress, Pirkis et al. (2006: 536) conclude with a militant call for action:

> The knowledge base regarding portrayal of mental illness in fictional films and television programmes is considerable, and it is timely to start using this knowledge to inform action. The mental health sector (policymakers, mental health professionals, and people with mental illness and their families) should collaborate with the film and television industries (producers, directors, scriptwriters, and actors) to minimise negative portrayal and maximise positive portrayal.

This statement treats the definition of 'positive' and 'negative' content and 'knowledge' about media representation in a positivist fashion. Psychiatry, it is implied, holds the key to 'accurate' representation which media images must be made to reproduce. Yet there are problems with this seemingly commonsensical approach to the analysis and amelioration of mental distress representations. In this chapter I shall critically examine some of the methodological and argumentational premises, as well as the cultural consequences of anti-stigma discourse, in order to prepare the ground for my later textual analyses.

Some preliminary qualifications should perhaps be made to the anti-stigma positions discussed above. First of all, public awareness of, and feedback about media texts' portrayals of madness have grown substantially in recent years, as I suggested in Chapter 1. Moreover, as I also argued in Chapter 1, many powerful pharmaceutical companies have a strong vested interest in promoting a more sympathetic awareness of mental health, as they attempt to create new markets for psychoactive drugs (Moynihan and Cassells, 2005; Patmore, 2006: 292–325). I also argue in this chapter that anti-stigma media criticism is rather

over-generalised and has tended to rely on a somewhat limited concep-
tualization of violence. Moreover, I suggest that anti-stigma discourse
can, in the process of critiquing popular images of mental distress, sometimes derogate the popular culture in which these representations are
found. Even the best and most prominent texts in this area – Wahl's
1995 book *Media Madness* (which concentrates on the US media) and
Greg Philo's (and the Glasgow Media Group's) *Media and Mental Distress*
(1996, which focuses mainly on the UK) – are vulnerable, I believe, to
these objections.

In *Media Madness*, Otto Wahl discusses the ubiquity of inaccurate and
stereotypical representations of mental distress in the mass media, ref-
erencing a vast array of popular films, music, television shows, novels
and cartoons. These include confusions over psychiatric terminology
(for example, 'psychopathic' and 'psychotic'), the use of stigmatising
language in relation to mentally ill people ('nutter', 'whacko', etc.),
the depiction of mental distress as insuperable, and, particularly, the
identification of mental distress with violence and criminality in popular film and literature. Wahl argues that while audiences often accept
and sometimes even enjoy these inaccuracies, some of those who suffer from, or know someone who is suffering from mental distress find
them insulting and offensive. The range and conviction of Wahl's book
is impressive and its cultural salience helped to it to win the 1996
Gustavus Myers Center Book Award for an outstanding book on human
rights in North America. The book's continuing relevance is underlined
by its influence on later studies on media and mental health issues
(e.g. Morris, 2006) and by subsequent survey findings about the deleterious impact of stereotypes of mental distress on the perceptions of
both adults (National Mental Health Association, 2000) and children
(Wilson et al., 2000).

Adopting quite different methodologies, the best and most substantial British research on the subject is the content analysis and audience
reception work of the Glasgow Media Group in *Media and Mental Distress*
(1996). Like Wahl, the Glasgow Media Group argue that mental distress
stereotypes are widespread in the media and can have deleterious effects
on the lives and well-being of sufferers and their families (Philo, 1996).
In addition to the book's influence among anti-stigma campaigners, the
Glasgow group's novel approach to focus group methodology – which
involved encouraging people to write their own news articles based
on newspaper headlines about stories involving mental distress – has
strongly influenced audience research scholarship within Media Studies. Less valuable and influential texts than these would be easier targets

of criticism. Yet it is precisely because these texts are so successful and so widely cited by other scholars working in this area that I would like to use them to illustrate some methodological and argumentational weaknesses typical of the 'stereotype critique' school of research, with a particular emphasis on the ways in which the correlation between madness and violence has been deployed by anti-stigma critics. This chapter attempts to describe and explain some of those weaknesses and to elaborate their implications for the analysis of media representations of mental distress.

The question of form: Madness and the popular media

As I have already indicated, Otto Wahl (1995) enlists a vast range of popular texts and genres to support his arguments about the treatment of madness in the media; but this ambitious inclusivity incurs a risk of over-generalisation. Susan Sontag (1966) long ago warned of the dangers of mining texts for thematic meaning while disregarding their textual and aesthetic qualities. By concentrating on 'positive' and 'negative' 'messages' about distress – terms which suggest a simplistic processual approach to media criticism – Wahl's approach tends to sideline the question of how these messages are conditioned by media form, narrative conventions, mode of address and other aesthetic considerations. For example, Wahl argues that newspaper stories that link mental distress and violence contain the same stock characters as those found in popular fiction such as *American Psycho* (1991) and *Red Dragon* (1993), namely 'insane killers who prey on multiple innocent victims' (Wahl, 1995: 70). It is certainly true that there are many such overlaps between the treatment of stories in the press and the handling of fictional accounts; but there are also differences. The particular conventions of different media forms will inflect the representation of mental distress in quite distinct ways: short newspaper stories, unlike fictional representations, cannot be expected to offer complex explorations of the issues they report. On the other hand, the news media have a representational responsibility not expected from popular fiction. Without further research that takes account of such generic or formal differences, the usefulness of any comparison between newspaper stories and popular fiction is bound to remain limited.

Exigencies of genre and form will inevitably condition any text's 'message' about mental distress. For example, the book and the film of Patrick McGrath's novel about a schizophrenic, *Spider* (McGrath, 1990; Cronenberg, 2002), offer two quite different perspectives on the hero's distress. This can be illustrated through a comparison between the respective endings of the two texts. The novel ends with the protagonist's chillingly detached resolution to commit suicide. At the end of the film, on the other hand, the schizophrenic protagonist Dennis Clegg enters the room of his landlady, whom he mistakenly identifies as his detested stepmother, with a hammer; Clegg recognises his delusion before going through with the attack, however, and is afterwards committed to a psychiatric institution. In comparing the book with the film version of *Spider*, it would be hasty to discuss the 'progressiveness' or otherwise of either of these texts without reference to its particular media form. The novel relies on first-person narration that is relatively hard to reproduce in film. Cinematic representation, however, demands that psychological experiences be 'visibilised' in particular ways (see Gilman, 1985; Cross, 2004), which explains (if not excuses) the dramatic and arguably sensationalist hammer scene at the end of Cronenberg's film. Understanding the book's or the film's portrayal of madness requires attention to the specificities of media forms, and the history of representation within each of them. The problem with many previous critiques is not that they are wrong, but that they are rather over-assimilated and cannot always do justice to the narratological, formal and generic constraints and determinations of the texts they discuss. As Graeme Turner (1986: 14) notes in relation to film,

> analyses of film made by literary critics, psychologists or sociologists, often see film as an unproblematic medium. They ignore the necessity of enquiring very deeply into its structures in order to understand what a specific film, or film generally, might do.

I am not alone in raising these kinds of questions about the need to study representations of mental distress in their generic and formal contexts. In his recent study of the representation of mental illness in television documentary, Cross (2004: 202) notes of the Glasgow Media Group's work by Philo, Henderson and McLaughlin:

> Philo, Henderson, and McLaughlin (1993) ignored aesthetic differences between film and TV while noting that negative stereotypes of mental illness are dominant across a range of visual media. Indeed, they collapsed all distinctions between children's cartoons, teenage drama, soap opera, and films shown on TV. These elisions conveniently avoid the question of whether similarities in representations

of mental illness are more significant than the differences arising from the particular genres and forms being employed.

This criticism might also be levelled as other, more recent works on media and madness, such as Patrick Fuery's *Madness and Cinema* (2004), which, for all its theoretical sophistication, tends to bundle together films which differ significantly in origin, popularity and genre. Of course, this generalising tendency may well be a necessary aspect of early studies in the relatively under-researched area of media and mental distress. In any fledgeling area of academic enquiry, ground-breaking texts are often wide-ranging in their scope and therefore inevitably subject to endless refinement and revision by subsequent critics with narrower textual focuses or disciplinary interests. My comments on anti-stigma media criticism are not intended, therefore, as absolute criticisms – and in any case, many stereotypes of mental distress do indeed transcend formal and generic boundaries. Rather, they are meant only to indicate that future studies of media representations of madness should take more account of formal and generic differences between texts, and should consider how different media forms and genres perform particular kinds of social function, or engage particular audiences with distinctive tastes and expectations.

Another problematic aspect of Wahl's book – and of anti-stigma discourse in general – is its tendency to reinforce conservative notions about the cultural value of popular texts. When discussing horror films, in particular, Wahl echoes traditional moralistic concerns about the corrupting influences of a violent and artistically impoverished youth culture. During a discussion of the *Friday the 13th* series, for example, slasher films are denounced not only for their misrepresentation of mental distress, but also for their violent anti-feminism, their graphic violence and the predictability of their plots (Wahl, 1995: 70). These judgements seem rather dismissive, however, of a whole genre of films. Wahl is quite right to bemoan the hackneyed and insulting recurrence of the figure of the 'insane murderer' in many violent horror films. Yet he goes a good deal further, expressing disgust with all such 'slasher' films and the frequency of violence in popular media texts. This response to the violence of these films is certainly not new; the same tendency is evident in earlier studies of mental illness and violence in horror film, such as Fleming and Manvell's *Images of Madness* (1985). But the *tout court* dismissal of the slasher subgenre ignores the potentially progressive aspects of these films, such as the survival of the 'final girl', which Clover (1992) regards as a progressive aspect of slasher films. Instead, the slasher film is derided as worthless, sensational and (the ultimate utilitarian insult) 'gratuitous'. Moreover, there is no allowance that violence might some-times be positive or even a progressive expression of social inequality (a point to which I shall return later). Finally, the related dismissal of the slasher film as 'predictable' is valid only if one regards predictability or repetitiveness as negative attributes. If one does so, however, then one must also, as Carol Clover (1992: 9) points out, discount many works of art, including most orally performed literature 'from the Greeks through to the late Middle Ages and beyond'. In the end, then, Wahl's criticism of the over-represented link between mental distress and violence is char-acterised by a rather bowdlerised conception of popular culture. While it is never as wholly negative about popular culture, *Media Madness*'s broadsides are sometimes too close for comfort to the Frankfurt School's dismissal of popular culture or even to the diatribes of the self-appointed conservative guardians of 'high culture', such as Allan Bloom (1987). There are distinct traces here of a conservative rhetoric of moral panic over popular culture.

Media Madness certainly presents a powerful case against the stigma-tisation of distress in popular texts; but greater attention to textual detail and to questions of cultural form would have ensured that popular culture was not homogenised and stigmatised in the process. Unfortunately, the somewhat over-generalised nature of Wahl's critique risks unintentional complicity with reactionary tirades against popular culture and may underestimate the progressive aspects of popular repre-sentations of mental distress – especially in often vilified genres such as horror film.

Reframing aggression: Reflections on the madness / violence debate

For many media critics, campaign groups and watchdogs, the most prob-lematic aspect of the media representation of madness is its frequent association with violence. This association has a long history. The heroes of the medieval romances are typically designated in Middle English by the adjective *wo(o)d*, derived from the Anglo-Saxon Woden, a god whose name, like that of his Norse equivalent Odin, connotes both madness and destructiveness. Today, all forms of media frequently present men-tally distressed people as violent. In film and television drama, for exam-ple, they are often presented as unpredictable (and often 'incurable') killers, sometimes with a remarkable degree of clinical implausibility. Such images may often create the misleading impression that people in psychological distress are to be feared (Wahl, 1995: 56–86). The Glasgow Media Group has made some of the most incisive investigations into the media's presentation of mental distress. In a content analysis, television and press reporting, magazines and children's literature as well as fictional television including soaps, films and dramas was studied for a period of one month. Philo (1999: 54) and his team concluded that

> Overall in the coverage, the category of 'violence to others' was by far the most common, outweighing the next most common ('advice') by a ratio of almost four to one. We also found that items linking mental illness and violence tended to receive 'headline' treatment, while more sympathetic items were largely 'back page' in their profile, such as problem page letters or health columns.

The group suggests that mental distress and violence are frequently associated, if not explicitly connected, in media texts. Put simply, one of the major contentions of anti-stigma discourse is that media images of madness imply a link, or at least a correlation between mental distress and violence that does not in fact exist.

Violence is undoubtedly a prominent feature of news reports that mention mental distress. Tabloid newspapers frequently label violent offenders 'psychos', whether or not mental distress is a factor in the story. Even when the reporting is not sensationalist, insanity is often headlined in news stories about violent acts. BBC1's 6pm television news bulletin on 25 February 2005, for example, reported how John Barrett, a paranoid schizophrenic, killed 'hours after he walked out of a secure psychiatric institution'. As this example suggests, arguments in the media about mental distress and violence often take a truncated or enthymemic form with the unspoken premise that people suffering from mental distress are more violent than others. Sometimes this premise is articulated explicitly. In July 2004, for instance, the conviction of Sion Jenkins for the murder of his foster daughter Billy Jo was quashed by the Court of Appeal (a second trial ended in acquittal in February 2006). In an ITV Lunchtime News interview on 16 July 2004, a friend of Mr Jenkins, canon Stuart Bell, averred that 'it would require somebody of dreadful psychiatric instability to commit the murder that led to Billy Jo's death', a remark supporting Jenkins' allegations that a 'schizophrenic' man had taken to wandering behind the Jenkins' family home prior to the murder.

In response to such media reporting, anti-stigma critics point to the lack of evidence linking mental distress to violence. Some critics even question why an individual's mental health status – as opposed to her age, height or socio-economic status – is mentioned at all in news reports of violent incidents (Shain and Phillips, 1991). Yet the picture is rather more complicated than this, since a correlation between some types of mental distress and violence *has* been demonstrated in several studies. Wahl, for example, fully acknowledges a body of American research showing a correlation between violent behaviour and diagnosed mental illness (Wahl, 1995: 79; Krakowski et al., 1988; Swanson, Holzer and Ganju, 1990; Link et al., 1992; Link and Stueve, 1994) and British research on the subject has returned similar findings (Shaw et al., 2006). Even psychiatric professionals eager to destigmatise madness cannot entirely deny the correlation. The Canadian Mental Health Association (2003), for example, notes that 'studies have found that the rate of violence (defined as threatening, hitting, fighting or otherwise hurting another person) for people with mental illness is 3 to 5 times the rate of the general public', while rightly pointing out that such figures must be adequately contextualised. Although they rightly de-emphasise the role of mental distress in absolute figures for violence and note that much of the violent behaviour of people with mental distress can be explained by co-factors such as substance misuse, Walsh and Fahy (2002) nonetheless acknowledge that patients with untreated 'psychotic illnesses' are statistically *relatively* more prone to violence than those without them: 'Our interpretation of these and other impressive epidemiological studies is that patients with psychotic illness alone have a modest increase in risk for violent behaviour.' Of course, as Wahl points out, a correlation is not a cause and there is no reason to assume that mentally distressed people who act violently always do so because of their condition. Yet the correlation between mental distress and violence cannot be ignored altogether; mental health professionals need to be aware, for example, that psychiatric patients may present an increased risk of violence, however small (Friedman, 2006: 2066). Responding to Walsh and Fahy's article, the medical researcher Tom Clark (2002), in a letter to the *British Medical Journal*, notes that 'an established association exists between mental disorder and violence that cannot be explained by cofactors.' While disagreeing with many of his other views about mental distress, it is hard to disagree with E. Fuller Torrey (1994) that a subgroup of people with severe mental distress is relatively more prone to violence than others.

This association is often disavowed, however, in academic and public debate. In an indignant letter published in the British regional newspaper the *Wrexham Mail*, John Reardon (2000) complains that the film

Me, Myself & Irene (Peter Farrelly and Bob Farrelly, 2000), which stars American comedian Jim Carrey as a violence-prone schizophrenic State Trooper, misunderstands psychiatric categories and reproduces stereotypes of violent insanity. The first complaint – that the film reproduces the popular confusion between schizophrenia and split personality – is certainly fair and justified from the standpoint of psychiatric classification. The second complaint – that the link between violence and mental distress is a 'great myth' – is more problematic. Here the letter-writer appeals to the corpus of psychiatric and sociological research on the subject: 'There has been no study to my knowledge', he states, 'that has shown that the rate of violence among the mentally ill varies significantly from that of the general population' (Reardon, 2000: 1). Even from a strictly psychiatric perspective, however, this is not quite true.

The suggestion that the mental distress-violence correlation is a 'great myth' appears even in the most *August Medical Journals*. The Walsh and Fahy editorial in the *British Medical Journal* reports that schizophrenics self-report violent episodes considerably more frequently than those with no psychiatric disorder, even when co-factors such as substance abuse are taken into account (Walsh and Fahy, 2002). Nevertheless, the editors themselves rather nervously avoid this potentially dangerous conclusion by entitling their piece 'Violence in society: contribution of mental illness is low'. In a world beset by terrorism and other forms of violence, it is certainly worth noting that the contribution of mentally distressed individuals to the statistics for total violence is minimal; nonetheless, this has little to do with whether the mentally distressed are *relatively* more violent than control groups. Similarly, Wahl (1995: 80) points to the undisputed yet somewhat irrelevant fact that the vast majority of those with mental distress are not physically violent.

Such slippages between relative and absolute statistics suggest that the empirical evidence showing a correlation between mental distress and violence is slightly embarrassing for anti-stigma critics. This may explain why the research on this matter is often passed over in silence. The Glasgow Media Group's (Philo, 1996) otherwise ground-breaking work on the media stereotyping of mental distress does not refer to sociological research on the relationship between violence and mental distress. Moreover, those commentators who *do* pronounce on the topic tend to sidestep uncomfortable findings. Thus a 1997 *Daily Telegraph* article quotes a statement made by the professor of psychiatry Louis Appleby that the threat posed by sufferers to the general public is 'largely a myth' and that 'most killings are in fact committed by people without mental illnesses' (Hall, 1997: 4). The equivocation of Appleby's first comment – that the threat to the public is 'largely' mythical – is hardly reassuring and the second point could be seen as a *non sequitur*. Well-intentioned as they are, neither of these points refutes the correlation between mental distress and physical violence. Other academic anti-stigma writers dismiss the correlation between mental distress and violence with only the most cursory reference to a single authority (Shain and Phillips, 1991: 71). Many critiques of the representation of mental distress, then – even those which take a seemingly hard-headed content analysis approach – seem to rely on dubious argumentation or a questionable representation of available evidence.

Even if one questions standard arguments about the link between mental distress and physical violence, however, one might still argue that the media *over-represents* mentally distressed people as violent, showing them as more violent than they are in real life. Wahl notes that 'the rare instance of a dramatic crime committed by a person with a mental illness is highly likely to make the papers' (1995: 85). This may explain why, in a survey of the German public, 64% said that they had read about a person with a mental illness who had committed a violent crime, and 50% about someone who became addicted to prescribed drugs, but only 17% had read about persons with mental illnesses who became able to lead a normal life by taking their medication (Hillert, Sandmann and Ehmig, 1999). Shain and Phillips's (1991) content analysis noted that mentally distressed people are over-represented as violent in news reports. However, the notion of over-representation must be clarified here. Many of the studies cited compare the incidence of stories about violent madness in the media with the incidence of violence in reality; unsurprisingly, they find that there is over-representation. Yet for this over-representation to have significance, one would have to show this over-representation to be greater than one would find in relation to individuals who *do not* have a diagnosed mental illness. It seems quite likely, after all, that individuals *without* a diagnosis of mental illness are *also* over-represented as violent in news reports, in accordance with the time-honoured news media principle: 'if it bleeds, it leads'. The same seems likely to be true of fictional media forms, in which both sufferers and non-sufferers are frequently presented as violent; indeed, since the 1960s the Cultural Indicators project has demonstrated the general over-representation of violence in the media (Signorielli, 1990; Perse, 2001: 198). In other words, individuals with mental distress may not be *uniquely* over-represented as violent; perhaps all we can safely conclude, therefore, is that violence is a major component of contemporary media culture and a prominent news value.

In view of these difficulties, it may be useful to widen the focus of the madness/violence debate. Following the Marxian precept that social life determines consciousness, we can consider violent thoughts and behaviour as the product not simply of personal derangement, but of social conditions. These conditions may relate to one's family context: it is well known, for instance, that those who physically or mentally abuse others have very commonly themselves been victims of violence (Lewis et al., 1988). There is also, as suggested in Chapter 1, a clear link between violence and poverty: physical and mental abuse, for example, is particularly common in low-income, 'low-status' families (James, 1995: 48; Godsi, 2004: 177). More generally, as also suggested above, people suffering with mental distress often belong to a lower social class than those who do not; their higher rates of violent behaviour might therefore be explained in terms of their frustration or anger at their lack of social power. A full discussion of this topic is beyond the compass of a book about media representations; but it is clear that anti-stigma critics should keep in mind the social contexts of violent mental distress.

Understanding violence as a response to social coercion is strategically useful, dislodging the stigmatising notion of violence as an individual act of evil. Such a politicised conception of violence is already common in cultural studies approaches to media analysis. As eager as any critic to find signs of 'resistance' in violent popular media texts, John Fiske (1989: 134) writes:

> Represented violence is popular (in a way that social violence is not) because it offers points of relevance to people living in societies where the power and resources are inequitably distributed and structured around lines of conflicting interests. Violence on television is a concrete representation of class (or other) conflict in society.

In many popular culture texts, too, this political dimension of madness is implicit, as a brief consideration of a well-known film will illustrate.

In Martin Scorsese's *Taxi Driver* (1976), Robert de Niro plays an ex-Vietnam veteran, Travis Bickle, who descends into violent paranoia. Bickle struggles to earn a living in a society which he sees as exploitative and decadent – although, *à la* Georg Simmel's 'The Metropolis and Mental Life' (1950), he remains outwardly cool and detached. Bickle is childlike and naïve, alienated from the sophisticated bourgeois milieu inhabited by the object of his infatuation, Betsy. He eventually finds relief from his alienation, however, through his heroic attempt to 'rescue' a prostitute, Iris. In the film's legendary 'mirror scene', Bickle addresses an imagined adversary while rehearsing acts of violence; he later vents his frustration at political hypocrisy by slowly kicking over a television set that is broadcasting a political debate. At the end of the film, Bickle shoots a presidential candidate and Iris's pimp, before turning his gun on himself.

Bickle is both homophobic and racist and his perverse heroism is tinged with a self-pitying supremacist fantasy of suffering whiteness (for a discussion of this theme in Hollywood 'muscle men' movies see Dyer, 1997). Nevertheless, the film sets his mental deterioration against the backdrop of a brutal urban jungle, so that neither the madness nor the violence appear simply as moral failings, but rather as responses to social alienation. In the background of the mirror scene, significantly, is a poster of the sanctimonious politician Charles Palatine, a representative of the privileged ranks from which Bickle is excluded. Bickle himself, meanwhile, places the blame for his violent inclinations onto others; as his voice-over in the mirror scene reminds us: 'here is a man who would not take it any more'. Like so many reactionaries, Bickle sees the solution to his plight in terms of a righteous outburst of violence against a society in which he can find no place for himself. This seems to be the reasoning of many mass murderers, from the Hungerford killer Michael Ryan to the Virginia Tech gunman, Seung-Hui Cho, who see furious revenge against a putatively 'corrupt' society as the ultimate solution to the cruelty or neglect they have experienced.

Bickle's vengeful violence is neither heroic nor excusable; yet it is evidently born out of frustration at his sense of powerlessness and alienation, in turn reflecting the anti-authoritarian ethos of 1970s Hollywood cinema. Moreover, as Judith Williamson (1986: 158) notes, despite the film's gory conclusion, its most violent image is not visual but verbal and is spoken by Scorsese in his cameo role as a jealous husband as he fantasises about exacting gruesome vengeance on his unfaithful wife. *Taxi Driver* thus raises the thorny question of whether Bickle is really any madder, or even more violent, than those around him. As R. D. Laing (1990: 27) put it long ago:

> When I certify someone insane, I am not equivocating when I write that he is of unsound mind, may be dangerous to himself and others, and requires care and attention in a mental hospital. However, at the same time, I am also aware that, in my opinion, there are other people who are regarded as sane, whose minds are as radically unsound,

who may be equally or more dangerous to themselves and others and whom society does not regard as psychotic and fit persons to be in a madhouse.

A politician, from this point of view, can be seen as a more irrational and dangerous individual than most of those given a psychiatric diagnosis. Furthermore, irrational violence is not only a feature of individual behaviour, but is integral to the structure of capitalist social relations, as film and media texts often show. In the British film *This Is England* (Shane Meadows, 2006), the psychological deterioration of the racist skinhead Combo and the senseless violence of his gang are presented alongside footage of the Falklands Conflict and suggestions that Combo may have experienced violence personally in the form of child abuse. The film thus gestures towards the interconnectedness of political/social violence and personal experiences of distress. In a world of class conflict and imperialist warfare, gang violence is understandable, if inexcusable. In still other cases – such as in self-defensive situations – the use of physical violence may indeed be morally justifiable, or even necessary as a tactic for resisting or overcoming injustice.

Whether in society or in media texts, however, provoked, defensive or resistive violence is seldom considered by anti-stigma writers – perhaps because such violence often, as in the films mentioned above, obliquely expresses working-class grievances that it is more comfortable to ignore. Instead, anti-stigma critics and campaigners tend to conceive of violence as a manifestation of evil: as one Internet anti-stigma campaigner opines: 'violence is not a result of mental illness, but a result of moral corruption' ('Violence and Mental Illness', 2002). Yet radical theorists have often pointed out that this is an unwarranted generalisation. As Reinhold Niebuhr (1941: 171–2) put it long ago in his classic work *Moral Man and Immoral Society*:

> one error is the belief that violence is a natural and inevitable expression of ill-will, and non-violence of goodwill, and that violence is therefore intrinsically evil and non-violence intrinsically good. While such a proposition has a certain measure of validity, or at least of plausibility, it is certainly not universally valid.

Violence can have many causes, not all of which imply moral corruption. As Niebuhr (1941: 176) goes on to point out, the equation of violence with immorality ignores both the violence of social oppression and the possibilities of violence as a legitimate response to it (see also

Franks, 2006: 142–3). As Slavoj Žižek (2008b: 174) writes, 'to chastise violence outright, to condemn it as "bad", is an ideological operation par excellence, a mystification which collaborates in rendering invisible the fundamental forms of social violence.' The premise that violent people are inherently evil is often exploited by the tabloid media; but that is hardly grounds for anti-stigma critics to accept it as the basis for their own arguments.

Indeed, I would argue that anti-stigma writers yield too much ground to their opposition: having assumed that violence (and illegality – see Wahl, 1995: 18) is a priori undesirable, nothing remains for them but to doggedly deny any correlation between mental disturbance and violence. Critics in this field tend to rely on an uninterrogated definition of violence as interpersonal physical aggression and they see this, through the lens of an absolutist deontology, as necessarily immoral. This rather attenuated liberal definition of violence, however, might be extended to encompass not only individual acts of aggression – justified or otherwise – but also non-physical, structural or institutional forms of coercion such as verbal abuse, imprisonment or unemployment – forms of violence that are congealed as 'constituted power' (Hardt and Negri, 2000) and to which the mentally distressed are themselves often subject. As Karen Boyle (1999: 9), drawing on the work of Suzanne Kappeler, writes:

> Violence – on and off screen – is an interactional *behaviour* not an isolated, individualised *act*. On-screen, as in life, violent behaviours are not confined to physical blows, but include verbal abuse, harassment, intimidation, threats, imprisonment and other behaviours by which the abuser enforces – or reinforces – their power and control of others.

Violence can therefore have social as well as interpersonal manifestations and can have coercive or liberatory force. Further distinctions can be made here. The question of whether violence is rewarded or punished, for example, further complicates the critical evaluation of mediated violence; Donnerstein, Slaby and Eron (1994) have suggested that media representations of violent acts that are unjustified yet rewarded are more likely to be imitated. As David Trend (2007: 4–5) writes:

> It matters what type of character commits the violence, why, and with what kind of consequence. Is the violence committed by a hero or a "good guy"? Is the action justified or rewarded? Does the violence cause pain and suffering? [...] Do we sympathise with the victim?

The implications of some of these points can be illustrated by a concrete example. A German study (Angermeyer and Matschinger, 1995) showed that media reports of two attempts on the lives of prominent politicians by persons with a 'mental disorder' led to a marked increase in 'negative' attitudes among the public towards mentally distressed people. The study ignores, however, the ideological context of the attacks. It is highly likely that the capitalist media will report attacks on politicians in a negative way no matter who the perpetrators are, given the high esteem in which the media generally hold politicians. From a perspective which understands capitalist politicians as the representatives of a structurally violent system, however, the motivation for such attacks seems more understandable. To be clear, this observation serves neither to excuse nor endorse assaults upon politicians; it simply demands that one be sensitive to *who* is violent, *towards whom* and *in what context*. Media representations of violence cannot be understood in isolation from social and institutional structures and the ideological investments of media organisations.

Adopting a more expansive definition of violence might help to eradicate the moral blame attached to the violent actions of distressed individuals. Only by understanding and – where appropriate – destigmatising violence itself can we understand and destigmatise the violence that is sometimes perpetrated by mentally distressed persons. It should be possible, then, for anti-stigma critics to accept that mental distress *does* correlate with violence and that this acceptance *does not* necessarily entail a negative moral judgement upon sufferers.

Of course, some media representations of violent madness do indeed warrant condemnation. In an episode of Stephen King's gothic mini series *Kingdom Hospital* shown on British television (BBC2, 8 August 2004), a sadistic doctor called Klaus Gottreich is referred to as a 'lunatic' and 'totally insane' and as having 'certain theories about pain'. Klaus is a cardboard cut-out monster, rather than a 'realistically' drawn character with understandable psychological motivations; there is no justification for his actions. Although Klaus is ultimately punished, the presentation of his madness is problematic, since it connects 'insane violence' with evilness. One may contrast this with a scene that occurs towards the end of David Cronenberg's film *Spider*, in which Clegg, the delusional 'schizophrenic' protagonist, enters the bedroom of his landlady at night with a hammer, before realising that his intended victim is not the 'evil stepmother' he mistakes her for. The abject Clegg elicits our sympathy throughout the film, however, and his potential act of violence is intelligible in the light of his profound mental confusion.

Clearly, then, the ethical acceptability of media images of 'mad' violence is highly context-dependent and possibly quite hard to determine. For example, an episode of the American television drama *Medium* (BBC1, 6 December 2005) centres on a series of interviews conducted by the psychic heroine, Allison, with a doctor who has been incarcerated in an insane asylum for the rape and murder of a female patient. The doctor suffers from auditory hallucinations; 'they used to call them possessed', the doctor's psychiatrist observes sardonically. It transpires, however, that the doctor is not mad, but is indeed possessed by an 'evil soul'. The drama's initial association of mental distress with unprovoked violence is problematic from an anti-stigma standpoint. On the other hand, the revelation that the murderer is possessed rather than mad throws doubt upon the psychiatrist's glib assumption that the doctor's violent behaviour is reducible to mental distress and could therefore be argued to undermine the common sense equation of madness with badness. It is not entirely clear, therefore, how the audience is intended to 'read' the doctor's mental distress, especially after his diagnosis is retracted. Clearly, evaluating fictional media representations of madness and violence is often far from straightforward.

The foregoing discussion may have methodological as well as hermeneutical implications, since the contextualisation that is needed to interpret examples of screen violence is not always in evidence in quantitative content analysis approaches. Content analyses investigating the prevalence of violence in the media have tended to extract categorical content from the contexts which give it meaning (for further critiques of the potentially abstract nature content analysis, see Sumner, 1979; Dyer, 1982; McKee, 2003). The cross-media content analysis research of the Glasgow Media Group (1996), for example, distinguishes between 'Violence towards self' and 'Violence towards others'; but these discriminations do not take account of the formal, narrative and ideological complexities that invariably shape the meaning of any particular textual example.

The problem with 'accuracy': Beyond psychiatric verisimilitude

So far this chapter has pointed to some of the pitfalls of anti-stigma media criticism, which can be over-generalised, tends to derogate popular culture and is premised upon a rather abstract, individualistic and depoliticised conception of violence. Another, related problem is that it often overvalues the importance of medical accuracy, treating media texts as psychiatric case studies rather than complex cultural symbols. Psychiatric criticism typically judges media stereotypes of madness as 'incorrect' or 'mythical', while ignoring the wider thematic and ideological dimensions of the text – rather like the literal-minded historian who evaluates a costume drama solely in terms of its fidelity to the archival record. According to the typical terms of anti-stigma criticism, media stereotypes of the violent or social incompetent mad person must be rooted out and replaced with more 'accurate' images of the mentally distressed as competent and independent subjects. This is a rather inflexible critical strategy, in which cultural prejudice is sought out and nominated for replacement by psychiatric truth. For a number of years now, however, media critics have expressed impatience with stereotype research; as Martin Barker (1989: 206) rather wearily put it 20 years ago, the search for media stereotypes has become 'a small industry in its own right'. Since the myth-busting approach to media representations of mental distress has become hegemonic, it seems timely to raise some difficulties with this general paradigm.

Much of the recent theorising about stereotypes has emphasised the dangers of prizing verisimilitude or 'truth to life' as the sole criterion for judging the validity of media images. Myra Macdonald (1995: 14) writes that

> There are [...] a number of problems in relying on stereotypes as a critical tool. First, this approach suggests that the ideal would be for the media to re-present reality as truthfully and accurately as possible. [...] This begs at least two questions: whose version of reality is to be given priority, and what happens in those instances, such as advertising or film, where the producer's intention is not to represent reality but to conjure up an appealing fantasy world.

As Macdonald implies, one cannot and should not assume that realism is among the aims of any media text. Beyond the concern with realism, we must also consider how madness functions narratively and metaphorically. As already suggested, madness in many narrative fictions symbolises social alienation or political resistance, even in genres that anti-stigma critics have typically vilified, such as horror film. Indeed, the question of verisimilitude overlaps with considerations of cultural value. Because psychiatric critics often conceive of realism as the royal road to representational accuracy, broadly realist films such as *Shine* (Scott Hicks, 1996) or *A Beautiful Mind* (Ron Howard, 2001) have garnered significant critical acclaim and are typically said to offer 'serious' studies of mental distress. Yet it would be wrongheaded to dismiss the representation of madness in 'fantastical' films such as *Donnie Darko* (Richard Kelly, 2001) or *Gothika* (Mathieu Kassovitz, 2003) simply because these films eschew a realist aesthetic. The symbolic import of madness in these films, as I argue later, exceeds and to some extent contests psychiatric discourse, metaphorising madness as social or political subversion. The narrow focus on realism leads to what the Marxist theorist Ernst Bloch (1995) terms 'half-enlightenment' – a rationalistic dismissal of all mystification and superstition that confounds scientific criteria. For Bloch, half-enlightenment deludes itself that truth can be obtained solely by eliminating error rather than showing what is positive and attractive about problematic ideologies or texts. A more adequate mode of critique, in Bloch's view, identifies distortions in an ideological text, but then goes on to read that text closely for critical salience or liberatory potential.

Too keen an emphasis upon 'accuracy', moreover, can result in the creation of new stereotypes that fail to acknowledge the inevitable differences within any minority group. I shall argue later that while films such as *Shine* and *A Beautiful Mind* have presented new, upbeat and celebratory narratives of madness, they also tend to present recovery from madness as an all-too-triumphant breakthrough into truth and enlightenment. In the light of this, it is important to consider the possible outcomes of a total purge of 'negative' media images of madness. As Ella Shohat and Robert Stam (1994: 204) saltily remark:

> The privileging of positive images also elides the patent differences, the social and moral heteroglossia (Bahktin's term signifying 'many-languagedness'), characteristic of any group. A cinema of contrivedly positive images betrays a lack of confidence in the group portrayed, which usually itself has no illusions concerning its own perfection.

Shohat and Stam are pointing here to what Pierre Machery calls the 'normative fallacy', as described by Homi Bhabha (1984: 105):

> [T]he demand that one image should circulate rather than another is made on the basis that the stereotype is distorted in relation to a given norm or model. It results in a mode of prescription criticism which Macherey has conveniently termed the 'normative fallacy', because it privileges an ideal 'dream-image' in relation to which the text is judged.

In the same vein, Judith Williamson (1986: 158) highlights the potential dangers of worthiness in 'progressive cinema', asking:

> Should films show the world as it ought to be or as it is? For what seems to be demanded more nowadays by those with ideals of liberation is a cinema of the superego: as if to make a 'sensitive' or 'progressive' film now, you have to show people *being* sensitive and progressive.

From their rather different perspectives, all of these critics raise doubts about whether unsympathetic media depictions of marginalised social groups are *always* unwelcome. Jack Nicholson's Obsessive Compulsive Disorder (OCD) sufferer in *As Good As It Gets* (James L. Brooks, 1997), for example, is a homophobic, hence unlikeable character. Yet does this in itself make it an unacceptable image of distress – especially as media images of madness are, in general, increasingly sympathetic? The concern here is that the wholesale eradication of one set of stigmatising images may lead to the normalisation of other, equally stereotyped 'positive' images.

In seeking to overcome this representational dilemma there may be theoretical lessons to be learned from the paradigm shifts that transformed anti-sexist and anti-racist cultural studies in the 1970s. In the wake of its second wave, for instance, feminism had to accommodate various challenges to the binaristic framework of 'good/accurate' and 'bad/inaccurate' images that had theretofore prevailed (Pollock, 1977). By introducing the notion of 'difference' and challenging essentialist definitions of femininity, post-structuralism provided a theoretical framework for thinking about issues of representation beyond these polarities – even if this shift has itself proved deeply problematic (Fenton, 2000). Similarly, cultural practitioners and critics concerned with the representation of visible minorities struggled for many years under the yoke of the 'burden of representation', which involved an unusually intense obligation – conspicuous in the social-issue content and documentary-realist style of the 1960s and 1970s 'cinema of duty' (Bailey, 1990–1991) – to represent every aspect of minority experience 'correctly' and 'responsibly'. More recently, however, as some of the burden of representational correctness has lifted, cultural explorations of ethnic identity have escaped the confines of social realism and are increasingly mediated through popular generic forms, such as romantic comedy, resulting in hybridised, even internally contradictory representations of racial identity (Malik, 1996). In the same way, studies of

images of mental distress cannot rest upon essentialist psychiatric definitions of mental distress that take no account of the differences between
sufferers in terms of, for example, class, gender, race or even personal
morality: it is perhaps no bad thing, indeed, if *some* mentally distressed
characters in film and television dramas, for example, are unsympathetic. The task of media criticism is not to replace one set of images of
the mentally distressed with another or to expect every media representation of mental distress to conform to a preconceived representational
paradigm, but to understand how images of madness are differentially
inflected in ideological ways.

Prizing verisimilitude as the sole criterion for judging the validity of
media images also risks neglecting questions of mediation. As Shohat
and Stam note (1994: 178):

> While these 'stereotypes and distortions' analyses pose legitimate
> questions about social plausibility and mimetic accuracy, about neg-
> ative and positive images, they are often premised on an exclusive
> allegiance to an esthetic of verisimilitude. An obsession with 'real-
> ism' casts the question as simply one of 'errors' and 'distortions', as
> if the 'truth' of a community were unproblematic, transparent, and
> easily accessible, and 'lies' about that community easily unmasked.

The allegation of 'misrepresentation' begs the question of who is warranted to vouchsafe the truth about madness. Appeals to notions of
'real' or 'true' madness in order to provide the 'missing' information
ignore the contexts of production and consumption that necessarily
shape media representations of distress. As Michael Pickering (2001: 15)
puts it in his book *Stereotyping*:

> The provision of additional information is not in itself a wrong
> move, but it cannot be offered as a guarantee of the reality of what
> has otherwise been falsely represented. While the definition of that
> reality is always part of what is at stake in any construction of it,
> the necessary struggle over the meanings of cultural representations
> cannot depend on straightforward appeals to empirical truth out-
> side the circuits of interpretation in which they are mediated and
> negotiated.

Since mental distress is constructed partly through the media, we cannot
simply smash through the media's ideological mystifications to reveal

the truth about it. As Žižek (1999: 47–9) reminds us, ideology is consti-
tutive of reality, rather than a screen separating us from it; thus madness
is always already ideologically constructed through psychiatric, media
and other cultural discourses.

Critical realists are often troubled by the supposedly anti-realist implications of such arguments. Interestingly, one of the keenest critics of
stigmatising images of madness – Greg Philo – has also been one of
most vocal critics of post-structuralist understandings of the status of
truth as a discursive effect (Philo and Miller, 2000). Philo argues that
post-structuralists want to put the skids under truth, a long-familiar
charge among radical critics of postmodernism (Callinicos, 1989: 145–7;
Eagleton, 1996). I would agree that the slipperiness of truth in much
post-structuralist theory is deeply problematic. Moreover, in the mid
1990s the concerns of these critical realists were understandable, particularly in relation to the anti-realist polemics of Jean Baudrillard (1994),
which at that time held near-canonical status in cultural studies. Yet
the caveat that truth is always ideologically/discursively inflected does
not constitute a rejection of truth claims. As I have shown in my earlier discussion of the correlation between mental distress and violence,
the evaluation of empirical evidence about mental distress is important;
nonetheless, we must also recognise that media images of distress are
discursively conditioned rather than simple distortions or reflections of
biomedical truths.

Finally, I shall conclude this section by registering a quite practical objection to the assumption that media images of madness should
conform to psychiatric criteria: namely, that the dissemination of the
medical model does not necessarily reduce the stigma of mental distress.
In his assessment of the pros and cons of using the 'illness model' of
mental distress, Len Bowers (2000: 158) suggests that the medical model
'facilitates the treatment of "mental illness" in a non-stigmatising,
humane manner'. Yet the evidence to support this assertion is far from
unambiguous. The medicalisation of distress has been argued by Kirk
and Kutchins (1999), for example, to increase the stigmatisation of sufferers; some research even suggests that 'doctors stigmatize psychiatric
patients more than the general public do' (Lawrie, 1999: 129). Farina
et al. (1978) and Fisher and Farina (1979) showed that those with psychological problems who conceptualise themselves as having a 'disease'
are more likely than those who do not to feel helpless about their
recovery and to abuse drugs or alcohol. Evidence from electric-shock
experiments, meanwhile, suggests that while the public is less likely to

blame sufferers with disease diagnoses, they tend to treat them more harshly than those who have been given psychosocial explanations for their problems (Mehta and Farina, 1997). More recently, a review article by John Read et al. (2006) also challenges the assumption that the 'mental illness is an illness like any other' approach is the most effective way to tackle stigmatisation. Read et al. note that 'knowledge' about mental distress is often equated with the espousal of an illness paradigm. Through a meta-analysis of international research, however, they show that most members of the public prefer psychosocial explanations of distress to biogenetic ones and that biogenetic beliefs and diagnostic labelling are positively related to prejudice, fear and a desire for distance from the mentally distressed. They conclude that anti-stigma campaigns should avoid decontextualised biogenetic explanations as well as terms like 'disease' and 'illness'. Accordingly, I avoid these terms in this book, preferring to situate media images of madness in their social, political, formal and generic contexts rather than measuring them against medical definitions.

Conclusions

Set against the many well-intentioned analyses that several media critics have provided to help combat undesirable representations of those with mental distress, the arguments advanced in this chapter may seem churlish. Nonetheless, I hope to have suggested here that there are some quite serious problems with the anti-stigma paradigm, most of which relate to its lack of attention to questions of social power, ideology and difference. I have argued here for the need to re-examine the theoretical basis of anti-stigma criticism. Research in this area needs to take more honest account of the evidence about the correlation between mental distress and violence. Anti-stigma critics would also, I believe, benefit from widening their often rather narrow definition of violence. This is not to argue that the association between mental distress and violence is never problematic; it is simply a plea for more adequate contextualisation of media images of violent madness. Moreover, critics should not make violence – even violence towards others – the *sole* category by which they judge media texts, irrespective of those texts' formal, generic and narrative features. I have also suggested here that existing critiques of images of madness are over-reliant on psychiatric verisimilitude as the criterion for judging representational acceptability – a concern compounded by research suggesting that biomedical understandings of mental distress may not, in any case, reduce stigmatisation. In view of the problematic nature of the psychiatric understanding of madness, we must scrutinise carefully the premises and conclusions of the prevailing arguments about the stigmatisation of mental distress, linking discussions of representational accuracy to wider considerations of power and ideology.

3
The Suffering Screen: Cinematic Portrayals of Mental Distress

Madness has always held a popular appeal as a visual spectacle. In medieval culture, the 'difference' of the madman (madness was largely a male preserve in the literature of the period) was often figured forth bodily. Like Nebuchadnezzar – the biblical king transformed into an ox as a punishment for his sin of pride – the mad heroes of the Middle Ages often metamorphosed into animals, as in the medieval Celtic legend *Buile Suibhne*, or, like King Herod in the medieval mystery plays, ranted and raved in the streets. In fact, as Foucault (2001: 65) notes, up until the nineteenth century, mentally distressed people were considered 'monsters' – that is, etymologically, 'beings or things to be shown'. As is well known, this literary objectification of madness was paralleled by early modern institutional practices. At London's Bedlam hospital in the eighteenth century, for instance, the insane could be viewed in their cells for a sum of money and the spectacularity of madness was often reflected in ballads about distracted folk heroes and heroines (Porter, 1987).

In an increasingly visual culture, people are likely to form their understanding of mental distress through its cinematic figurations. This might give us cause for concern, since contemporary cinema can be seen as continuing the historical othering of madness. Just as the popular media typically exaggerate certain behavioural and sartorial distinctions between men and women in order to reify gender difference, so cinema often stresses the senses in which mentally distressed people look and act differently to others. Over time, filmmakers and audiences have thus developed quite particular expectations of how mad characters ought to look. Otto Wahl (1995: 38) describes how patients at Oregon State Hospital were considered for walk-on parts as asylum patients in the classic anti-psychiatry film *One Flew Over*

the Cuckoo's Nest. The film's production team famously decided, however, that these patients were not sufficiently 'mad-looking' for the
parts and they were not cast for the film. The stereotype of wild-eyed
and erratic mad people anticipated by the casting team of *One Flew
Over the Cuckoo's Nest* ultimately rests, of course, upon ancient cultural traditions outlined above. As suggested in Chapter 2, however,
one must also consider texts about mental distress in relation to their
immediate generic contexts. Drawing on an analysis of characterisa-
tion and narrative structure, each section of this chapter investigates
how a single genre typically represents the causes, manifestations and
treatments of distress and how sympathetically each genre represents
mentally distressed characters. Horror film has often been seen as the
most problematic cinematic genre and I therefore devote a section of
this chapter to its discussion. In addition, I shall consider the representation of mental distress in drama, comedy, romance and action adventure
films, since these genres are the most popular with audiences of all types
(Fischoff, Antonio and Lewis, 1998). I shall also examine the biopic,
which has become an extremely popular subgenre of film drama in
recent years.

Overall, the chapter supports the argument of Jacqueline Zimmerman
(2003), whose historical survey of Hollywood films concludes that
cinema has generally treated mad characters sympathetically. On the
other hand, Zimmerman pays little attention to the ways in which
images of madness are filtered through the discursive lenses of class, gender and race. A consideration of these categories, I argue, yields rather
less optimistic conclusions.

Truly, madly, deeply: Mental distress in the romantic drama

Perhaps more than other film genre, romantic drama illustrates the life-
affirming yet problematic nature of contemporary cinematic narratives
of distress. Following the enormous success of *When Harry Met Sally*
(Rob Reiner, 1989), romantic drama enjoyed a resurgence in popularity
during the 1990s. The representation of mental distress in these films
brings the politics of gender, in particular, into sharp focus. In Mike
Figgis's *Mr Jones* (1993), for example, Richard Gere plays a bipolar man
who is 'saved' by the love of his female psychiatrist, Libbie. The film
evinces a remarkably detailed understanding of bipolar disorder and its
treatment; but it also illustrates a problem alluded to in Chapter 2 –
namely, the tendency to sanitise madness through the narrative trope
of redemption: the blossoming romance between Mr Jones and Libbie

at the end of the film implies that sanity can be restored through the power of romantic love.

The same message is conveyed in two highly successful mid-1990s mental distress films: *Shine* – in which pianist David Helfgott emerges from a severe mental breakdown caused by creative exhaustion and paternal abuse with the help of his partner – and the Obsessive Compulsive Disorder (OCD) comedy *As Good As It Gets* (James L. Brooks, 1997). A variation on the theme is offered in Nick Cassevette's *She's So Lovely* (1997), in which the impulsive Eddie Quinn leaves a psychiatric facility in which he has been imprisoned for shooting a policeman to rescue his ex-wife from her boorish and violent new partner. The treatment of mental distress in *Shine* and *She's So Lovely*, in particular, is generally progressive: both films imply that those with diagnosed mental illnesses are kinder and gentler than many of the people around them. Moreover, all of these films suggest that romantic love may offer sanctuary from alienated social relations or abuse. Indeed, it seems commonsensical to suppose that the experience of love may help many people to overcome some forms of psychological distress, although the implication that serious mental distress can be resolved through the love of a good woman has proved less than convincing to psychiatrists (Rosen and Walter, 2000). The distribution of this theme is also notably determined by gender: while the male heroes of these films manage to combine psychiatric 'breakthrough' and romantic success, film heroines, as we shall see later, are generally less fortunate.

This gender distinction is particularly apparent in the myriad teen-romance melodramas that followed in the wake of Fox's successful early-1990s American teen television drama *Beverly Hills 90210*. The 'troubled', alienated teen is, of course, a staple character type in the teen-romance genre (Banks, 2004); many of these troubled teens are female – well-known television examples include Jen Lindley in *Dawson's Creek* (WB, 1998–2003) and Marissa Cooper in *The O.C.* (Fox, 2003–2007) – so that female mental distress can be said to be a particular thematic concern of the genre. Yet compared to their male counterparts, these film characters often seem insipid, tragic or helpless.

In *Mad Love* (Antonia Bird, 1995), bipolar Casey is broken out of a 'secure' psychiatric unit by her straight-laced boyfriend Matt in an act of rebellion against stifling parental and psychiatric authority. The couple determine – to paraphrase their own words – to 'make their own rules'. While on the run, the couple steal a car and drive recklessly towards Mexico – a location associated, not least through iconic films such as *Thelma and Louise* (Ridley Scott, 1992), with freedom from the restrictions of American society. Rebellion is overtaken by realism, however, when Casey's depression deepens. After some brief telephone conversations with Casey's mother, Matt comes to accept that his girl-friend's increasingly erratic behaviour requires psychiatric intervention and the couple eventually decide to return to the hospital where Casey's family and psychiatrists are anxiously waiting. In the remarkably simi-lar *Crazy/Beautiful* (John Stockwell, 2001), Kirsten Dunst plays a spoiled rich girl, Nicole, who falls in love with a talented and industrious, yet poor, Latino boy, Carlos. Nicole fears inheriting the psychological con-dition that lead to her mother's suicide (and subsequently to her father remarrying to Nicole's icily aloof stepmother). Carlos is torn between his love for the highly erratic Nicole and his ambition to perform well at school and eventually to enter the United States Naval Academy. Over time, however, Carlos becomes a steadying influence upon Nicole and enables her to live a happier life.

There are some differences between the heroines of the films dis-cussed here. While Casey in *Mad Love* has serious psychological prob-lems, *Crazy/Beautiful*'s Nicole seems less-psychologically disturbed than simply rebellious, seemingly in response to her uncaring stepmother and her distant, neglectful father. In conversation with Carlos, Nicole's father reveals that his daughter has attempted suicide several times, yet these attempts are not depicted. In fact, the only visible indication of Nicole's psychological distress in the film occurs near the beginning, when she takes her medication. Both *Mad Love* and *Crazy/Beautiful*, however, frame the heroine's distress in terms of passionate emotional excess that transgresses adult norms.

In both films, too, any transgressive potential in the elopement is quickly contained. Casey's voluntary return to the hospital in *Mad Love* is arguably appropriate given her level of distress; yet there can be no doubt that her headstrong rebelliousness has been defeated. In *Crazy/Beautiful*, meanwhile, 'mad' rebellion is recuperated through a particularly conservative narrative closure: Nicole is reunited with her father and Carlos makes the transition from ambitious outsider to pro-tector of the state by joining the Annapolis Naval Academy as a pilot. Both films end, then, with the reunion of the biological family and the endorsement of other institutional forms of authority, from psy-chiatry to the military. Similarly, in Peter Werner's television movie *On the Edge of Innocence* (1997), a 'mad' teenage couple who slough off parental and psychiatric authority are ultimately forced to recog-nise their illnesses and face up to their responsibilities. Like modern-day morality plays, all of these films use the theme of madness to illustrate the irresponsibility of teenage transgression – and particularly of errant femininity.

A similarly didactic message is discernable in the Australian film *Angel Baby* (Michael Rymer, 1995), which charts the course of a passionate romance between a young schizophrenic couple, Harry and Kate, which initially seems to challenge bourgeois norms, before coming up against several harsh realities. Harry and Kate determine to live autonomously and to raise a child together, against the advice of their close family members (Harry's brother and sister-in-law) and psychiatric professionals. Eventually the couple decide to stop taking their anti-psychotic medication and to break out of a psychiatric institution, a decision that ultimately has tragic consequences.

The film certainly presents mental distress sympathetically. Harry is thoughtful and 'good with children', as his strong relationship with his nephew suggests. Moreover, the presentation of two schizophrenics sharing a romantic relationship is commendable, as mentally distressed people in films are often presented as alienated individuals. At the same time, the film's unusual musical score, which includes Arab music and other 'world music' from David Byrne and Brian Eno, encourages us to read the couple's relationship as mildly idiosyncratic. As the film progresses, several scenes foreground the peculiarity of the schizophrenic couple in the eyes of well-meaning psychiatric professionals and family. When Harry first takes Kate to his brother and sister-in-law's house for a meal, for example, the conventional social awkwardness of the situation is exacerbated by Kate's lack of proficiency with her cutlery. Chatting after the meal, meanwhile, a breathlessly manic Kate shocks Harry's sister-in-law with the information that Harry is 'the best lay I've ever had. I swear he's got a sideways movement from hell. If you strapped electrodes to his nuts he could light up the city'. Kate, in particular, is indifferent towards the etiquette of polite society and, by extension, distinctions of social class. Thus *Angel Baby* is a kindly yet critical treatment of a couple's ill-fated desire to live like 'ordinary' people. Harry's brother and sister-in-law attempt to sanitise Harry and Kate's relationship by inducting them into middle-class values and practices. While Harry and Kate are treated sympathetically by most of the film's characters, however, the film nonetheless slowly shifts our sympathies towards the long-suffering relatives and the medical authorities as the couple begin to endanger themselves through increasingly reckless behaviour.

Ultimately, the film judges the relationship between the two schizophrenics to be doomed. While Kate's baby is born, Kate dies during labour, consistent with the tragic destiny of many women in mental distress films, such as *The Hours* (Stephen Daldry, 2002) and *Sylvia* (Christine Jeffs, 2003) – and, incidentally, in many non-Western films about mental distress, such as the Japanese film *Picnic* (Shunji Iwai, 1996). In the final scene of the film, Harry contemplates jumping from a bridge that the couple used to visit. Despite its romantic theme and its initially sympathetic view of the young lovers, then, *Angel Baby* finally emphasises the dangers of ignoring medical counsel and depicts the dire consequences of ceasing or refusing medication. As the promotional tagline for *Angel Baby* puts it, the schizophrenic couple are: 'In Love, In Deep, In Danger'. For all the film's charm, the unmistakable message is that prospective 'mad lovers' – like the teenage protagonists in *Mad Love* and *Crazy/Beautiful* – must heed the advice of psychiatric authority or suffer severe punishment. The same premise governs the remarkably similar British romance *Some Voices* (Simon Cellan Jones, 2000), whose promotional tagline warns that 'love is not the only drug'. My point here is not that psychiatric intervention is always oppressive, either in film or in reality; it is simply that psychiatric imperatives loom large in romantic film drama – and that female characters seem to bear the greater part of the responsibility for observing them.

Aleks Horvat's character-driven drama *Sweethearts* (1996) reproduces many of the key themes of romantic dramas about mental distress, albeit slightly more progressively. The narrative of the film centres on a blind date between Arliss, a conservative neurotic in his early 30s seeking his 'ideal woman' and a rapid-cycle bipolar sufferer, Jasmine, a thoughtful and witty woman who – to Arliss's understandable concern – turns up to the date carrying a gun. During their conversation in the 'Asylum' bar, Jasmine explains that she sees her madness as an integral part of her identity and discusses the intricacies of her psyche. Indeed, the film's presentation of mental distress is highly self-consciousness. Although Jasmine has recourse to the medical model to explain her condition ('essentially, it's a chemical imbalance in the brain'), she also criticises drug therapies, complaining to Arliss that the side effects of the various drugs she has tried 'are just as bad as the episodes themselves'. The film also counters what anti-stigma campaigners hold to be the stereotypical association between mental distress and aggressive violence to others, when it transpires that Jasmine intends to use her gun on herself rather than Arliss.

Sweethearts refuses the conventional happy ending of the teen romance. Jasmine vows throughout the evening to kill herself the following day, although both Arliss and the audience are unsure at the end of the film as to whether she has gone through with her pledge. This indeterminate ending may explain why *Sweethearts* was never released theatrically and instead went straight to video. Classical Hollywood romantic dramas, from *Gone With The Wind* to *Casablanca*, featured complex and even downbeat narrative closures; yet contemporary romantic cinema has normalised the happy ending and filmmakers ignore this generic convention at their peril. Indeed, while the film offers an unusual take on the theme of 'mad love', the commercial fate of *Sweethearts* bespeaks the difficulty of delivering atypical narratives of mental distress in the post-classical period of film-making. Moreover, despite its thought-provoking indeterminacy and its awareness of its own status as a 'mental distress film', *Sweethearts* nonetheless reproduces the stereotype of the tragic heroine. It is true that, alive or dead, Jasmine leaves a positive legacy for Arliss, who ends the film disturbed by events, but less emotionally repressed and more accommodating towards women who do not conform to his 'ideal type' of partner; yet Jasmine's possible suicide reinforces an unfortunately common sexist motif of romantic film drama.

Enter the auteurs: Korine, Kerrigan, Cronenberg

In contrast to the narrative and thematic conventionality of romance drama, 'authored' drama films in recent years have offered some extremely challenging and ideologically complex images of madness; some of these merit fuller and perhaps slightly deeper textual analysis here. In itself, of course, auteurism is no guarantee of ideological progressiveness. It is true that, following the break-up of the studio system in the 1960s, writer-directors increasingly created idiosyncratic visions that often exploited mental distress for satirical purposes; Stanley Kubrick's *Dr Strangelove* (1964) is the pre-eminent example. Yet while cinematic images of mental distress became more fragmented and subjective in nature, they were not always more progressive in their presentation of mental distress: Roman Polanski's *Repulsion* (1965), whose frigid, hysterical and violent heroine begins to imagine the walls of her apartment crumbling around her, is a case in point. Many recent films directed by auteurs explore mad masculinity with equally startling if politically dubious results.

Harmony Korine's *Julien Donkey-Boy* (1999) is a grainy film shot mainly on hand-held cameras, mostly according to the tenets of the Dogme 95 group. Played by Ewen Bremner, Julien is a 'schizophrenic' in a dysfunctional working-class family consisting of a domineering and abusive father – a German émigré played by Werner Herzog – a brother who dreams of being a professional wrestler and a sister who is pregnant with Julien's child. Julien's identification as a donkey, like the avian twitching of the hero of Alan Parker's *Birdy* (1984), signals his alienation from human society through the ancient trope of bestial transformation.

Bremner based his portrayal of Julien on his meeting with Korine's schizophrenic uncle Eddie and he convincingly mimics the rapid delivery and obsessive patterns of 'schizophrenic' speech. Korine's disorientating jump cuts and sequences of still shots create a fractured collage of images that reflects both Julien's psychological chaos and the mayhem of his family life. Discussing the editing techniques of the French New Wave, Fuery (2004: 86) notes that the jump cut disrupts the established sequence of montage and therefore 'stands for [...] psychosis', rather as the schizophrenic's invention of new words represents her construction of her fractured world. The jump cut invites us to experience the protagonist's mental state, so that 'the spectator is more like the psychotic who enters this world order (and there understands it), and less like the analyst who attempts to distance himself/herself from the created world order (who attempts to interpret it).'

Despite the superficial incoherence of the narrative, certain key themes emerge in *Julien Donkey-Boy*, including a critique of the schizophregenic family, recalling R. D. Laing's (1965) attribution of schizophrenia to familial dysfunction, and of phallocratic tyranny. In contrast with Julien's bullying father, the women in the film – Julien's fondly remembered dead mother and his sister – are nurturing and supportive. In a particularly moving scene, Julien talks on the telephone to his sister, who disturbingly pretends to be their dead mother. The film also frequently cuts to a grainy image of a graceful ice skater, which seemingly represents Julien's idealised memory of his mother (the recurring image of the ice skater seems to have been borrowed from Kinugasa Teinosuke's 1926 avant-garde film *A Page of Madness*, a film which darts even more bewilderingly between objective and subjective worlds).

As well as attempting to reproduce the subjective perspective of its hero, *Julien Donkey-Boy* depicts public reactions to mental distress. In one of the film's more documentary-like scenes, Julien wanders the streets, talking to himself, as members of the public either ignore or stare at him (as in other Dogme films, none of these members of the public was aware of the filming since DV spy cameras were used). The scene is filmed continuously and with natural sound without the jump cuts or still images found elsewhere, producing a powerful sense of realism. Here is a very unusual attempt, then, to convey the reality of stigmatisation within a fictional narrative.

The film also contains several comic scenes. In one of these, Julien threatens an imaginary Adolf Hitler with a shotgun in front of a full-length mirror; after a few minutes of threats, Julien reveals that he is 'only joking', drops his weapon and offers the phantasmal Führer a cup of tea. In its imitation of the classic mirror scene from *Taxi Driver*, the scene attests to the film's self-consciousness about its representation of madness. Moreover, the scene hints cleverly at the causes of Julien's distress. Julien describes his imaginary Hitler, for example, as having eaten 'his mother's titties', suggesting that Julien's mother died of breast cancer; but his fixation on the figure of Hitler also implicates his authoritarian father as another cause of his distress.

Far more obviously problematic – and in stark contrast to what could be seen as the film's sensitivity towards the stigmatisation of madness elsewhere – is Julien's casual act of violence in the film's opening scene, in which he accidentally kills a young boy during a petty squabble over some turtles. The bleak start of the film is mirrored by its ending. When his sister miscarries her baby, Julien steals the dead foetus from the hospital and takes it home, where he clutches it as he cowers under the sheets in the foetal position, seeking sanctuary, as he does throughout the film, in his identification with his mother. Thus a film that begins with an apparently motiveless killing ends in death and apparent despair.

The contrast between this ending and the triumphal conclusions of many other mental distress films, such as *Shine* and *A Beautiful Mind*, could not be starker – a fact not lost on Korine (1999), who comments in an interview on the Tartan Video DVD release that:

> I wanted to do a film about someone who was mentally ill, but I wanted to do it justice because usually when you see these characters portrayed in the movies, it's always, like, the cute, lovable eccentric, you know, the cute schizophrenic, and I think that's really crap. I hate that, you know. I wanted to show a guy with blood on his underwear, hitting himself on the head, jumping out of windows, I wanted to show what's it's really like and the horror of schizophrenia.

Korine's complaint that public images of madness are bloodless and saccharine constitutes an implicit critique of 'politically correct' discourse about mental distress. In contrast to campaigners' calls for more 'sensitive' representations of madness, Korine privileges spectacular and shocking images in the name of a violent verisimilitude. In view of some of the bowdlerised and worthy treatment of madness in many other films discussed in this chapter, it is easy to agree with Korine that many contemporary films 'sanitise' madness; after all, as argued in Chapter 2, people with diagnoses of schizophrenia are sometimes violent. Yet it is the senselessness of Julien's killing of the young boy that is problematic here: although the incident seems to be an accident, it is difficult to discern much narrative explanation or psychological justification for its inclusion in the narrative and as such it seems merely exploitative.

Like *Julien Donkey-Boy*, Lodge Kerrigan's moving film *Keane* (2004) is filmed in live environments using only hand-held cameras and almost entirely natural lighting. After the apparent abduction of his daughter, William Keane, played by Damian Lewis, haunts the bus station where she was last seen, muttering to himself. The attempt to mimic schizophrenic speech here is unusual, recalling Kerrigan's earlier portrait of serious mental disturbance, *Clean, Shaven* (1994), which begins with a series of abstract sounds and images. Throughout much of the film, the camera is trained on Lewis's face in medium close-up and, like Keane himself, is in constant motion, creating a sense of restless intensity that mirrors the protagonist's mental turmoil (Thomson, 2005: 95). The busy indifference of the crowds swelling around Keane in the bus station scenes also emphasises Keane's psychological alienation. Only when Keane befriends another young girl of a similar age to his daughter does his condition improve; at the end of the film, there is a suggestion that he may have come to terms with the guilt he feels for the loss of his daughter. Like *Julien Donkey-Boy*, *Keane* is an aesthetically innovative representation of mental distress; unlike Korine's film, however, *Keane* offers a gripping and intense insight into a tortured mind without resorting to sensationalised scenes of violence.

Cult horror director David Cronenberg's *Spider* (2002) is based on a 1992 novel by Patrick McGrath. Its hero Clegg is discharged from an institution for the criminally insane in 1988 – at the advent of the Conservative government's community care programme – and ends up living in a halfway house. Here Clegg tries to piece together his previous life, in particular the childhood events from the 1950s that led to the death of his beloved mother. Clegg has convinced himself that his boorish father killed his mother and took a new mistress, a coarse prostitute (the mother and the prostitute are both played by Miranda Richardson). However, it slowly emerges that Clegg has spun a web of self-deceit to protect himself from the truth: that he killed his mother out of jealousy of his father. Thus *Spider* drama-tises Freud's Oedipus complex, concentrating on the child's emotional attachment to his mother. The film's psychological framework invokes Erich Fromm's (1963: 42) contention that while Freud rationalised the Oedipus complex as a sexual response, the 'real problem' is 'the depth and intensity of the *irrational affective* tie to the mother'. As in *Julien Donkey-Boy*, the protagonist's madness here is a reaction to the dysfunctional family, and, in particular, to the loss of a beloved mother.

The adaptation of *Spider* from novel to film highlights how the spe-cific formal exigencies of the two media forms can produce substantial differences in the presentation of character and theme. In McGrath's novel, the highly literate protagonist meticulously describes his psychi-atric and personal history, as well as his frightening delusions of actually being a spider, in the first person. Time constraints, however, necessitate the omission or reduction of much of this information in the film. Cro-nenberg does not even attempt to reproduce the novel's narratorial tone via a voice-over (a common technique in literary adaptations for the screen, such as *Girl, Interrupted*) and Clegg's muffled subvocalisations are barely intelligible. Cronenberg also eschews the obvious opportunity to visibilise Clegg's delusions through the lurid corporeal metamorphoses that characterise his many 'body horror' films.

Despite its elliptical narration, the film allows the audience to progress from observing Clegg to participating in his desperate efforts to untan-gle past from present and fantasy from reality. This transition is achieved through the intercutting of scenes of Clegg's waking life with daydreams and flashbacks. Rather like Dennis Potter's *The Singing Detective* (1986), in which memory, fantasy and reality also commingle, *Spider* invites the audience to participate in its protagonist's self-analysis through the narrative technique of internal focalisation, in which fragments of memories are audio-visually rendered as dreamlike hallucinations. In one scene, for example, Clegg sits in a café and, prompted by a wall poster of a verdant landscape, experiences a hallucination of a con-versation with two elderly gardeners – presumably friends of Clegg's from an earlier time. Some details of this hallucination recall elements of Clegg's current life, while others feed Clegg's paranoid fantasy: the bucolic setting of this particular hallucination, for instance, reappears later in Clegg's delusion that his father has killed his mother and stored her body in the shed on his allotment. Branigan's (1992: 101–3) definition of internal focalisation in audio-visual narratives is useful in understanding the technique used here:

> Focalization (reflection) involves a character neither speaking (narrating, reporting, communicating) nor acting (focusing, focused by), but rather experiencing something through seeing or hearing it. Focalization also extends to more complex experiencing of objects: thinking, remembering, interpreting, wondering, fearing, believing, desiring, understanding, feeling guilt. [...] In internal focalization, story world and screen are meant to collapse into each other, forming a perfect identity in the name of a character. [...] Internal focalization is more fully private and subjective than external focalization. No character can witness these experiences in another character. Internal focalization ranges from simple perception (e.g., the point-of-view shot), to impressions (e.g., the out-of-focus point of view shot depicting a character who is drunk, dizzy, or drugged), to 'deeper thoughts' (e.g. dreams, hallucinations, and memories).

The use of sound in *Spider* is also noteworthy. Literary works sometimes attempt to represent the sounds heard by, or made by mentally distressed protagonists. Paul Abelman's (1957) classic novel about schizophrenia, *I Hear Voices*, for example, begins with the narrator's experience of a buzzing sound ('Can that be flies or machines?'). Experimentation in film sound, however, tends to be the preserve of avant-garde directors; Krzysztof Kieślowski's use of 'natural' sound springs to mind. While auditory hallucinations do signify mental turmoil in films as diverse as Anatole Litvak's *The Snake Pit* (1948) and Erick Santamaria's early slasher film *Playgirl Killer* (1968), they have not featured prominently in mental distress films. In many recent films, however, the audience is made to share the confusion of voice-hearing. Ray, the protagonist of *Some Voices*, for example, hears indistinct whispers at times of acute distress. In *Spider*, as in *Keane*, the protagonist's mental confusion is conveyed by his own muffled voice. By inviting the audience to share Clegg's subjective experiences through hallucinations and idioglossic monologue, *Spider* confounds the narrative realism that typically characterises the mental distress film.

Indeed, films like *Spider*, *Keane* and *Julien Donkey-Boy* attest to one of the most significant changes in the representation of mental distress in recent years: the shift in narrative point of view from the third to the first person. Mental distress films, it seems, increasingly aim to get 'inside the heads' of their subjects. For many conservative critics, this drift towards subjectivism sails close to spurious relativism. Eric Cox (2003) damns the producers of Hollywood films about mental distress for precisely this reason:

> They compare mental disease favorably with mental health, or they insist on making the movie as depressing as possible in the mistaken assumption that the audience must experience the protagonist's version of reality for her story to have any meaning.

Cox correctly implies that many mental distress films seem to privilege the first-person perspective; yet he ignores the potential of subjective points of view to counteract the more traditional objectification of sufferers.

At the end of *Spider*, the adult Clegg enters the bedroom of the matron in charge of the halfway house with a hammer, convinced that the matron is the 'evil stepmother' he believes replaced his mother. Yet McGrath's novel does not contain any hammer scene, ending instead with Clegg's chillingly nonchalant determination to commit suicide after smoking his final cigarette: 'One last thin one, one for the road, then it's out with the sock, out with the keys, and off up to the attic for me!' (McGrath, 1990: 221). The film's hammer scene provides a more visually dramatic climax. Although Clegg mercifully recognises his delusion before he proceeds with the attack, the linkage between madness and violence in the film's hammer scene would be regarded as problematic by anti-stigma critics. However, as I argued in Chapter 2, arguments about the preponderance of violence in media representations of distress are far from conclusive; moreover, Clegg's profound mental disorientation makes it hard to blame him for his actions.

The original and challenging presentation of madness in *Spider* has not won universal praise for the film. In a review of the film, Sean Axmaker (2003) complains that 'Fiennes' portrayal of a man's absolute isolation is impressive but so complete that he becomes an empty vessel defined entirely by his story.' Similarly, Roger Ebert (2005: 642) expresses his disappointment that while we may care for Clegg, 'we cannot identify with him because he is no longer capable of change and decision. He has long since stopped trying to tell apart his layers of memory, nightmare, experience and fantasy.' Yet the fact that Clegg aborts his attack surely indicates that he has started to comprehend the extent of his self-delusion. Not only does Clegg change, but the audience is invited to share his dawning consciousness of his past actions; it is only regrettable that such complex and engaging treatments of mental distress are so rare – and that they seem usually to feature only white, male protagonists.

Madly famous: Madness in the biopic

The biopic has become an extraordinary popular and successful sub-genre of film drama in recent years. Billy Bob Thornton, who both directed and played the mentally disabled Karl Childers in the film *Sling Blade* (1996), notes that Oscars voters often favour dark and socially relevant dramas, 'like examining the life of an alcoholic or Jack Nicholson suffering from OCD. These are important issues, there's something to that worth looking at and, I think, it helps humanity in general. The academy appreciates that as well' (cited by Strauss, 1998). Indeed, the Oscars system has become an important mechanism for promoting Hollywood biopics with 'serious' themes. Stephen Daldry's *The Hours*, for instance, won the 2003 Golden Globe for Best Dramatic Film and garnered nine Oscar nominations, with Nicole Kidman winning the Oscar for Best Actress for her depiction of Virginia Woolf. As this suggests, biopics also gain prestige from the actorly qualities they are presumed to showcase. As Mark Lawson (2007: 28) notes:

> At the Oscars, two kinds of film have tended to be disproportionately honoured: the biopic (*Walk the Line, Capote, Erin Brockovich*) and the movie dealing with physical or mental stress: *Rain Man, Boys Don't Cry, Shine, The Pianist*. The reason for this is that voters can be absolutely certain that acting is taking place, a harder judgement when someone is playing closer to their own appearance and delivery.

It is unsurprising, therefore, that biopics with mental distress themes, such as *A Beautiful Mind* and *Shine*, have accrued considerable cultural capital. The following section examines the representation of distress in these films and explores some of its ideological implications.

Biopics based on books tend to come with a ready-made cultural value. James Mangold's *Girl, Interrupted* (1999), based on the autobiography of writer Susanna Kaysen, is a critically lauded exploration of a young woman's mental breakdown in the 1960s, which won Angelina Jolie an Academy Award for Best Supporting Actress as the fractious Lisa. Lisa and Susanna develop a passionate attachment which leads to the couple's joint escape from the institution. Susanna is diagnosed with 'borderline personality disorder', a condition described by Susanna herself as clinically nebulous and which the film attributes to Susanna's sexual molestation by her teacher. Since the 1960s saw the exponential growth of the women's liberation movement, it is fitting that the film foregrounds the association between madness and patriarchal power. When Susanna is committed to a mental hospital, for example, the distracted and indifferent attentions of an arrogant male psychiatrist are offset by the kindlier ministrations of a female therapist.

Yet the film is problematic in several respects. Like *One Flew Over the Cuckoo's Nest*, *Girl, Interrupted* problematically parades 'patients with funny habits'– a staple trick of films set in psychiatric institutions (Wahl, 1995: 30). It also seems to trade on the racial stereotype of the 'Mammy', as the black nurse played by Whoopi Goldberg dispenses pearls of wisdom to the self-pitying Susanna. Like the friendship between the mentally impaired Henry and his black friend in Mike Nichols' *Regarding Henry* (1991), the relationship between Susanna and her nurse point to a larger problem of racial representation in the mental distress movie: namely, that only white characters seem capable of possessing tortured subjectivity and inwardness. Moreover, the potentially transgressive force of Susanna and Lisa's relationship is ultimately recuperated: a proto-lesbian kiss between the pair happens under the influence of psychoactive drugs in the psychedelically painted camper van of a group of hippies, casting the couple's intimacy as a temporary aberration.

Girl, Interrupted, like many other biopics, also reinforces a somewhat voluntaristic understanding of madness as a problem that can be transcended simply through force of will and as an individual 'journey' into enlightenment. This theme of 'living for oneself' looks forward to Mangold's later biopic of the troubled country singer Johnny Cash, *Walk the Line* (2005). It also points backwards to the films of the 1950s, such as *Fear Strikes Out* (Jimmy Mulligan, 1957), which is based on the autobiography of baseball star Jimmy Piersall: Piersall has a breakdown when he was unable to live up to his domineering father's ambitions for him; he eventually realises, however, that he cannot 'live for' his father and takes up baseball again – this time on his own terms. The theme of authentically being 'true to oneself', while undoubtedly influenced by the strong existentialist currents and nascent counter-cultural themes of the late 1950s, also accords nicely with the competitive individualism of capitalist ideology. Like *Fear Strikes Out*, *Girl Interrupted* sets up mental distress as a reaction against an adult authority whose stipulations are initially contested, but finally accommodated. Where *Fear Strikes Out* posits baseball as the route to autonomy, *Girl, Interrupted* suggests writing as the path to self-knowledge.

The most celebrated biopic of recent years is *A Beautiful Mind* (2001), which won the Academy Award for Best Picture in 2001. The film concerns Harvard mathematician John Nash's struggle for sanity. The sense of Nash's professional struggle conveyed in Sylvia Nasar's (2002) biography of the academic is here eclipsed, however, in favour of a sensational symptomology, including Nash's vivid hallucinations of a CIA agent. Moreover, like many of the romantic dramas discussed above, *A Beautiful Mind* offers the near-statutory Hollywood happy ending, prompting Sam Khorrami (2002: 117) to note sardonically that 'we learn that a good woman can help a man overcome any difficulty, even including paranoid schizophrenia.' Critics have also expressed concerns over the film's historical revisionism, in particular its convenient glossing over of Nash's racism and snobbery and his arrest for soliciting homosexual sex, as though the audience could not tolerate the depiction of these elements (Taylor, 2001; Khorrami, 2002). Consequently, the film sails close to hagiography, as suggested by its title's quasi-allusion to *Hamlet*: 'O, what a noble mind is here o'erthrown'. *A Beautiful Mind* is also typical of many recent mental distress films, such as *Angel Baby*, in emphasising the dire consequences of neglecting psychiatric counsel: in the grip of a delusion after he abandons his medication, Nash is physically violent towards his wife and almost drowns his baby in the bathtub – scenes summarised wearily by journalist Matthew Bond (2002: 66) as the 'what-happens-when-he-stops-taking-the-medication stuff'.

A Beautiful Mind's exploitation of the 'struggling genius' theme is not unique in the biopic. The 1996 biopic *Shine* presents the story of David Helfgott, a gifted pianist, played by Geoffrey Rush, who suffered with psychological problems for most of his adult life. While Shine traces the origins of Helfgott's distress to his abusive childhood, it also implicitly links his instability to his creative drive. *Quills* (Philip Kaufman, 2000), also starring Rush, this time as the incarcerated eighteenth-century writer the Marquis de Sade, also reinforces the concept of the creative artist as an oppressed genius, even though de Sade is merely labelled as mad as a political expedient. Indeed, these films attest to the perseverance of a stereotype whose historical origins and contemporary resonance merit brief consideration here.

The perceived link between greatness and madness has an ancient pedigree. The Platonic association of madness with creativity was revived in the Renaissance and expressed by Shakespeare's Duke Theseus in *A Midsummer Night's Dream*: 'The lunatic, the lover, and the poet / Are of imagination all compact'. In the post-Romantic era, 'genius' came to be defined as a brilliant yet flawed personality: the greater the genius, the more marked the 'lapses' (Negus and Pickering, 2004: 159). As such, madness became attractive to many aspiring artists. Susan Sontag (1991: 109) notes of the Romanian fascist writer Emil Cioran that

> syphilis-envy figured in his adolescent expectations of literary glory: he would discover that he had contracted syphilis, be rewarded with several hyperproductive years of genius, then collapse into madness. This romanticizing of the dementia characteristic of neurosyphilis was the forerunner of the much more persistent fantasy in this century about mental illness as a source of artistic creativity or spiritual originality.

This supposed alliance between madness and genius contributed to the aura of artists from Vincent van Gogh to Jackson Pollock. Madness strongly influenced the exquisitely unbalanced sensibility of Modernist artists and even became a key theme in the work of Modernist writers such as Thomas Mann. More recently, the myth of the mad genius has often attached to film producers: Francis Ford Coppola was rumoured – wrongly, it would seem – to have suffered three breakdowns during the making of his masterpiece *Apocalypse Now* (O'Hagan, 2007: 11).

Indeed, madness and genius are closely interrelated in contemporary Western media. The last decade has seen an explosion of self-help books attesting to the giftedness of mentally distressed people, ranging from autobiographies such as actress Patty Duke's *A Brilliant Madness* (1999) to psychological investigations such as Kay Redfield Jamison's *Touched with Fire: Manic-Depressive Illness and the Artistic Temperament* (1996). Besides *Shine*, *A Beautiful Mind* and *Quills*, many recent biopics associate madness with artistic, literary or academic genius or with increased spiritual insight. *Pollock* (Ed Harris, 2000) depicts the depression of the eponymous Abstract Expressionist painter, while *The Hours* (Stephen Daldry, 2002), *Sylvia* (Christine Jeffs, 2003) and *The Aviator* (Martin Scorsese, 2004), present the tortured lives of Virginia Wolf, Sylvia Plath and Howard Hughes respectively.

The popularity of these narratives among Western audiences indicates the continuing appeal of the 'tortured genius' stereotype – and its ideological utility. As narratives about individuals who struggle through adversity, such texts uphold a particularly American tradition of voluntarism, which developed out of the 'the stern Protestant sense of loneliness – the outcome of the inevitability of the divine decree – and from the fact that the American state did not initially provide strong institutional support, thus leaving individuals to their own resources'

(Illouz, 2003: 137). Heroic mental distress biopics seem to support and extend neo-liberal discourses of meritocracy and competitive individualism. Such narratives doubtless carry a particular appeal for audiences in 'post-traditional societies' (Giddens, 1991), in which subjects increasingly abandon long-established lifestyle scripts structured by class or kinship affiliations in favour of individualised modes of self-fashioning. 'Mad genius' films spectacularly dramatise the inherent psychological risks of artistic self-construction, while reassuring audiences that, far from being a barrier to 'success', madness may in some sense constitute a rite of passage leading, ultimately, to social and/or professional recognition. Mania, in particular, is undergoing just such a cultural revaluation in modern American culture; the much-lauded creativity of 'manic' artists is now often compared to the creativity of 'manic' CEOs, reinforcing the ideology of meritocracy (Martin, 2007).

The meritocratic message is, of course, inflected by distinctions of social class. The troubled individuals whose lives these biopics chart are typically petty bourgeois celebrities: writers, musicians and artists (indeed, the term 'genius' itself is generally reserved for artists and intellectuals and seldom applied to bus drivers or refuse collectors). The behaviour of the male and female characters in these narratives is also strongly influenced by stereotypes of gender. This has long been the case in film drama. Frank and Eleanor Perry's 1962 film *David and Lisa*, for example, presents two troubled teenagers with quite different characteristics: David is rational if eccentric, while Lisa is incoherent, petulant and infantile (*Angel Baby*, discussed earlier, offers an analogous gender bifurcation). In the biopic, however, this gender split is particularly apparent. Whereas biopics with male protagonists, such as *Shine*, *A Beautiful Mind* and *Pollock*, present heroic psychological 'battles' culminating in enlightenment, those about mad women, such as *Sylvia*, *Iris* (Richard Eyre, 2002) and *The Hours*, offer darker, tragic visions of personal struggle that often end in death.

The aestheticisation of female death and madness continues the nineteenth-century trope encapsulated in Edgar Allan Poe's aphorism: 'the death of a beautiful woman is, unquestionably, the most poetical topic in the world.' Sylvia Plath was quite aware of this fetishisation of tragic femininity, writing in one of her poems: 'The woman is perfected. / Her dead / Body wears the smile of accomplishment'. Yet whereas the achievements of the protagonists in *Shine* and *A Beautiful Mind* are lauded in the film itself, *Sylvia* is quite unforthcoming about Plath's work, while *The Hours* and *Iris* reveal little about the achievements of their subjects (Walsh, 2003). Even Susanna's successful writing ambitions in *Girl, Interrupted* are presented as therapeutically useful, rather than the artistic strivings of a 'genius'.

In films about famous women, then, the heroism or nobility that might attach to psychological struggle tends to be vitiated by tragedy, melodrama, hysteria and death. This conclusion supports Griselda Pollock's (1987) argument that the artist has been constructed historically through bourgeois norms of masculinity that permit men, but not women, to move between the public and private spheres, as well as Christine Battersby's (1989) contention that genius has traditionally been defined as a combination of masculine and feminine qualities attainable only by men. It also resonates with sociologist Joan Busfield's (1996: 234) finding that

> men's 'disruptions' and difficult behaviour have typically been viewed as the product of agency and, consequently, as behaviour for which they are to be held responsible. In contrast, women's disruptions have often been seen as something outside a woman's control for which agency has been denied.

While the mad men of contemporary cinema are often represented as active heroes struggling against psychiatric adversity, mad women are more typically represented as the passive victims of their disordered psyches. This distinction within the biopic is reflected in cultural assumptions about the gendered distribution of genius: in a list of public nominations for 'top ten geniuses' conducted by a consulting firm in 2007, only 15 of the 100 most commonly mentioned figures were female (Williams, 2007: 13).

Real crazy guys: Madness and masculinity in film comedy

What may not be evident from the foregoing discussion is the distinctly comic tinge of many cinematic representations of mental distress. Comic elements and moments can of course emerge even in the most sombre film drama: the verbal and behavioural idiosyncrasies of David Helfgott in *Shine* or John Nash in *A Beautiful Mind*, for instance, are often regarded by other characters as winsome rather than threatening. While such idiosyncrasies may provide light relief from otherwise gloomy subject matter, however, their treatment is potentially stigmatising, encouraging the audience to laugh at – rather than with – the protagonist. The following section focuses on the treatment of madness within the genre of film comedy, where this potential problem is magnified. Since the genre features mainly male protagonists, this section also discusses the gendered nature of comic films about distress.

The representation of distress in film comedy has often attracted censure from psychiatric critics on grounds of medical inaccuracy. The screwball comedy *Me, Myself and Irene* (1999) and its promotional materials confuse Dissociative Identity Disorder (previously known clinically as Multiple Personality Disorder) with schizophrenia. As noted earlier, however, the persistence of the etymologically unfortunate term schizophrenia is itself partly to blame for this; moreover, to evaluate such images of madness solely in terms of psychiatric accuracy is itself problematic. More troublingly, perhaps, in posters advertising the film, the star Jim Carey was captioned with the phrase: 'from gentle to mental', implying that those with 'schizophrenic' symptoms are somehow psychologically bifurcated between good and evil, a prevalent media stereotype (Philo, McLaughlin and Henderson, 1996: 76). Finally, the hero's puerile behaviour throughout the film makes him a laughing stock with few redeeming characteristics. While it would be stretching representational correctness too far to expect all characters in mental distress films to be likeable, it is fortunate that relatively few comic representations of mental distress are of this type.

Other comedy films exploit the device of 'patients with funny habits', as discussed in relation to *Girl, Interrupted*. In Steve Pink's riotous comedy *Accepted* (2006), a group of college rejects decide to turn an abandoned psychiatric institution into a decidedly alternative higher education institution, in which students are encouraged to indulge their interests rather than study a traditional curriculum. Some of the students are clearly coded as psychologically disturbed and the Attention Deficit Disorder sufferer Abernathy is freakishly hyperactive throughout. Such films rather lazily exaggerate and ridicule the symptoms of psychological distress.

Notwithstanding such problems, some cultural contextualisation of the theme of comic madness is useful here. Historically, social anxieties and prejudices surrounding mental distress have often been negotiated through comedy. Many medieval plays and poems include a mad hero whose role is partly to provide comic relief. King Herod, a stock villain in the medieval mystery plays, unfailingly appears as a raving maniac, whose egregious abandonment of God-given reason served as a dreadful moral admonition (Doob, 1974). Yet even in the didactic literature of the Middle Ages, the comic madman was not exclusively a villain to be mocked and vanquished; he could also challenge, or at least test the limits of official ideologies. The central character of Adam de la Halle's early thirteenth-century French satirical play *Le Jeu de la Feuillée*, for example, is a comic madman who exhibits both the symptoms of the modern 'schizophrenic' and the craziness of the court buffoon licensed to mock the pretensions of the powerful (DuBrock, 1974). Twentieth-century cinema has continued many of these traditions. Thus Milos, in the Czech New Wave classic *Closely Observed Trains* (Jiri Menzel, 1966), suffers from psychological disturbance leading to a suicide attempt; yet he also belongs to the tradition of Holy Fools and recalls in particular the Renaissance figure of Simplicius Simplicissimus: an unwilling and unwitting hero who is considered mad or eccentric by a crazy world.

The films of the Spanish director Pedro Almodóvar, in particular, connect with this satirical tradition of madness and highlight some of the problems involved in determining the ideological import of comic images of madness. In Almodóvar's comedy of manners *Women on the Verge of a Nervous Breakdown* (1988), the heroine Pepa is threatened with a gun by her lover's ex-wife, who has, we learn, recently left a mental institution. Later in the film, the ex-wife attempts to shoot Pepa's lover. Pepa and her friend pursue the violent wife in a road chase to prevent the shooting, all the while referring to her as 'loopy', 'crazy' and 'mad'. The menacingly discordant music accompanying the chase scenes reinforces the ex-wife's dangerous instability. Finally, as if to bring the film's representation of mental distress to a stigmatising crescendo, the ex-wife asks to be taken back to the institution which she has recently left, 'where I belong'. *Women on the Verge* seems to reproduce stereotypical assumptions about madness, reinforcing its association with irrational femininity and violence. Yet the film's semiotic excesses indicate that its discourse of madness must not be taken at face value. The overloaded language, absurd melodrama and cartoonish visual style and pacing seem to constitute a parody of soap opera melodrama, in keeping with Almodóvar's reputation as a politically progressive filmmaker whose anarchic films upset traditional gender roles and attack the mores of the Spanish middle classes.

Almodóvar returned to the theme of madness in *Tie Me Up! Tie Me Down!* (1990), in which a callow young handyman named Ricky is discharged from a psychiatric hospital and kidnaps a drug-addicted pornographic film actress whom he naively claims is the 'woman of his dreams'. Ricky's mental instability is established throughout the film via the recurring leitmotif of the musical refrain from *Psycho*. He keeps the actress tied up and beats her, but also buys drugs to feed her addiction, until she falls in love with him. At first blush, *Tie Me Up! Tie Me Down!*, like *Women on the Verge*, hardly seems a sympathetic depiction of mental distress. Yet the absurd intensity of Ricky's desire to achieve a 'normal' bourgeois life with the actress through violent means – and her equally preposterous acquiescence – suggest a satirical import (similarly, Kieran Galvin's dark Australian comedy mental distress comedy *Puppy* (2005) over-emphasises the signifiers of forced restraint and medication for satirical ends). Rikki Morgan (1995: 118) adds that *Tie Me Up*'s cultural lineage provides grounds for reading the anti-hero's mad actions ironically:

> The critical discourse of the madman is a tradition in Spanish cultural production, reaching back to such mythical protagonists as Calderón de la Barca's Segismundo in *Life's a Dream* (1635) and Cervantes' *Don Quijote de la Mancha* (1605). Ricky's deluded 'logic' and the convergence of 'madness' and 'normality' in his reasoning have a critical function in that they cast the pursuit of socially accepted norms as madness: the discourse of the 'madman' thus reveals the 'madness' of 'normality.'

The farcical derangement of Almodóvar's characters is best understood, then, in the historical context of satirical social commentary.

Hollywood films also deploy comic madness for satirical purposes. Like *Girl, Interrupted*, *Crazy People* (Tony Bill and Barry L. Young, 1990) parades 'patients with funny habits'; yet the film's premise – that telling the truth in an advertising agency is a 'certifiable' sign of madness – gently mocks the ethical fraudulence of the advertising industry. In *What About Bob?* (Frank Oz, 1991), the supposedly disturbed Bob, played by comic actor Bill Murray, encroaches upon, and finally usurps the family and professional lives of his neurotically officious psychiatrist Leo. Bob, it transpires, is more insightful about human psychology than his shrink and becomes much loved by the psychiatrist's wife and children. After interrupting Leo's stuttering performance in a television interview and stealing the show, Bob becomes a best-selling author in the field of psychiatry. As Bob prospers, Leo's mental state deteriorates, so that the erstwhile psychiatrist ends up weaving a wicker basket in a psychiatric ward. Madness, in *What About Bob?*, is validated as an inseparable part of human life that is all too often repressed in the name of a bluff, macho rationalism. Significantly, too, the exuberant spirit of *What About Bob?* elevates the film above the mean-spiritedness of *Me, Myself and Irene*: we laugh with, rather than at the protagonist.

As a film which light-heartedly challenges accepted distinctions between madness and normality, *What About Bob?* has much in common with later 1990s 'madcap' films, such as *Patch Adams* (1998) – a film based on a true story of the eponymous psychiatrist – in which Robin Williams plays the young doctor whose unconventional laughter therapies undermine the earnest egocentricism and emotional frigidity of professional psychiatry, a theme continued in the Robert de Niro vehicles *Analyse This* (1999) and its sequel *Analyse That* (2002). These films contribute to a broader trend of psychiatric denigration in Hollywood cinema over the last 40 years – a theme to which I shall return in the conclusion of this chapter. As well as valorising mental distress and symbolically challenging psychiatric hegemony, many of these comedies implicitly critique the psychic costs of patriarchal ambition. *The Kid* (Jon Turteltaub, 2002), starring Bruce Willis, for example, offers a typically Romantic critique of alienated masculinity. Russell Duritz is a brash, self-satisfied image consultant who has lost his child-like *joie de vivre*. His confident machismo is unravelled, however, through a series of apparent hallucinations of a child. When the child turns out to be real, Duritz begins to unlock his repressed instincts for fun. As in *What About Bob?* – in which the patient collaborates with the psychiatrist's wife and children – the cold instrumentality of patriarchy is broken down by the innocent spontaneity of youth.

Anthony and Joe Russo's *You, Me, and Dupree* (2006) contains another variation on the theme of the patriarch in crisis. After a series of humiliations at the hands of his dropout buddy Randy Dupree, up-tight architect Carl Peterson begins to lose control of his job, his marriage and his physical and mental health. At the film's climax, Peterson indulges in a wild fantasy that Dupree has usurped his career and his marriage. Gradually, however, he comes to accept that Dupree embodies an openness and authenticity lacking in his own personality. Peterson learns to relinquish his anxiety over his career, to trust his childish side and is taught by his idiot savant friend – in Dupree's own peculiar psychobabble – to 'embrace his inner "ness"'. At the end of the film, Peterson is reunited with his wife, while the anarchic Dupree, rather like the anti-hero of *What About Bob?*, finds commercial success as a self-help guru.

While such films are open to charges of mawkishness, they certainly promote the 'softer' conception of masculinity inherent in the notion of the 'new man' which has been a constant theme in popular culture since the 1980s (Beynon, 2002). Through scatological or carnivalesque comedy, films such as *What About Bob?*, *Patch Adams*, *The Kid* and *You, Me and Dupree* pathologize and destabilise the patriarchal obsession with success and control and advocate self-reflection and emotional sensitivity. Some comedy films even take on the stigma of mental distress directly. *Lars and the Real Girl* (Craig Gillespie, 2007), for instance, tells of a young man who suffers delusions after the death of his father. When Lars brings home his 'girlfriend', a plastic doll named Bianca, to meet his parents, he is met with consternation but is ultimately accepted, like Bianca, by the wider community. As Lars accommodates himself to reality, Bianca 'dies' and is given a funeral at which the townspeople grieve. *Lars and the Real Girl* thus wittily exploits the essentially public, social spirit of comedy (as opposed to the classically private nature of tragedy) to destigmatize mental distress.

As all of these films hint, the 'wisdom of fools' contains a liberatory aspect. Yet these critiques of social stigma, patriarchy and masculinist psychiatry are often nonetheless delivered from a conservative ideological perspective. By emphasising the redemptive power of friends and family, these films tend to locate the solution to mental disquiet in the cosy *gemeinschaft* of the middle-class lifeworld and to ignore the ineluctable, structural pressures of capitalism and patriarchy. While the pressures of wage labour, for example, are sometimes implicated as sources of mental distress – especially in *You, Me and Dupree* – these films advocate moral rather than social transformation, or being 'true to oneself' as the solution to life's problems. Moreover, the endings of both *What About Bob?* and *You, Me and Dupree* posit involvement in the self-help industry as a route to riches and happiness and thereby equate psychic well-being with a distinctly capitalist notion of success.

Moreover, for all the winsome charm of these films, their sensitive, suffering subjects are exclusively white and middle class. Comic films about mental distress are thus problematically androcentric. As Lynne Segal (1990: 2) puts it, 'it is because "manhood" still has a symbolic weight denied to womanhood that men's apparent failings loom so large – to men themselves and those around them.' What might be called the 'Woody Allen syndrome' is evident in many of the films I have discussed here: it is typically white males, it seems, who suffer from neuroses. This gender bias is given an unsavoury twist in Gore Verbinski's bleak comedy *The Weather Man* (2005), which details the family troubles of a hard-pressed, lugubrious white-collar divorcee, David Spritz (a name shortened, we learn, from Spritzer, invoking the stereotype of self-hating, neurotic Jewishness). An unpopular television weather presenter, Spritz frequently has fast food thrown at him in the street, pines for his ex-wife and considers his overweight daughter to be a social failure. As his sense of despair grows, Spritz starts to experience bizarre hallucinations of his daughter's vulva, framed in extreme close-up – seemingly for comic effect – which seem to link his neuroses to a fear of femininity. Since the narrative is focalised from Spritz's perspective, the audience experiences what Judith Williamson (1986: 197) calls 'identification in passivity', whereby, although we see through the eyes of a self-pitying and misogynistic hero, we are nonetheless made to feel that he is a hapless victim of circumstance.

The figure of the long-suffering hero arguably instantiates a broader representational shift in comedy films. In her discussion of the gender politics of romantic comedy in the mid-1990s, Kathleen Rowe (1995a: 185) argues that romantic comedies of the classical Hollywood period were organised around the relationship between a co-equal couple, whereas more recent comedies offer far less sympathy with female suffering and instead privilege 'a beleaguered and victimised masculinity', a conclusion that contradicts some of the more optimistic, whiggish assessments of cinematic gender representation, such as David Gauntlett's *Media, Gender and Identity* (2002). Insofar as it marginalises female suffering, the rise of the neurotic male as a melodramatic subject in recent comedy films cannot be seen as an unproblematic progression towards more 'sensitive' images of masculinity.

Comedy film has allowed several male actors (Jim Carrey, Robert de Niro, Billy Crystal, Bill Murray, Adam Sandler) to develop and explore 'mad' or crazy personae across a series of films. Actresses, however, are afforded far less performative latitude and comedies involving mentally distressed heroines are few and far between. Historically, comedy films have featured psychologically distressed female leads. For example, the 1944 comedy musical *Lady in the Dark*, a film which combines a deep faith in Freudian psychotherapy with a misogynistic premise based loosely on the Electra complex, features a madcap heroine. Liza Elliot, played by Ginger Rodgers, is a 'stressed-out', career-focused magazine editor who rejects her fiancé's marriage proposal and seeks therapeutic assistance in overcoming her growing feelings of indecisiveness in relation to the tension between her romantic life and her public role. At the start of the film, Elliot is undermined by her ambitious junior colleague, Charlie Johnson, who is eager to snatch her job and who believes Elliot to be 'too masculine' ('you have magazines instead of babies'). Elliot's psychotherapy sessions seem to corroborate Charlie's belief. As a result of her treatment, she experiences repressed fantasies in which she is a glamorous socialite, adored by men and envied by women – an image at odds with the business-suited formality of her waking self. She also learns from her therapist that her rejection of a marriage proposal was the result of the unconscious identification she has made between her suitor and her father. In a direct analogy with Virginia Cunningham in the slightly later *The Snake Pit*, Elliot comes to understand that, as Virginia is instructed, 'husbands are not fathers' and eventually to accept the possibility of marriage; simultaneously, she learns to work under the stewardship of Johnson. While Elliot does not immediately resign from her job and fall into the arms of a husband-protector, the film's unmistakable message is that if women *are* to have careers, they ought to understand that their proper place is not at the top of the ladder.

For all its sexism, *Lady in the Dark* at least gives a 'funny woman' centre stage. Unruly women were, however, gradually excluded from post-war American cinema as part of the effort to reconstruct myths of feminine domesticity and in response to the more direct ideological struggles over gender and power in the 1960s (Rowe, 1995b: 193; King, 2002: 131). The few funny women in contemporary films – of whom Bridget Jones is the most notable – are distinctly hapless individuals. In one scene in *Bridget Jones: The Edge of Reason* (Beeban Kidron, 2004), for example, the hapless heroine – distracted by the thought that she may be pregnant – ineptly slithers down a Swiss ski slope, landing in an improbably located pharmacy. Using wild-hand gestures, she attempts to ask the pharmacist for a pregnancy test kit. Unable to understand her, the pharmacist concludes, in subtitled German, 'I think that her problem is psychological', while another customer mockingly observes that 'there's nothing a pill can do to help her'. According to the common wisdom of the villagers of Mitteleuropa, it seems, mental distress is as incurable as it is amusing; moreover, here as elsewhere in the *Bridget Jones* films, the heroine is an object of ridicule. Her position at the 'edge' of reason – rather like Almodóvar's women on the 'verge' on a nervous breakdown – codes her as 'decentred', unstable and 'out of control' and less responsible for her fate than the men who vie for her attentions. Andrei Konchalovsky's quirky comedy *House of Fools* (2002), to take another example, is set in a mental institution during the Chetchen–Russian War, setting up a satirical if well-worn ironic contrast between the 'madness' of war and the comparative sanity of the patients. In this, the film harks back to *One Flew Over the Cuckoo's Nest*; yet unlike the decisive and subversive hero McMurphy in Forman's film, the heroine of *House of Fools* is a wistful, Ophelia-like figure. Indeed, the neurotic female protagonists of film comedy are generally seen as not-responsible individuals who are unable to take charge of their destiny. Just as male characters monopolise the category of 'genius', they are also granted greater narrative agency than female characters in film comedy.

Recent comedy films about mental distress offer some progressive perspectives, then, on gender politics. Male characters struggle to overcome patriarchal prejudices and dysfunctional behaviour, while their female partners and families frequently embody the 'solid', often conservative values of faith and community that will eventually recall errant masculinity to its senses. These films may well attest to a shift from the Freudian focus on the 'problem' of femininity in 1940s cinema to an arguably postmodern problematisation of masculine subjectivity. This is not necessarily a progressive shift, however, since film comedy seemingly depicts only white, middle-class men as mentally distressed, reinforcing the hegemonic discriminations of the wider cinema of madness.

Violent villains and guilty girls: Mental distress in the action and thriller genres

For obvious reasons, the often violent and maniacal villains of action films have attracted considerable attention from anti-stigma critics. As psychiatric critics point out, Hollywood actioners perpetuate diagnostic confusions between psychosis (which can be defined loosely as serious and disabling mental distress) and psychopathy (a personality disorder leading to anti-social and immoral behaviour now known clinically as Dissocial Personality Disorder). While psychosis involves mental disorientation, psychopaths can be well organised and clear-thinking and are generally in good health; yet many action and thriller film villains combine these qualities in a way that is not only implausible, but also stigmatising.

Wahl (1995: 19) notes that in Thomas Harris's serial killer novel *Red Dragon*, the killer Francis Dolarhyde is highly organised, holding down a responsible job, yet becomes psychotic when involved in scenes of violence. Recent thrillers continue to hedge their diagnostic bets in their creation of screen villains. In the film version of *Red Dragon* (Brett Ratner, 2002), for example, Dolarhyde's dichotomous behaviour replicates that described in the film's source. In D. J. Caruso's *Taking Lives* (2004), meanwhile, Ethan Hawke plays a 'psychopath', James Costa, an art dealer whose *modus operandi* involves adopting the identity of his most recent victim. Despite planning his crimes in a consummately methodical fashion throughout most of the film, Costa becomes psychotically uncontrolled just before he commits his murders. I argued in Chapter 2 that psychiatric accuracy may not always be the most relevant concern in the evaluation of representations of mental distress.

Yet there is more at stake here than mimetic plausibility or the simple confusion of psychiatric terminology: the conflation of psychopathy and psychosis tends to imply that sufferers of mental distress are ruthlessly immoral. In Wachowski brothers' *The Matrix Revolutions* (2003), for instance, the weasel-like villain Bane, after brutally slaughtering a medical orderly, attacks Trinity, who describes him as 'psychotic' and 'out of his mind'. Another obnoxious thriller villain is the smooth-talking yet 'criminally insane' leader of the rebel prisoners, Cyrus 'the Virus', in Simon West's *Con Air* (1997). Cyrus, like Hannibal Lecter in *The Silence of the Lambs* (Jonathan Demme, 1991) is superficially charming and refined in his disapproval of commonplace vulgarities, but also appallingly brutal when the occasion demands. There is a clear class aspect to these representations. Many action-film villains – Bane, Cyrus 'the Virus', and perhaps even James Costa, who merely *poses* as a middle-class art dealer – are coded as proletarian brutes. Like the tattooed redneck Early Grace in *Kalifornia* (Dominic Sena, 1993), these characters lack any backstory that might explicate their 'insane' violence and instead appear as frighteningly unpredictable monsters. These characters might in turn be argued to embody social anxieties about the violent potential of working-class masculinity.

Action films seldom offer images of empowered femininity (Churchwell, 2007). In fact, to find substantial treatments of mentally distressed heroines in any comparable genre, one must turn instead to psychological thrillers. In recent years, a number of these have mobilised the theme of mental distress in quite progressive ways. Often the heroines of these thrillers must contest male psychiatric authority to rescue family members. The heroines of both *The Forgotten* (Joseph Ruben, 2004) and *Flightplan* (Robert Schwentke, 2005), for example, are accused of imagining the loss of their children; both manage, however, to overcome the conspiracies against them. Similarly, in *Premonition* (Mennan Yapo, 2007), a troubled housewife, Linda, tries to alter the future after experiencing intimations of her husband's death, but struggles to convince others that she is not mad. Consigned to a psychiatric institution, Linda is treated with lithium by her callous psychiatrist Dr Roth. Adding to the sense of menace, Roth is played by Peter Stormare, an actor who is cast in a similar role in Jeff Buhler's *Insanitarium* (2008) and is associated with screen villainy through his roles in *Fargo* (Joel Cohen, 1996), *Constantine* (Francis Lawrence, 2005) and the television serial *Prison Break* (Fox, 2005–). In all of these films, then, madness serves a broadly feminist agenda, while psychiatry is synecdochal of patriarchal oppression.

Yet even in *Premonition*, mental distress is only an incidental theme; where it is narratively more central, this feminist dimension is less apparent. David Lynch's riddling *Mulholland Drive* (2001) depicts the psychological disintegration of a struggling Hollywood would-be, Diane. Diane's sexual and professional jealously of her more successful actress friend, Camilla, leads her to embark on a course of murderous revenge against her peer. Much of the film's narrative reflects the desperate fantasy that Diane has constructed for herself. In order to escape the harsh reality of her rejection by both Hollywood and Camilla, Diane imagines a 'perfect' Hollywood existence in which she, rather than Camilla, has power and success.

Mulholland Drive is a highly original and thought-provoking film; yet its presentation of Diane's descent into madness is problematic. There are suggestions throughout the film that Diane has experienced sexual abuse as a child: for example, at a Hollywood audition session, Diane plays a scene between an abuser and a child so well that she leaves her audience stunned. Yet insofar as this suggested backstory is intended to explain Diane's lesbian sexuality, it might be seen to pathologise lesbianism as aberrant; moreover, Diane's plan to murder her friend associates lesbianism with violence, invoking a long-standing Hollywood stereotype (Kessler, 2003). In the film's finale, Diane meets the statutory fate of mentally distressed women in cinema, when, wracked with guilt for her crime and her failure to succeed as an actress – and seemingly tortured by horrific memories of her childhood abuse – she shoots herself in the head. To be fair, Lynch metes out a similar fate to the *male* hero, Fred Madison, of his preceding film, *Lost Highway* (1997). Yet, as suggested earlier, such ghastly and tragic endings are most often reserved for female characters.

A case in point is *A Tale of Two Sisters* (Ji-woon Kim, 2003), a Korean psychological thriller which garnered considerable critical acclaim internationally. The film is narrated by a young girl, Su-mi, who pieces together the events leading up to her incarceration in a psychiatric ward. Su-mi is initially presented as a protective older sister to Su-Yeon; yet she is an unreliable narrator. As she strips away the layers of self-delusion, she recalls that she might have saved her sister had she not been so preoccupied with her hatred for the girls' reviled step-mother. Like *Mulholland Drive*, *A Tale of Two Sisters* charts the heroine's gradual emancipation from self-delusion; and as in Lynch's film, a tragic mood prevails at the end of the film, as Su-mi languishes guiltily in hospital.

The gendered nature of Diane's and Su-mi's tragic fates is thrown into relief when compared with two psychological thrillers featuring delusional *male* protagonists: *The Machinist* (Brad Anderson, 2004) and *Secret Window* (David Koepp, 2004). In the former film, Trevor Reznik is factory worker who seeks to overcome his guilt for his part in a hit and run accident by inventing a fantasy world in which he rescues those around him. While tormented for the duration of the film with insomnia and hallucinations of a diabolical double named Ivan, Reznik in the end comes to the redemptive recognition that Ivan is a product of his guilty conscience (fittingly, the film references Dostoyevsky throughout – Reznik attempts to read *The Idiot* and *Crime and Punishment* throughout the film, while the name Ivan references *The Brothers Karamazov*). In *Secret Window*, meanwhile, Mort Rainey murders his ex-wife and her new partner in a jealous rage, while under the influence of his malevolent alter ego (or rather superego, given his moralising tone and Quaker hat), John Shooter. *Mulholland Drive, A Tale of Two Sisters, The Machinist* and *Secret Window* all attest to the recent popularity, inside and outside Hollywood, of mindbender and Dissociative Identity Disorder films. Yet males prove more resilient than females to psychological crisis in these films. While Reznik eventually finds relief from his guilt and Rainey is restored to his 'normal', albeit disagreeably supercilious personality after his crimes, Ji-woon Kim's Su-mi and Lynch's Diane are granted no such respite. (Incidentally, it is also difficult to ignore the ways in which class status is linked to particular aspects of madness in these films. Reznik and Rainey are clearly mentally distressed, for example; yet the most violent aspects of their madness are projected onto the figures of the thuggish Ivan and the Southern psychopath John Shooter, respectively.)

Perhaps the most abject image of mad femininity in contemporary film occurs in the kidnap thriller *Don't Say a Word* (Gary Fleder, 2001). The film's hero, played by Michael Douglas, is Nathan Conrad, a psychiatrist who attempts to extract a numerical code from a hysterical, near-catatonic patient, Elizabeth Burrows (Britanny Murphy), in order to locate his kidnapped daughter. Diagnosed with post-traumatic stress disorder (PTSD), Elizabeth experiences flashbacks of her father's murder at the hands of his fellow conspirators during a jewel heist. Conrad establishes that Elizabeth is also mimicking other psychiatric conditions in order to remain in hospital, beyond the reach of the film's villains. While extensive psychiatric mimicry by a PTSD sufferer stretches credibility to the maximum, Elizabeth is a sympathetic character, not least because she eventually helps Conrad to locate his daughter. Yet she is hardly powerful. Like many nineteenth-century hysterics (Showalter, 1987a: 160–1), Elizabeth is mute, communicating only via hand gestures. Her theatrical, coquettish flirtation with Conrad also recall accounts of female psychiatric patients in the nineteenth century, whose hysterical attacks were dramatically staged, sometimes after coaching, for the approval of psychiatric investigators such as Charcot (Showalter, 1987a: 147–154). Elizabeth conforms to long-standing stereotypes of the beautiful, innocent, wide-eyed madwoman; she spends much of the film shivering, wrapped in a blanket or in Conrad's jacket – a symbol of her subordination to her therapist – singing mournful songs of childhood.

Indeed, *Don't Say a Word* draws upon patriarchal fantasies of femmine vulnerability. In an attempt to coax the code from Elizabeth, Conrad gives her his daughter's comic book, blackboard and rag doll, gifts which serve both to identify Elizabeth with Conrad's missing daughter and to infantilise her. As Gretchin Bisplinghoff (1992) notes, historically the doll motif has played a key role in cinematic constructions of mad femininity:

> the repeated choice of the doll image (*Snake Pit; Rain Tree County; Freud; Whatever Happened to Baby Jane?; Suddenly Last Summer; Sisters; A Safe Place; Frances;* etc.) automatically operates to place the woman within the female role at her most regressive.

Conrad's sexual fantasies, as well as his professional standing, are dependent on feminine passivity. In an early seduction scene, for example, he enters the bedroom he shares with his wife Aggie, who is immobilised with her leg in plaster, playfully noting that she is 'totally exposed – and quite vulnerable'. Despite its jocularity, the scene consolidates Conrad's authority over the 'vulnerable' women around him. For Elizabeth, meanwhile, Conrad is clearly a substitute for her murdered father, an identification strengthened when, in the conclud-ing scene of the film, Elizabeth reaches out to touch the hand of Conrad's daughter, whom she helps to rescue. Elizabeth is thus rein-tegrated into the patriarchal order by her therapist, much as Freud or Charcot's female patients had to be seen to be 'saved' by their psychiatric masters.

Indeed, *Don't Say a Word* resurrects images of female lunacy first consolidated in the nineteenth century, when women were held to be weaker and therefore more susceptible to mental affliction than men. As Elaine Showalter (1987b) notes, this misogyny finds expres-sion in Romantic theatrical and pictorial representations of *Hamlet*'s Ophelia. Showalter (1987a: 13) also discusses the popular Romantic figure of Crazy Jane, a servant girl who wanders the windswept land-scape, plaintively commemorating her lost lover, so that 'for Romantic writers, Crazy Jane was a touching image of feminine vulnerability and a flattering reminder of female dependence upon male affection.' *Don't Say a Word* reproduces this stereotype of ethereal, dependent femininity with particular blatancy.

The sexual undertones of Elizabeth's behaviour towards Conrad invoke another stereotype of the mental distress film: that of the 'female patient as seductress' (Seale, 2002: 103). Her behaviour recalls both the promiscuity of Lisa in *Girl, Interrupted* and Virginia Cunningham's obsession with her psychiatrist in *The Snake Pit*. Yet while Virginia Cunningham at least manages to break free from her obsession, Elizabeth, at the end of *Don't Say A Word*, seems more dependent than ever on her psychiatrist. Brittany Murphy's prior film role, Daisy Randone in *Girl, Interrupted*, commits suicide after being sexually abused by her father; yet while Daisy's alienation from her family leads to a tragic fate, Elizabeth is saved by her acceptance of a properly filial role within the patriarchal family structure – a peculiarly Victorian theme. As Fuery (2004: 161) notes, cinematic representations of hysteria hark back to a pre-Freudian notion of family and marriage as preventatives for hysteria and Fuery's description of female film hysterics as 'outsiders to the family, envious of such a structure, desiring to be part of it', clearly applies to Elizabeth.

Into the shadows: Madness in the horror film

Despite the violence of action-film villains, it is horror cinema that has received the most sustained criticism from anti-stigma campaigners. The 'otherness' of mental distress is particularly apparent in early horror cinema. In W. F. Murnau's classic Expressionist vampire film *Nosferatu* (1919), for example, the deranged estate agent Knock delights in the plague that ensues from the spread of vampirism across Europe – a terri-fying symbol of the blood-letting of the First World War. Repeating the mantra 'Blood is Life!', the wild-eyed Knock attacks his doctor, before being restrained. Such an image of madness, heavily influenced by the melodramatic theatrical traditions of the nineteenth century, is hardly likely to strike a contemporary audience as an accurate representation of mental distress. Yet the key problem with this portrayal is not so much its lack of verisimilitude – something guaranteed, one might argue, by its early date – or even its violence, but its unequivocal association of madness with moral depravity.

The contemporary treatment of madness in horror cinema is seldom so overtly stigmatising; yet particular trends in horror film have given critics cause for concern. Since the 1980s, the stock character of the deranged and often misogynistic killer in the 'slasher' genre has met with much critical protest (Wahl, 1995: 111–2). Susan Faludi (1992) has argued that the 1980s was a politically regressive decade whose media products reflected a rolling back of the feminist advances of the 1960s and 1970s. It should not perhaps surprise us, therefore, that the treatment of mental distress was so problematic during this decade, featuring nominally mentally distressed killers such as Jason Vorhees, of the *Friday the 13th* series, who prey on multiple female victims (although the less well-known 1980s *Sleepaway Camp* slashers featured a young female killer, Angela Baker). Particularly nauseating is the backstory of the *Nightmare on Elm Street* films' Freddie Krueger, known as the 'son of a hundred maniacs', since his mother was raped and tortured by psychiatric patients. In the light of such details, it is unsurprising that anti-stigma campaigners often latch onto the horrific image of the 'axe-wielding psycho' as the emblem of all that is wrong with cinema's portrayal of mental distress.

The lazy recourse to mental distress as a gruesome explanatory backstory to these film series is inexcusable. Yet similar slasher films are still made. In Richard Valentine's neo-slasher film *Bloody Mary* (2006), for example, a group of workers and patients in a psychiatric hospital feed nubile teenage girls to a witch who dwells in the tunnels beneath the institution in which she was once a patient. The association of madness here with not just violence, but primordial, chthonic malevolence, together with the presentation of the mental hospital as a gothic chamber of horrors are both deeply problematic. Yet there is a danger of over-emphasising the importance of the slasher genre within the history of the mental distress film. The slasher movie has suffered declining commercial fortunes since the 1980s, when the enormous popularity of video rentals inaugurated a moral panic around so-called video nasties.

Moreover, contemporary slashers are also more likely than their 1980s predecessors to offer a psychological rationale that mitigates if not excuses the crimes of the killer. At first glace, the hulking, grunting killer Kane in the gothic teen gore-fest *See No Evil* (Gregory Dark, 2006), for example, is over-coded as a brute, recalling Foucault's description of madness in the classical period as rooted in the threat of predatory, murderous bestiality (Foucault, 2005). Yet the moral responsibility for Kane's killing spree eventually shifts to Kane's manipulative mother, a religious zealot who, we learn, has kept her son in a cage and tormented him for many years. The real villain of the piece, we come to understand, is Kane's brutalising mother. If there is misogyny here, it perhaps inheres less in the madman's acts of violence against teenaged girls than in the explanation supplied for them; as Deborah Jermyn (2003: 54) notes, 'domineering mothers [...] are often constructed as the root cause of the male psychopath'.

It is also difficult to sustain the argument – sometimes rather slackly touted in anti-stigma circles – that horror films are centrally concerned with mental distress. As Fuery (2004: 25) says of the slasher subgenre: 'these films may hint at the madness of the killers, but more often it is the themes of revenge, sexual transgression, and (occasionally) the supernatural that define the narrative and explicate the events.' Indeed, horror protagonists are often presented as mad only to be vindicated later in the story when their supernatural powers are revealed. In Katt Shea's *The Rage: Carrie 2* (1999), for instance, Rachel is suspected to be suffering from hereditary mental distress by her school counsellor; yet it quickly becomes clear, to the audience at least, that Rachel is actually in possession of devastating telekinetic powers. One should perhaps not overstate the case here: the psychiatric institution in which Rachel's mother is incarcerated is certainly a rather frightening place. Yet the horrific events of the film are not attributed to mental distress.

One could go even further and argue that those horror films in which madness *does* constitute a central theme are sometimes quite progressive. I would like to develop this point through a brief case study of Mathieu Kossovitz's 2003 film, *Gothika*. In the film, Halle Berry plays Dr Miranda Grey, a hard-nosed psychologist who awakes from a catatonic state to find herself a patient in the bleak, fortress-like psychiatric institution where she used to work, accused of having murdered her husband – the boss of the institution – with an axe. Miranda now finds that her one-time charge, Chloe, is a fellow patient. Chloe, who is being abused by a local law enforcement officer, Sheriff Ryan, teaches Miranda to see things from the perspective of the patient and helps her to uncover ongoing sexual abuse within the institution. Assisted by Rachel, the ghost of a murdered girl, Miranda escapes from hospital and gradually discovers that her husband, the head of the institution, tortured and killed Rachel with the help of the sheriff. At the end of the film, Miranda is reunited with Chloe outside the institution, only to discover that she is now able to see the ghosts of many other murdered children. This ending alludes to Caliban's 'Be not afeard. The isle is full of noises' speech in Shakespeare's *The Tempest*. Like her namesake in that play, Miranda has become a compassionate creature, newly attuned to a 'brave new world that has [dead] people in't'.

In the years since its release, *Gothika* has achieved notoriety for its predictable set design, hackneyed horror lighting effects and plot holes and narrative absurdities. For example, to allow Miranda to pursue her investigations, the ghost, Rachel, must twice break Miranda out of prison in order to return her to the location where the murder took place; yet such a formidable entity as Rachel could easily have revealed to Miranda why she had killed her husband as soon as she had committed the act. While Miranda's pattern of return and escape from the hospital lacks clear narrative rationale, however, it underscores her struggle against institutional power, reinforcing the film's anti-sexist premise. One could argue, in fact, that *Gothika*'s scant regard for realism is a key element in its melodramatic subversiveness. Gary Morris (2006: 37) complains that the hospital's high level of security is 'unnecessary', suggesting the violence of its patients. Certainly, some of the patients played by extras who appear in the background of many shots are othered by their strange appearance and eccentric behaviour. At the same time, however, the hospital patients are not generally portrayed as violent so much as oppressed; it is partly by emphasising the 'unnecessary' constraints of the hospital that the film vindicates the patients and indicts the institution as the real source of violence.

According to the conservative critic Eric Cox (2003), '*Gothika*'s premise rests on the idea – popularized in the 1960s by French historian Michel Foucault and Scottish psychiatrist R. D. Laing – that the distinction between sanity and madness is an artificial social construct.' Cox goes on to complain that the film privileges madness as a 'lifestyle choice'. Cox's second point seems wrongheaded, since none of the characters chooses madness. Yet Cox is correct to argue that the film postulates madness as socially constructed. For Foucault (2005), medieval and early modern people found a truth in madness that was later suppressed in the Great Confinement of the seventeenth century; for better or worse, *Gothika* revives this conception of madness as a pathway to truth and enlightenment.

Gothika critiques the psychiatric reliance on pharmaceutical treatment. In an early scene, Miranda objects that Chloe is receiving a dangerously high dosage of drugs (presumably, in the light of later revelations, to facilitate her sexual abuse). Moreover, both of the film's principal female characters are both initially regarded as mentally disturbed before being finally vindicated. Like James Cameron's *Terminator 2: Judgement Day* (1991), in which Sarah Connor is incarcerated in a psychiatric unit for her supposedly 'delusional' beliefs, *Gothika* presents madness as part of an expedient patriarchal plot. It is the film's two male villains who are truly delusional, in particular Miranda's husband, a symbolic father who twice asserts his belief that he is a god – first as a joke, later in earnest. By suggesting the radical constructedness of 'mental illness' and the sordid motivations underpinning its attribution, *Gothika* underscores the ease with which psychiatric labels can be mobilised in the service of patriarchy.

In an interview available on the Dark Castle DVD release of the film, Halle Berry explains that her mother was a psychiatric nurse for 35 years and that she 'was a great source of information for me and my journey was to discover what one would feel as reality slowly starts to slip away'. Berry expresses her actorly challenge here in terms of psychiatric verisimilitude; but this seems peculiarly irrelevant, for at least two reasons. First, the premise of the film is that Miranda's supposed madness is in fact an awakening to a new reality beyond the rationalist, male-dominated world of psychiatry. Far from losing her grip on reality, the incarcerated Miranda gradually apprehends the truth about her supposed crime. Secondly, *Gothika* is neither intended to be, nor intelligible as a sociological or psychiatric study of mental distress. Miranda slips into and out of 'mental illness' with alarming ease (as does Chloe, who is discharged from hospital at the end of the film with little explanation, leading us to suppose that she was never mad in the first place). Moreover, the ghost of Rachel seems to control the onset of manic episodes in both Miranda and Chloe: this is particularly evident in the scene in which Rachel 'possesses' Miranda, throwing her body off the walls of her solitary confinement cell in order to convince the guards to unlock the cell door and thereby facilitate Miranda's implausible second escape. Madness in *Gothika*, then, functions as a convenient narrative device.

Madness also serves to condense the film's key theme of female solidarity. The film is framed, in fact, by two conversations between Miranda and Chloe – the first inside the institution, the second outside of it. In the first of these, Miranda, still a psychologist, refuses to accept the truth of Chloe's abuse at the hands of a prison guard. In the final scene, Miranda and Chloe finally communicate on friendly and equal terms. The film implies that the only way Miranda could truly understand Chloe's plight is by sharing her experience of being institutionalised and held to be insane. As Chloe states somewhat ponderously at the end of film: 'Everyone thought we were crazy, but we were seeing the truth; more than they could see.' The film's climax contains a distinctly anti-sexist twist, too. When Sheriff Ryan attacks Miranda towards the end of the film, the audience expects Miranda's sceptical but supportive colleague Pete to come heroically to the rescue. Yet Pete arrives too late and it is Rachel who materialises to save Miranda from death, rendering Pete pathetically ineffectual. The film's finale thus constitutes a wholesale rejection of institutional patriarchy in favour of sisterly solidarity.

Clearly, *Gothika* forgoes psychiatric verisimilitude, combining antipsychiatric perspectives with supernatural fantasy in the service of ideological critique. In doing so, it draws upon a tradition of proto-feminist nineteenth-century literature in which attributions of madness are exposed as part of a cynical psychiatric strategy for the containment of unruly femininity (Tomes, 1994: 358). This tradition includes Elizabeth Packard's (1973) experiences of wrongful incarceration in nineteenth-century America and the Victorian 'sensation novels' – a genre reviled by respectable literary critics of the period – which challenged patriarchal values through the themes of madness, incarceration and sexual deviance and which often featured women wrongly diagnosed by male characters as insane (Shuttleworth, 1993). The same themes are explored cinematically in George Cukor's Victorian-set thriller about patriarchal oppression and madness, *Gaslight* (1944). *Gothika's* revaluation of female madness and critique of patriarchy also has contemporary analogues in the horror genre. In the post-*Buffy* Sarah Michelle Gellar vehicle *The Return* (Asif Kapadia, 2006), for instance, the heroine Joanna experiences hallucinations and inexplicably cuts herself; but we soon learn that she is acting out messages from a murdered woman upon whose killer Joanna finally takes revenge.

Richard Kelly's horror/thriller *Donnie Darko* also exploits the theme of madness for subversive effect. Set in the late 1980s, this high school movie combines a critique of the social mores of the Reagan era with a time-travel storyline. Donnie is held to be eccentric by his family and peers because of his fascination with the radical possibilities of quantum physics and his precocious rejection of his social milieu, which is characterised by corrupt politicians, degenerate classmates, a banal and degraded popular culture, and an imbecilic, authoritarian teacher who spouts New Age platitudes. Under the influence of visions of a man in a bunny costume, Donnie commits a variety of mischievous and violent acts directed against his school and against a local motivational speaker and paedophile, Jim Cunningham.

The film also gently sends up psychiatry. Donnie takes an unspecified psychiatric medication and attends regular therapy sessions with a female therapist, Dr Thurman. Although she is a sympathetic character,

Thurman tells Donnie's parents that their son is paranoid and recommends increasing his medication. In the film's terms, this advice is erroneous, since Donnie's contrarian tendencies are eventually vindicated and his hallucinations persist despite his medication. The sense of the young hero as a beacon of sanity in an insane world is reinforced at the end of the film, when Gary Jules' cover version of Tears for Fears' 1983 single 'Mad World' plays over a montage depicting the misery of several of the film's characters, many of whom have destroyed their lives through their own misdeeds.

Donnie Darko is just one of a clutch of ludic mindbender films, including *Twelve Monkeys* (Terry Gilliam, 1995), *The Butterfly Effect* (Eric Bress and J. Mackye Gruber, 2004), *The Darkroom* (Michael Hurst, 2006) and *Abre los ojos* (Alejandro Amenábar, 1997), later remade by Tom Cruise as *Vanilla Sky* (2001), in which madness is associated with an ability to travel in time or to access alternative universes. Many of these films have a subversive subtext. Jack Starks, the hero of *The Jacket* (John Maybury, 2005), is a veteran of the first Gulf War who is discharged from the army after being shot in the head by a terrified Iraqi child. He subsequently develops Gulf War Syndrome, suffering from 'amnesia' and 'acute psychological suppression'. After his discharge, Starks is committed to a hospital for the criminally insane after being wrongfully accused of shooting a police officer. Diagnosed as delusional, he is subjected to a banned drug treatment by the sadistic Dr Becker and confined for long periods in a body drawer of the hospital morgue. Becker's fiendishness is complemented by that of his assistant, Nurse Harding, whose very name – like that of Nurse Ratched in *One Flew Over the Cuckoo's Nest* – connotes sadistic malice. Nevertheless, during his 'therapies', Starks is able to project himself into the future to discover the solution to his and others' problems.

Psychiatric accuracy is hardly the aim of *The Jacket*; rather, the film comments obliquely on the psychological consequences of warfare. Amid the confusion of the film's brief opening night-time scene in Iraq, Starks expresses his alienation from the military action in which he is taking part, muttering: 'none of this is our problem'. In conversation with the hospital's sympathetic female psychiatrist, meanwhile, Starks explains that 'the real events that have happened to me have been fucked up, not my mind.' Like Sam Mendes' *Jarhead* (2005), *The Jacket* explores the stresses endured by soldiers during and after the first Gulf War. Yet the film also refers backwards to a long tradition of mental distress films about veterans, such as *Birdy* (Alan Parker, 1984). Like Travis Bickle and the troubled Vietnam veteran John Rambo in

First Blood (Ted Kotcheff, 1982), Starks is a loner who is ignominiously dumped back into society having served his military purpose. It is this inhumanity that constitutes the true horror of *The Jacket*.

Conclusion

Writing in the mid-1990s, Otto Wahl (1995: 58) suggested that:

> Film portrayal of mentally ill villains has not diminished in the 1990s. Many of the films [...] have focused on disturbed criminals. These include, for example, *Blue Steel, Miami Blues,* and *Henry: Portrait of a Serial Killer.* Innocent victims have been menaced by disturbed babysitters (*The Hand That Rocks the Cradle*), sinister tenants (*Pacific Heights*), unstable fans (*Misery*), psychopathic secretaries (*The Temp*), troubled children (*The Good Son*), traumatized football fans (*Ace Ventura, Pet Detective*) and even obsessed police officers (*Unlawful Entry*).

Fifteeen years later, cinematic images of madness are not, I would argue, as uniformly abominable as this quotation implies; or at least, they are problematic for rather different reasons than is usually supposed among anti-stigma critics.

In contrast to the films listed above by Wahl, many of the most innovative mental distress films are not high-grossing Hollywood films, but independent productions. Films such as *Spider* (Capitol Films), and *Keane* (Canary Films) present formally innovative and moving depictions of human loss and struggle, evoking the subjective experience of madness through visual and auditory hallucinations, while stretching and testing the formal conventions of classical narrative realism. Although its representation of violence seems exploitative, even *Julien Donkey-Boy* (391 Productions) also artfully explores the difficulties faced by individuals suffering serious mental distress. These innovative films play a vital role in refreshing the store of cultural images of madness.

This chapter has also attempted to reclaim some progressive potential for previously neglected film genres. Critics have tended to castigate cinematic representations of mental distress belonging to the less-prestigious film genres, such as horror. Yet a number of horror films from the last few years, including *Donnie Darko, Gothika* and *The Jacket*, represent a more progressive trend in the representation of madness. In these texts, psychiatric verisimilitude is eschewed and the trope of madness is instead employed in the service of social commentary and the critique of patriarchy, reviving and reworking long-standing satirical traditions. As in many of the comedy films concerning mental distress, such as *Patch Adams* and *What About Bob?*, the oppositional import of madness is often combined with highly critical representations of psychiatric power, which – at least in its masculine incarnations – is typically viewed as brutal or unjustified.

Although horror films and 'low-brow' comedies about mental distress can be critically redeemed, it remains the case that the public acceptance of contemporary films about mental distress is often related to a film's literary provenance or credentials. Many of the 'serious' dramatic mental distress films – *Shine, Girl, Interrupted, Spider,* and *A Beautiful Mind* – are based on books and consequently have a rather higher cultural value than other films. The serious, even sombre tone of many of these films, as well as their broadly realistic aesthetic, no doubt indexes their status as 'quality dramas' and thus of their suitability for nomination for Academy Awards. Yet many of these treatments, pre-eminently *A Beautiful Mind*, seem to have airbrushed unpleasant realities out of the narrative or bowdlerised their literary antecedents. The problem with 'message-based' filmmaking is that it can result in a rather saccharine, hagiographic picture of distress; in the cases of *Shine* and *A Beautiful Mind*, at least, one is inclined to agree with Samuel Goldwyn's remark that the delivery of messages should be left to Western Union.

The rise of more 'positive' representations of madness also bolsters psychiatric hegemony. Most of the films discussed above articulate a Freudian/Modernist commitment to the notion of a 'true self' that is crystallised through the near-statutory 'happy ending'. As Burr and Butt (2000: 196) explain, 'Modernist thought penetrates our everyday thinking when we "discover" how we "really feel" about someone or something.' Cinematic treatments of madness typically end with a final 'reveal' in which the heroine or hero rolls back the layers of psychic repression to become aware of its self-division and the psyche is healed, or – as is often the case in films with female protagonists – is driven beyond madness into death. This preoccupation with the revelation of an authentic self reinforces not only the ideological values of individualism and self-reliance, but also the authority of psychiatric discourse, which is grounded in the notion of the transparent, rational cogito whose purity must be re-established through psychiatric intervention.

More specifically, many of these films reinforce the pre-eminence of medication as a treatment method. Psycho-pharmaceutical drugs can be helpful to many people suffering from mental distress, although there are, as noted earlier, serious and widespread doubts about their efficacy and sometimes deadly 'side-effects'; one might also question whether pharmaceutical drugs are always the only or most suitable ones for their purpose. In contemporary film, however, pharmaceutical intervention is often seen as the first, rather than the last recourse in the treatment of mental distress. Films that question this faith are few and far between; the animated film *Persepolis* (Vincent Paronnaud and Marjane Satrapi, 2007), whose heroine attempts suicide after being prescribed anti-depressants by a glib psychiatrist, is a rare exception.

This cinematic faith in psychiatry in general requires some brief historicisation and qualification. The rise of the 'madness film' in the 1940s coincided with psychotherapy's peak in popularity and with a determination to return women to a domestic role. Perhaps the best-known of these films is *The Snake Pit*, in which the hospital is a frightening environment. Virginia Cunningham is terrorised by an overbearing male psychiatrist and the vengeful Nurse Davis. Nonetheless, like many Hollywood films of the time, *The Snake Pit* ultimately bolsters the credibility of psychiatry as a healing discipline. Both the electro-shock treatment and narco-synthesis which Virginia receives in hospital are seen as a terrifying but ultimately effective treatments, and – as in *Lady in the Dark* and Irving Rapper's *Now, Voyager* (1942), a middle-class psychodrama in which a shy daughter sloughs off her childish neuroses to assume her 'proper' role as wife and lover – psychotherapy sessions gradually bring the heroine from the darkness of ignorance into the light of self-understanding. Up until the 1960s, indeed, psychiatrists in the movies, as in life, were the 'authoritative voices of reason, adjustment, and well-being' (Gabbard and Gabbard, 1999: 75).

This changed with the advent of the so-called anti-psychiatry movement inspired by Esterton, Szasz and Laing. Both Samuel Fuller's *Shock Corridor* (1963) and Robert Rossen's *Lilith* (1964) question the power relations inherent in the enforcement of distinctions between madness and sanity. And although both the surgical practice of lobotomy and electroconvulsive therapy (ECT) were in decline when the film was made in 1975, *One Flew Over the Cuckoo's Nest* is also deeply critical of psychiatric practices – even although, as Fleming and Manvell (1985: 53) note, the film does not present such a radical perspective on mental distress as the novel upon which it is based. Hollywood films in the post-1960s period project scepticism not just about Freudian psychoanalysis, but also, more generally, about psychiatry and its social and political functions. Films as various as *Angel Baby, Don't Say A Word* and *Gothika* all present the psychiatric institution as a prison, while a sceptical or hostile take on psychiatry is widespread in Hollywood cinema from *Birdy* to *The Jacket*. Even early psychiatry is criticised in the historical film *Quills*: the film's sadistic alienist, Dr Royer-Collard, draws upon eighteenth-century reservations about the nascent psychiatric profession (Peterson, 1982); but it also resonates with post-1960s anti-psychiatric perspectives. Indeed, the 'thoroughly evil psychiatrist' has become a common film stereotype (Clara, 1995: 7). Screen psychiatrists are often incompetent, too. Comparing Alfred Hitchcock's *Psycho* (1960) with its 1998 remake by Gus Van Sant, Mark Welch and Twilla Racine (1999) note that the psychiatrist at the end of the 1960 version is as authoritative and confident as Bates is shy and neurotic; in the later version, however, it is the psychiatrist who is hesitant and diffident, while Bates is brashly arrogant.

Yet psychiatry has retained its credibility in the cinema by means of a deft hegemonic twist. While the 'evil psychiatrist' remains a staple of horror and psychological thrillers and male psychiatrists in film comedy are incompetent, cinematic psychiatry has generally become more patient-focused, 'softer' and 'feminised'. In *K-Pax* (Iain Softley, 2001), for instance, a kindly male psychiatrist unravels the repressed past of Prot, a man who claims to be an alien from a planet where emotions are redundant; in the process of helping Prot, the psychiatrist overcomes his own emotional repression. Yet the benign authority of psychiatry is embodied most commonly by *female* screen therapists such as Dr Susan Lowenstein, the mild-mannered friend-cum-analyst who pacifies the aggressive, hyper-masculine Tom Wingo in *The Prince of Tides* (1991) and Dr Sonia Wick in *Girl, Interrupted* (1999). As Elaine Showalter (1997: 59) notes:

> The old-style authoritarian shrink, modeled on a stern Charcot or a bullying Freud, has been replaced by a softer, more approachable figure. Rather than a shaman or guru, the image of the therapist is changing into that of a comforting friend. The therapist's role is more and more to affirm, support, and endorse the patient's narrative, to provide a 'safe space' for disclosure, and not to challenge the truth or historical reality of the patient's assertions.

This shift supports Žižek's (1997) theory of the decline in the postmodern imaginary of judgemental and repressive social authority (the Lacanian 'big Other'). More prosaically, given the growing number of women entering the psychiatric professions since the 1980s (Parkhouse, 1991), it is unsurprising that contemporary culture typically presents female psychiatrists favourably and male psychiatrists as officious and uncaring. In several of the films discussed in this chapter – *Girl, Interrupted, Gothika* and *The Jacket* – a domineering and unsympathetic male psychiatrist is counterbalanced by a more compassionate and competent female therapist. Thus, while Morris (2006: 156) sees cinematic representations of psychiatry as confusingly diverse, it is arguable that they are patterned according to historical period and gender. Whereas the films of the post-war period lionised psychiatry as a means of restoring women to their proper station in life, contemporary films tend to critique oppressive, masculinist versions of psychiatry, while validating 'softer', 'feminised' forms of therapy.

The cinematic generosity towards female psychiatrists is not always extended, however, to mad women. It is true that several films, from *Gothika* to *Flightplan*, reverse the stereotype of the 'crazy woman' as part of a broadly feminist strategy. In comic treatments of mental distress, however, female characters are, quite simply, few and far between, while in romantic drama 'mad' girls who contest the social order through elopement are punished for their transgressions. Moreover, in Hollywood cinema, the tragic helplessness of female protagonists stands in stark contrast to the heroism or 'genius' of male characters.

This cinematic obsession with the figure of the 'mad genius' who overcomes all obstacles to achieve fame complements the meritocratic and voluntaristic ethos of neoliberalism. At a time of low social mobility in both the UK and US (Centre for Economic Performance, 2005), assurances that 'genius will out' and that willpower enables triumph over adversity seem particularly serviceable ideological messages. The classed nature of these messages is self-evident, albeit seldom discussed in analyses of madness and film: narratives of struggling mathematicians and musicians are culturally valorised, not least at the Academy Awards; working-class characters, meanwhile, are more likely to be constructed as villains or killers.

Finally, ethnic minority characters are conspicuous by their virtual absence from mental distress films. Visible minority characters often feature in cinematic depictions of communal or political struggle; yet they are less-commonly depicted as tortured or alienated individuals, perhaps reflecting a cultural bias towards images of tortured white subjectivity; even Halle Berry's Miranda in *Gothika* is merely held to be mad by others. There are, it is true, few visible minority characters in Hollywood lead roles in general, perhaps reflecting the racism of the Hollywood system. Nonetheless, the whiteness of cinematic madness is problematic. Visible minority people in society may have a more guarded attitude towards the psychiatric profession than whites: Elaine Showalter (1997: 9) quotes a *New York* magazine poll showing that 44% of New Yorkers living in Manhattan have sought psychological counselling, more than twice the percentage of residents who have done so in the predominantly black areas of Brooklyn, Staten Island, or Queens. Yet despite seeming to be less inclined or financial able to seek psychological counselling, visible minorities figure disproportionately in hospitalisation statistics (King et al., 1994; Harrison, 2002), suggesting that black heroines and heroes are significantly under-represented in films about mental distress.

4
Channelling Affliction: Television Discourses of Distress

The tripartite structure of classical Hollywood narrative film tends to mirror that of the 'equilibrium-breakdown-recovery' pattern of mental disturbance, making the feature film a particularly suitable format for the elaboration of psychiatric themes. Yet the relatively closed nature of cinema's narrative structures does not encourage representational diversity or ambiguity. Television's more segmented character has long been argued to produce more 'open texts' (Eco, 1979; Ellis, 1982). The relative fluidity of the medium – and its variety of genres – means that television offers an enormous diversity of images of mental distress; yet it also complicates the analysis of those images in several ways.

One problem is the sheer number of available texts: while it is feasible to survey many of the key mental distress films of the past 15 years, it is impossible to analyse every television representation of madness. To this problem of scope must be added the difficulty of deciding which television forms and genres to focus upon. Raymond Williams famously conceived of television textuality as a 'flow', rather than a series of singular and self-contained programmes. Within this flow, throwaway references to 'psychos' and 'nutters' abound, so that the analysis of television's representation of madness might encompass not only television programmes, but also advertisements, continuity links, schedule listings and even the columns of television critics and other television 'intertexts' (Fiske, 1989). A Channel 4 continuity announcer, for example, referred flippantly to the fearless reptile-handling TV zoologist Mark O'Shea as a 'madman' (16 September 2001) and studies by Wahl (1995), Philo (1996) and Wilson et al. (2000) show that terms like 'nutty', 'whacko' and 'deranged' are routinely used in television advertising in ways that arguably evoke a negative image of mental distress. Depending on the explicitness of their reference to mental distress, some of these examples are doubtless more problematic than others. In the UK in 2005, a frenzied cartoon character, Crazy Frog, appeared in television advertisements for mobile telephone ringtones, achieving considerable notoriety as a pop cultural 'meme'. Crazy Frog was not simply a 'wacky' figure, however, but seemed to reference the signs and symptoms of serious mental distress in a light-hearted way; his boggling pupils, for example, mimicked the side-effects of psychotropic medications.

Television continuity announcements, listings and episode sum-maries can also be problematic when they casually associate madness with destructive, malicious or unjustified forms of violence. Thus the BBC's Ceefax (5 November 2003) television guide lists an episode of *The New Adventures of Superman* in which 'a madman takes over a satel-lite weapons system in Metropolis and threatens to destroy the world.' Not only does this description associate mental distress with malicious violence; it also questionably presupposes the sanity of the 'normal' state of affairs, in which deadly weapons systems are kept 'safely' in the possession of state authorities.

Television news, too, often casually associates madness with reac-tionary forms of violence. An ITN evening news report by Nick Robinson on 15 September 2004 described an invasion of the chamber of the House of Commons by protesters claiming to represent the campaign group, Countryside Alliance. Robinson began the item as follows: 'They could have been terrorists, they could have been assassins, they could have been lunatics'. The archaism of 'lunatic', together with its associa-tion with terrorism and its final, emphatic position in Robinson's list of three slurs, combine to make this a stigmatising comment. More trou-bling than Robinson's remark because of its seeming lack of empathy in the face of evident human suffering is the behaviour of ABC's *World News Now* anchors Ryan Owens and Taina Hernandez, who laughed their way through a feature about comedy actor Owen Wilson's depres-sion and attempted suicide on 27 August 2007. The story was captioned with the subtitle 'Poor Owen'. 'He apparently tried to kill himself', noted Owens in mock reproach of his co-anchor, 'which is terribly serious, which is why you should not be laughing right now, Taina'. Follow-ing protests on the Internet, the pair apologised in a subsequent news broadcast. The difficulty of setting too much store by such remarks, however, lies in their very transience and, consequently, the difficulty of determining their proper context: defending her apparent laugh-ter over the Wilson report, Taina Hernandez, for example, claimed that she had in fact been giggling at a previous conversation with her co-anchor.

In view of such interpretative problems, this chapter does not focus on brief or casual references to mental distress, although these certainly pepper television output. Instead, it focuses on a selection of substantial treatments of mental distress in contemporary television dramas, soap operas, talk shows and documentaries. It seeks to address several questions about the representation of madness. For example, to what extent does the formal and generic diversity of television permit the exploration of mental distress from a variety of perspectives? Does television privilege social or biomedical paradigms of distress? Are there differences between US and UK television cultures treatments of distress? Does documentary, with its historical commitments to verisimilitude, present madness more 'realistically' than fiction? Most crucially of all, do television images of madness promote the same stereotypes – or uphold the same discriminations of gender, race and social class – as cinema?

For some critics, contemporary television primarily emphasises the otherness of those suffering with mental distress. As Nancy Signorielli (1993: 153–4) puts it:

> Mental illness is [a] ... topic that is presented quite problematically, particularly on television. Images of the mentally ill are stigmatized and sinister: Mentally ill characters, in contrast with reality, are most likely to be involved in violence, especially violence of a lethal nature. Moreover, they are often seen as failures and unable to cope successfully with life: They do not function either in the workplace or in the family.

Mentally distressed people on television, in other words, are often presented as unable to cope with the demands of family and working life. Thus television emphasises the difference or otherness of mentally distressed characters and their alienation from everyday life. A spectacular example of this occurs in season 2, episode 13 of David Lynch and Mark Frost's cult serial *Twin Peaks* (1990–1991), when Philip Gerard, also known as 'the one-armed man', is interrogated about the murder of the schoolgirl Laura Palmer and is asked if he suffers 'from schizophrenia, multiple personalities?'. Gerard, it transpires, is possessed by an evil spirit who was once a familiar of the serial's malevolent supernatural spirit Bob, a connection which reinforces stereotypical associations between disability, madness and evil. Through his physical disability as well as his implied schizophrenia, Gerard is over-determined as 'other'. Indeed, television characters are sometimes identified as mentally distressed through the incorporation of stigmatising visual iconography.

In a British television adaptation of Agatha Christie's novel *The Mystery of the Blue Train* (ITV1, 2006), for example, a very brief explanatory flash-back during the drama's denouement reveals the 'insane' wife of Rufus van Aldin sitting in semi-darkness wielding a pair of scissors – a detail absent from Christie's novel. The wife, a marginal figure in the story, does not feature either before or after this moment in the narrative; in the absence of other knowledge about her, the scissors and the darkness function as rather distasteful shorthand symbols for her insanity.

Nevertheless, some problematic assumptions underlie Signorielli's contention that television typically 'others' mental distress. For one thing, as I argue in this chapter, television often depicts mentally distressed people in recognisable social contexts and offers a greater variety of perspectives on psychological distress than film (although this may be particularly true of British television, rather than American television, which is Signorielli's main concern). A more fundamental objection to Signorielli's argument is that people with psychological problems *really do* encounter significant romantic and workplace prob-lems and that ignoring these genuine problems amounts to another kind of misrepresentation. Furthermore, to attack images of mentally distressed television characters as unemployed or unmarried is implic-itly to endorse a conservative definition of the 'normal', industrious, heterosexual human subject and to stigmatise the unemployed and the unmarried as social deviants. In this sense, Signorielli seems to fall foul of Machery's 'normative fallacy', as described in Chapter 2. Signorielli's objection that mentally distressed television characters do not function in the workplace or the family overlooks the possibility that such dys-functions might constitute a symbolic rejection of the roles demanded by work and the family under capitalism.

In Chapter 3, I argued that even 'unrealistic' representations of mental distress in film can challenge hegemonic definitions of normality. The same is true of television fiction, in which the realist aesthetic, especially in Britain, has been dominant. A British television play broadcast on ITV in 1967, *I Am Osango*, imaginatively explores the intersection between psychological distress and political oppression through the story of a welder who believes that he is an imprisoned African minister. Yet the television critic R. W. Cooper (1967: 6) opined that the play 'seemed too contrived for television, whatever its merits as a short story or radio play'. Cooper's comment seems to presuppose that television drama has stronger obligations towards representational realism than other media forms. In considering television images of madness, however, I sug-gest that there is no particular reason to privilege 'realism' over other aesthetic modes; we should consider television representations of distress in their generic contexts, rather than testing them solely against standards of realism.

'Look on the bright side: he may not be dangerous': Challenging stigma in television drama

In television drama, as in film, mental distress is increasingly positively presented. In recent years, many television dramas have been produced with the explicit aim of reducing the stigma of mental distress. This is particularly true of dramas intended for young adults, a group whose awareness of personal distress issues is a matter for public concern: a study in 2001 found that 60% of young people in the UK admitted to having verbally abused mentally distressed individuals ('Mentally ill abused by young', 2001).

Channel 4 has been particularly active in building mental health awareness among younger audiences. In June 2002, for example, the channel broadcast a 25-minute 'edutainment' drama entitled *Losing It*, whose explicit aims, according to Channel 4's website, were to help young people and those close to them to identify mental health and illness, overcome fear and stigma and develop emotional literacy. Supported by a Science on Stage and Screen Award from The Wellcome Trust, *Losing It* depicts a depressed teenager named Jude who attempts suicide owing to the pressures of schoolwork and the benign neglect of his parents. The increasing rate of suicide among young people, especially young men, makes the development of such dramas timely. The selection of a male protagonist, meanwhile, is also sociologically significant, since it is widely known that while depression is equally common in men and women, men are less likely than women to seek professional help; as Jude's female friend puts it, 'boys keep everything bottled up inside until they lash out.' *Losing It* also challenges several common stereotypes of madness, emphasising, for example, the normality of depression. Jude himself acknowledges that his life is, to all appearances, unremarkable: he has a comfortable, middle-class life and has generally performed well at school. The drama also illustrates that those suffering mental distress are more likely to be the victims than the perpetrators of violence: before attempting suicide, Jude gets involved in a fight in which he is badly beaten up.

For an edutainment film aimed at young adults, *Losing It* is remarkably sophisticated, artfully deploying the motif of invisibility. Eschewing the spectacular emphasis on physically abusive parents found in films such as *Shine* and *Julien Donkey-Boy, Losing It* attributes its protagonist's distress to the rather less dramatic cause of parental disregard – also a precipitating factor in the mental disturbance of Cassie in the teen drama *Skins*, broadcast on Channel 4's youth-oriented companion channel E4 (2007–). Neglected by his self-absorbed parents, Jude craves social acknowledgement, scrawling the words 'See Me' on his school exam paper (a phrase which, incidentally, was later the catchphrase of a Scottish Executive cross-media mental health campaign). When Jude's friend Tom meets a female blind date for the first time, she tells Tom that she has seen him before, to which Tom replies 'I'm not invisible then'. Tom's comment indicates that he shares Jude's basic human need for acknowledgement and recognition. *Losing It* thus presents mental distress as part and parcel of human life rather than monstrously other. This drama's theme of invisibility is apt: for many distressed young people, the loss of a coherent identity is often expressed in terms of becoming invisible to those around them, especially parents. As Anthony Giddens (1991: 60), drawing on Freud's description of the fort-da game in *Beyond the Pleasure Principle*, puts it, 'the child's exploration of its own disappearance is closely associated with the difficulty of grasping that the absent parent has not "gone for good" '. The sense of insecurity produced by alienation from parents is a major risk factor for teenage suicide (Huffine, 1991).

Another Channel 4 young adult drama, *The Illustrated Mum* (2003), is based on a young adults' book by Jacqueline Wilson which won the 1999 *Guardian* prize for children's fiction. It tells the story of a single mother of two called Marigold, who struggles to raise her two daughters while suffering with bipolar disorder. The older daughter, Star, loses faith in her mother, while the younger, Dolphin, is left to cope with household duties as Marigold's behaviour becomes increasingly manic. Told from Dolphin's perspective, the drama attempts to illustrate the everyday realities of stigmatisation; in one scene, for example, Marigold reacts aggressively to a taxi driver who unthinkingly calls her 'crazy'. It also shows psychological problems as a part of life whose consequences many children have to cope with unprepared.

Adult television drama has also pushed the anti-stigma agenda in recent years. 'Coming Out' (1995), an early episode of the ITV medical drama *Peak Practice*, charts reaction of a rural community to the arrival of a group of ex-psychiatric patients into the fictional village of Cardale. Broadcast just two years after the implementation of the National Health Service (NHS) and Community Care Act (the so-called Care in the Community Act), the episode dramatises the hostility often faced by ex-patients in the community: a notice reading 'No To Psychopaths in the Community' is pinned to a tree and a woman is hounded by children who scream 'loony', 'maniac' and 'freak' at her. Adding insult to injury, the ex-patients are wrongly blamed for an outbreak of Weil's disease during a public meeting. Yet one of the practice doctors, Jack Kerruish, delivers an impassioned speech at the meeting. 'This is where they belong', he tells the audience, 'not locked away in some decrepit Victorian institution'. As the title of this episode suggests, ex-psychiatric patients in this episode are seen, in quite crusading terms, as an oppressed social group who deserve the sympathy of the public and the advocacy of the medical profession.

Yet even stigma-busting representations of distress do not entirely avoid sensationalism. In another episode of *Peak Practice*, 'State of Mind' (1997), Clare becomes bipolar, endangering a patient by poking her eyes with her finger and eventually crashing her car into a wall. Yet mental distress in *Peak Practice* is seen as manageable with the aid of proper psychiatric medication. In 'A Matter of Principle' (1998), for instance, a regular character, Clare, fears that her lithium tablets are making her feel nauseous, but eventually discovers that medication is not the problem – she is pregnant. Ultimately, then, *Peak Practice* enshrines a medical, liberal and progressive view of mental distress.

Yet the medical profession is not idealised in British TV drama. Some dramas depict how medical authorities and institutions sometimes fail to exercise their duty of care. In a 2005 episode of the BBC1 medical drama *Casualty*, for example, a woman emerges from a persistent vegetative state after attempting to hang herself during a puerperal depression as her husband comments to the couple's son that 'daddy didn't do enough to help'. The husband also comments to the nurse that his wife's general practitioner (GP) considered that she would soon 'snap out of [her depression]', suggesting that the GP was also partly responsible for the suicide attempt. The episode portrays distressed individuals as more likely to harm themselves than others, while gently admonishing practitioners and family members to heed the signs of emotional disturbance in others. Other British dramas have attempted to depict the extent of institutional prejudices against distressed people. Thus, in series 4 episode 4 of Paul Abbott's BBC1 series *Clocking Off* (2003), a man attacks a care home nurse who has been bullying his mentally distressed brother; the police, however, prefer to believe that the patient is responsible for the assault. Thus British television drama, while typically framing mental distress in liberal medical terms, also acknowledges that the institutions caring for or dealing with sufferers are not infallible.

The complexities and inadequacies of the British psychiatric care system are given fuller treatment in Channel 4's one-off drama *Poppy Shakespeare* (2008), based on a novel by an ex-psychiatric patient, Clare Allan, which charts the struggles against bureaucracy of two women who attend a psychiatric day care centre. *Poppy Shakespeare* outlines the absurdity of a mental health system in which the disturbingly sane Poppy can only prove her sanity by first pretending to be mad. The drama shares with *Clocking Off* a rather bleak outlook on mental health care, as most of the day care centre staff are patronising or Machiavellian. Yet this disconcerting presentation of mental health care is partly justified in light of the massive underfunding of mental health services in the UK. Moreover, as a drama written by a service user, *Poppy Shakespeare* possesses a certain authenticity and authority.

Many US dramas also show a sympathetic attitude towards issues of mental distress. Several episodes of the 'missing persons' drama *Without A Trace* (CBS, 2002–), which has also proved popular in the UK on Channel 4, have featured storylines in which mentally distressed individuals go missing – a concept that allows the drama to emphasise the impact of mental distress on the friends and family left behind. One of these, 'Light Years', closely resembles the plot of the film *K-Pax*. An increasingly paranoid missing person, Teddy, believes he has been abducted by aliens and that he has an implant in his head. As the story unfolds, the detectives pursuing him discover that Teddy had been abused by his uncle after the death of his parents, causing him to recast the story of his abuse as an abduction fantasy.

Some scenes in 'Light Years' seem to ridicule or undermine delusional individuals. When Fitzgerald and Spade investigate a hideout for people who believe they have been abducted by aliens, they find themselves amongst a group of twitchy, paranoid men who seem to spend their time in semi-darkness, one of whom asks the FBI agents if they are 'the real Mulder and Scully'. Moreover, the episode's final scene, in which the exasperated investigation leader Jack Malone shouts at the hapless Teddy in order to make him understand the truth he has repressed, might also be read as discouraging towards those suffering from mental distress. Yet the episode's overall perspective on mental distress is kindly and Teddy himself is a likeable and admirable figure: during the course of a flashback sequence, for instance, he is seen gently encouraging a young child to tell him about the abuse the child has been receiving at the hands of his father (a clue for the audience that Teddy had suffered similar experiences at a similar age).

An earlier episode of *Without a Trace*, 'Hawks and Handsaws', contains a similar, sympathetic story of emotional distress. When Joe Gibson, a criminal defence lawyer, becomes seriously distressed and goes missing at the same time as a young girl, Jack Malone reminds his team of FBI investigators:

> Just because we're dealing with a schizophrenic doesn't mean we're dealing with a random, haphazard set of events. Delusions, which are one of the hallmarks of this disease, are defined as fixed, false beliefs. They're organized in a systematic fashion. [...] I believe there is a unifying theory to Joe's delusions.

For Malone, the key to solving the case is to discover the method in Joe's madness. In doing so, the team discover the missing girl, whom Joe has tried to protect, and apprehend the criminal responsible for her abduction. Like Teddy, Joe is a protector of others, rather than a danger to them.

Unlike 'Light Years', 'Hawks and Handsaws' inclines towards the medical view of schizophrenia as an 'illness'. Joe, it is implied, inherited schizophrenia from his father, who, Joe's sister confirms, developed the condition at Joe's age. Yet however one views this medicalisation, Joe is sympathetically regarded. Stigmatising attitudes towards Joe are voiced, but not necessarily endorsed by other characters. For example, agent Martin Fitzgerald observes frustratedly that the only evidence on which to base the arrest of the episode's villain rests on the word of 'a total nut job', while another agent, Vivian Johnson, summarises: 'OK, so he's paranoid and delusional and he's got a gun. That's not a great combination'. Yet this view of Joe's dangerousness is countered later in the episode, when Samantha Spade tells her boss Malone to 'look on the bright side: he may not be dangerous. Most schizophrenics aren't'. *Without a Trace* thus serves as an example of how television drama increasingly serves a broadly anti-stigma agenda, showing the kindness of people who suffer from mental distress, while dramatising the public misunderstanding and fear that often surround it.

Madness and social criticism in TV drama: Gender, class and race

While a great deal of television drama undercuts the stigmatisation of mental distress, there are still other dramas in which experiences of distress are linked to even more fundamental ideological or political contestations – particularly in the work of British television auteurs. For example, female madness is pitted against patriarchal hegemony in Andrew Davies' 1980s-set neo-heritage drama *The Line of Beauty* (BBC2, 2006), in which Catherine, the daughter of a wealthy Conservative Party politician, relentlessly mocks the class and racial bigotry of her loathsome parents. Peter Swaab (2007: 14) correctly notes that Catherine 'really hates and assaults the conservative culture prevailing around her. But she's mentally disturbed, her childlike clarity also a deficiency of balance', so that, 'the story gives you a really oppositional politics only in the context of mental illness'. Swaab implicitly devalues critique emanating from those suffering mental distress; yet there seems no reason to suppose that social criticism is any less salient when it is levelled by a 'mad' individual. On the contrary, the speech or behaviour of mentally distressed individuals often implicitly indicts social injustice as a cause of the distress. This is nowhere clearer than in Peter Kosminsky's Channel 4 drama *Britz* (2006). Sab, the best friend of the drama's heroine Nasima, is a British Asian woman placed under a control order on suspicion of being involved in terrorism. Having been body-searched by the police following her arrest and thereby lost her virginity, the humiliated Sab commits suicide. The difficulty here, as noted in relation to cinematic images of madness, is that while female distress is linked to what Swaab calls an 'oppositional politics', the potential of this antagonism is foreclosed by the all-too-conventional death of the heroine.

Mental distress in television drama is often metaphorical of class, as well as gender oppression. Stephen Poliakoff's meditation on social success and failure, *Friends and Crocodiles* (BBC1, 2005), charts the differing fortunes of a group of friends across two decades. Billionaire Paul spends the 1980s at his country mansion, entertaining assorted friends and hangers-on, including a disreputable ex-journalist named Sneath and a naive teenaged savant named Oliver. By the late 1990s, however, Paul has fallen on hard times. Encountering Sneath on a London bus, the dishevelled, down-and-out Paul drags Sneath – now a rising Labour politician – to a 24-hour café that is ominously located 'at the end of the [bus] line' in a dingy quarter of London. Amongst many other social dropouts in the café sits Oliver, now a withdrawn and depressed figure. The social and moral critique here is unmistakeable: while the poisonous Sneath has prospered, the generous Paul and the gifted Oliver are social outcasts. Where Catherine in *The Line of Beauty* voices a critique of 1980s conservatism, Oliver's desolation epitomises the alienation experienced by all those 'socially excluded' from the brave new world of meritocratic neoliberalism inaugurated by New Labour in 1997.

On the basis of the television texts discussed so far in this chapter, it would certainly be difficult to maintain that mental distress is routinely stigmatised. Some television drama treatments of the topic are more ambiguous, however. The anti-sexist potential of dramatic images of madness, for example, can easily tip into misogyny. In a 2003 episode of the BBC1 medical drama *Casualty* entitled 'Falling for a Friend', a young bipolar woman, Eve, befriends hospital nurse Comfort in a bar. As the two women spend the day together, Eve's behaviour becomes increasingly daring and outrageous. At the end of the episode Eve takes Comfort on a joyride which ends on the roof of a car park, from which Eve eventually falls to her death. 'Falling for a Friend' suggests that mania can be thrilling and even alluring to others. Eve and Comfort's behaviour scandalises social norms: the pair pretend to be prostitutes in a bar, for example, and leave a café without paying. Yet as so often occurs in narratives of female transgression, Eve – the episode's aptly named sinner – is spectacularly punished, her dramatic death implicitly reinforcing conservative media discourses about the damaging effects of female binge drinking and, more generally, the threat to the social order posed by unruly or 'excessive' female sexuality. The episode thus explores but ultimately forecloses the potential of madness as a feminist metaphor.

British television drama also offers few images of black or Asian sufferers of mental distress. *Poppy Shakespeare*, whose eponymous heroine is African-Caribbean, offers a rare exception; yet even here, Poppy plays second fiddle to the book's white narrator: rather than seeing the world from Poppy's point of view, we watch her through the eyes of her friend. Sharon Foster's one-off BBC drama *Shoot the Messenger* (BBC2, 2006) offers a more provocative perspective on black mental distress and is thus worthy of fuller analysis.

Shoot the Messenger is a provocative exploration of racial politics within London's African-Caribbean community. The drama's hero, Joe Pascale, is a well-meaning black schoolteacher whose efforts to 'make a difference' in the education of failing black pupils in an inner-city school result in unemployment, schizophrenia and homelessness. A tough disciplinarian, Joe loses his job after being wrongly accused of physical abuse by a black pupil, Germal. He is subsequently vilified as a racist by prominent members of the black community, becoming a middle-class martyr to political correctness. After his dismissal, Joe is discovered by social services cowering on top of a wardrobe in his flat; he is promptly taken to hospital and diagnosed with paranoid schizophrenia.

With the aid of psychiatric medication, Joe seems to recover swiftly and leaves hospital, but begins to blame the black community for his troubles. 'Everything bad that has happened to me', he reflects, 'has involved a black person'. He rails against black people's 'invented' names and their aspirationally 'white' fashions and their refusal to take responsibility for their problems. He is even punched at a party for suggesting that black people are obsessed with slavery. For Joe, black problems are caused by black people – a perspective that mirrors the real-life Labour government's emphasis on tackling gun-crime and other problems 'within the black community' through 'community leadership'. Moreover, Joe's critiques of the black community are dramatised through a number of stereotypical incidental characters, including a violent gun criminal and a self-hating fundamentalist Christian matriarch who rescues Joe from the street after his discharge from hospital.

After his rescue from the streets, Joe takes up employment at the Job Centre, where he encounters a further parade of black stereotypes, whom he admonishes in conspiratorial soliloquies to camera. When former pupil Germal visits the Job Centre, Joe delights in assigning him a distinctly proletarian job as an unskilled sanitation worker in order to 'teach him a lesson'. Although Joe's anger at Germal is understandable, his reaction to him and other Job Centre clients is tinged with class contempt. As the drama progresses, Joe softens and is moved to pity when Germal is admitted into psychiatric care. Yet his change of heart is qualified and ambiguous. In the film's final scene, Joe sits by the river and speaks to camera. Joe reveals that he doesn't retract *all* of the views he has expressed, but refuses to specify which opinions he now upholds and which he rescinds. Ostensibly, this is an admirably undogmatic ending, as the audience is invited to resolve for itself the debates raised by the drama; yet problematically, the drama refuses clearly to disavow Joe's racial and class hatred.

The paucity of television images of 'black madness' is remarkable given the racialised nature of mental health care in the UK. Pilgrim and Rogers (1993: 47–8) note the high frequency of hospital admissions for mental health problems among the African-Caribbean population. More recently, in a meta-analysis of studies of compulsory detention rates under the UK Mental Health Act, Glynn Harrison (2002: 198) notes that 'the evidence is now compelling that rates of compulsory detention in the UK are higher in those of African-Caribbean background and, to varying degrees, higher also in other ethnic minority groups'. In such a context, *Shoot the Messenger* must be commended for offering a rare-screen depiction of black mental distress. Germal's admission into care is a particularly moving moment which highlights the all-too-common fate of young black men in Britain.

Yet there are several problems with the drama's presentation of psychiatric issues. From the perspective of psychiatric plausibility, Joe's rapid recovery from serious mental distress is less than convincing. More importantly, perhaps, *Shoot the Messenger* obscures the reactionary nature of Joe's racist invective through the dark glass of his psychological disturbance. In contrast to the subversive force of madness in some of the texts discussed above, Joe's madness is a rather convenient excuse for his bigotry and Joe's conspiratorial addresses to the audience encourage us to share his view that the problems of young black men, symbolically culminating in Germal's hospitalisation, are essentially rooted in an irresponsible and backward-looking 'black culture'. In all, then, it is difficult unequivocally to welcome *Shoot the Messenger* as a pioneering depiction of black mental distress.

Dark fears: Madness in gothic and supernatural drama

Gothic and supernaturally themed television drama often exploits the theme of mental distress. In teen melodramas, as in adult horror and mindbender films, madness sometimes functions as a sensational symbol of disempowerment and abjection. In season 3, episode 9 of Warner Brothers' *Smallville* (2001–), for example, Lex Luthor's domineering father Lionel institutionalises his son and subjects him to electro-shock treatment, purely as a punishment. In a 2006 episode of *Smallville* entitled 'Tomb', meanwhile, Chloe tells Clark she has a hereditary mental illness and experiences a hallucination of her mother in a straightjacket. 'I've been waiting for you, Chloe', Chloe's mother ominously tells her daughter. 'You can't escape it. No women in our family ever have'. Chloe's anxious fantasies about her mother recall Nicole's fear of inheriting her mother's suicidal depression in the teen film *Crazy/Beautiful*. Both texts attest to the endurance of the Victorian psychiatric belief 'that most madness was hereditary: the mother was the strongest source, and the daughter the most likely recipient' (Summerscale, 2008: 80).

Sinister, gothic representations of mental distress also overlap with teenage anxiety in a 2002 episode of *Buffy the Vampire Slayer* entitled 'Normal Again', which is based on the earlier Dark Horse comic book treatment *Slayer Interrupted*. Here Buffy finds herself in a mental institution where she told that for the last six years she has not been the heroic demon slayer she thinks herself to be, but a schizophrenic lost in her own fantastical world. The asylum storyline itself, however, can be construed as a comforting delusion. In this fantasy, Buffy's dead mother and absent father are both present, so that the asylum delusion seems to symbolise the heroine's psychological regression: in the psychiatric hospital, Buffy is relieved of the onerous responsibilities of a demon slayer, even if her physical restriction by arm and leg restraints also suggests a certain emotional repression.

The asylum fantasy in 'Normal Again' deals with several of the key themes of teen melodrama, as identified by Miranda Banks (2004). First, it registers Buffy's fears of rejection by her parents. 'Back when I saw my first vampires', she explains to her friend Willow, 'I got so scared. I told my parents, and they completely freaked out'. Buffy explains further that her parents sent her to a clinic and only accepted her back when she pretended to relinquish her 'delusion' of vampires. 'I was only there a couple of weeks', she says: 'I stopped talking about it, and they let me go. Eventually, my parents just forgot'. Second, the romantic subtext invoked by Buffy ('when I first *saw* vampires') alludes to her romantic feelings for the vampire Spike, who is linked to her psychiatrist in the asylum fantasy through a number of visual cues (the doctor in Buffy's delusion is a negative image of Spike – a black male in a white coat, where Spike is a white man in a black coat, etc.) The asylum thus metaphorises the pressures experienced by teenage girls as they negotiate the transition between childhood and adulthood. Such treatments of mental distress may differ in style and intention from 'edutainment' dramas for young people, such as *Losing It*; nevertheless, they share a key theme with them: the teenager's anxiety about her relationships with romantic partners and parents.

Many adult television dramas also exploit the metaphorical potential of madness in a distinctly gothic register. In ITV1's popular and critically acclaimed drama *Afterlife* (2005–2006), for example, Andrew Lincoln plays a sceptical psychology lecturer who is forced to consider the unwelcome possibility that various apparently supernatural phenomena experienced by a psychic, Alison, are real, despite his initial assumption that Alison either is a fraud or is deluded. In the process, the lecturer must face some of his own long-repressed emotions relating to the death of his son. As in the film *The Kid, Afterlife* undermines the putatively 'masculine', narrow-minded obsession with reason, exposing the epistemological and emotional bankruptcy of male rationality and sanctioning traditionally marginalised 'feminine' intuition.

Similar themes predominate in the American supernatural drama *Medium* (NBS, 2005–), which has proved popular with British audiences on BBC2. *Medium* follows the progress of a mother-of-two, Allison

Dubois, as she helps the Phoenix district attorney to solve murder cases using her psychic powers. As in the British *Afterlife*, the heroine is often regarded as mentally disturbed on account of her unexpected insights. In one episode ('Time Out of Mind'), Allison has a recurring dream that she is Beverley, a woman incarcerated in a mental institution in 1959 for apparently murdering her daughter. After a series of dreams in which Allison encounters a bullying male psychiatrist and endures electro-shock therapy, she is able to unravel the mystery surrounding Beverley's case. Beverley, it transpires, did not in fact kill her daughter and Beverley's husband is exposed as a child molester and murderer. The denouement of the episode thus exposes psychiatry as a tool of patriarchal oppression, even if the 1959 setting lets contemporary psychiatry off the hook and reassures the audience that sexual and institutional violence against women are things of the past.

As in *Gothika*, madness in *Afterlife* and *Medium* serves as a screen or disguise for supernatural forces and madness is eventually exposed as no more than a label wielded by patriarchal psychiatrists against unruly women. To be sure, the depiction of women as channels for supernatural forces draws upon ancient misogynistic and essentialist assumptions about feminine irrationality. Yet irrationality is not derogated in these dramas; rather, these supernatural narratives undermine Enlightenment certainties about the supremacy of rationality. Indeed, while nineteenth-century psychiatry swept aside superstitious explanations of madness, postmodern television drama reinstalls faith in the supernatural at the expense of male psychiatric authority. As we have seen, then, mental distress is often treated sympathetically across various genres of television drama and is sometimes even mobilised in the service of social criticism.

Between realism and melodrama: Soap opera and mental distress in the UK and US

Compared to other modes of television drama, soap operas have always devoted much screen time to mental distress storylines (Fruth and Padderud, 1985: 387); they therefore deserve particularly close scrutiny. Soap can be seen as television's dominant dramatic genre (Nelson, 1997: 20). As Ien Ang (1985) argued long ago, soap opera narratives – particularly in the US – are typically couched in the register of melodrama and the pleasures of soaps inhere as much in their psychological resonance as in their social realism. It is not surprising, therefore, that soap opera writers often rely on emotional crisis as a narrative motor.

On the other hand, soap operas, especially in the UK and Australia, are steeped in the conventions of social realism. Because of this – and partly also for budgetary reasons – hallucinations, for example, are seldom rendered via subjective shots, as they often are in narrative films, which may feature extended fantasy sequences or internal focalisations. The madness of soap characters does not typically result in florid hallucinations and is usually quickly identified and contained by the unerring gaze of the close-knit community and its medical authorities.

Soap opera also generates a sense of realism by developing storylines over a relatively long period of time as part of an open-ended narrative structure. Narrative films about mental distress often move inexorably towards closure, often in the form of a sententious conclusion, 'happy ending' or simplistic resolution, tending to imply that serious mental distress is easily overcome. The neat narratorial *moralitas* at the end of James Mangold's *Girl, Interrupted* or the inappropriately screwball ending of Alan Parker's *Birdy* are cases in point. To take a literary example, Chris Sizemore, author of the psycho-biography *The Three Faces of Eve*, was advised by her publisher not to reveal the persistence of her mental distress on the grounds that this might interfere with the book's narrative resolution (Lloyd and Johnson, 2003: 19).

The 'unfinished' nature of soap narrative, on the other hand, can better convey the messy, protean and unpredictable nature of mental distress. Many television serials treat mental distress over extended periods of time: thus, in 2001, season 7 of the US medical drama *ER* charted the course of Maggie's bipolarity over six episodes, showing its consequences for both the patient and her family. Yet soap operas often develop such storylines over years rather than months, sometimes showing how sufferers' problem change over time. In September 2004, for instance, Cameron, in the British teen soap opera *Hollyoaks*, became suicidal during the build-up to his school exams (despite being a 'straight A' student), while in late 2005 and early 2006 the same character suffered from Obsessive-Compulsive Disorder (OCD). Soap opera narrative is also well suited to articulating representations of personal distress with quotidian social pressures such as marital breakdown or professional problems. The breakdown of *EastEnders'* Arthur Fowler, famously screened on BBC1 on Christmas Day 1986, for example, was the culmination of a long-running storyline involving Arthur's unemployment, petty criminality and sexual infidelity. Moreover, closure in soap opera mental distress storylines are often achieved not through some spectacular event, but through the gradual social reintegration of its troubled characters. Finally, because the soap stretches out indefinitely in time, its plot is continually in the process of construction, allowing audiences to offer feedback to the scriptwriters, either indirectly through polls or directly through online chat groups, fan clubs and magazines.

The mundanity of soap opera's thematic concerns, together with its extended form and quotidian *mise-en-scène*, make it a potential resource for psychological identification. Anthony Giddens (1991: 199) has speculated on the appeal of soap opera narratives to reflexive, post-traditional subjects in their quest to create a coherent 'narrative of the self' out of media resources. Storylines involving mental distress may thus play a role in helping audiences to negotiate the pressures of late modern lifestyles. This is as much a collective as an individual enterprise. Based on, and intersecting with, oral culture, soap operas are often the subject of talk and gossip (Brown, 1994) and their interpretation is 'collaborative' (Seiter et al., 1989), so that 'watching soap operas is a social act as well as an engagement with a narrative text' (Allen, 1985: 148). In this sense, soap operas can be seen as part of the mediated public sphere, helping to reflect and shape the social understanding of health and lifestyle issues.

Soap opera storylines have certainly attracted a great deal of comment from anti-stigma campaigners and other media programmes concerning mental distress. In Britain, a postnatal depression storyline in ITV1's *Coronation Street*, for example, was used to launch a debate about the topic on Five's daytime discussion programme *The Wright Stuff* (13 September 2006). This cultural visibility and public influence makes soap opera worthy of detailed attention. In this section, I want to survey briefly the treatment of mental distress in some well-known soap operas, focusing on questions of gender, class and race, the representation of psychiatric care and the influence, on British soap operas in particular, of public service values. I shall start, however, with a short discussion of the representation of distress in some of the top-rated American soap operas, all of which are now broadcast globally as well as in the UK, but which differ significantly from British soaps in their mode of address and in their depictions of the causes and treatments of distress.

In US soap operas, the victims of psychiatric conditions are usually female (Cassatta, Skill and Boadu, 1979) and storylines involving mental distress often invoke cultural anxieties around motherhood, paternity and guilt. In the late 1970s, for instance, *Days of Our Lives'* (NBC) Laura Horton became increasingly disturbed and eventually attempts suicide out of guilt at having concealed the true paternity of her son, Mike. A few years later in the same soap opera (1982), Daphne tells her son

Tony that he is not the son of her husband Stefano. As she does so, she starts to regress to her childhood, asking her nurse if she would like to 'come to [her] birthday' and if she can make a wish on the cake. These images of female madness are enmeshed with long-standing sexist paradigms which construct femininity through discourses of helplessness and innocence and, above all, anxieties around maternity. A few more recent examples will show the persistence of these themes.

Over several weeks in the summer of 1996, the CBS soap *The Bold and the Beautiful* portrayed the mental breakdown of one of its key characters, Brooke Forrester. Brooke receives the result of a paternity test showing that her daughter is not the child of her partner Ridge. Cancelling her wedding to Ridge, Brooke is stricken with guilt and travels to Barbados where she sleeps in an unoccupied house, stealing food to survive as she rambles around the island without purpose. During her wanderings, Brooke comes across two plastic dolls, which she starts to protect as though they are her two children, Rick and Bridget – a delusion rendered visually through the intercutting of shots of the dolls with shots of Brooke's real children.

Brooke's madness is constructed a 'spectacle' in several ways. Firstly, the Barbadian backdrop others Brooke's behaviour, signalling her separation from the 'normal' suburban milieu of the soap. Secondly, as Brooke's paranoia about her children grows, she exhibits the classically Victorian signs of female distraction, including wide eyes, wringing hands, unkempt hair and, until she is encouraged to talk by a young local girl, muteness – a key melodramatic signifier of the inexpressibility of a repressed truth (Brooks, 1974). These signifiers, together with her obsessive anxiety about her children and even the flowing, all-white dress which she wears during these scenes, cast Brooke as a stereotypically passive, fragile and innocent madwoman. And as in the film *Don't Say A Word*, the motif of the doll serves to infantilise the heroine.

Clearly, melodrama is the dominant aesthetic mode in Brooke's breakdown scenes. Peter Brooks (1976) argues that melodrama is concerned with the recognition of individual virtue in a world where appearances are always deceptive. Melodrama evokes a Manichean universe in which, hidden behind everyday appearances, a cosmic struggle between good and evil is being waged; it visibilises this other-worldly struggle that structures our existence through elaborate staging effects, heightened or exaggerated delivery, and a reliance on physical gesture rather than words. In *The Bold and the Beautiful*, Brooke's body becomes what Brooks calls a 'text of muteness', exteriorising what cannot be verbally expressed. Hysterical muteness is not restricted to female characters, as Matthew Modine's performance as a mute hysteric in Alan Parker's *Birdy* (1984) attests; yet it is a particularly common element in the repertoire of feminine madness from Freud's Dora to Elizabeth in *Don't Say a Word*.

Brooke's melodramatic performance of madness in *The Bold and the Beautiful* is mirrored in ABC's *General Hospital* by the character of Carly Alcazar, whose breakdown was first screened over the August and September of 2005. Carly has a history of mental distress in *General Hospital*. She suffered from postpartum depression in 1998 and was institutionalised after shooting her lover later in the same year. The proximal cause of Carly's breakdown in 2005 is her fear of losing her partner Sonny and her children Michael and Morgan to her long-standing love rival Reese. Yet Carly also suffers guilt for having slept with Reese's father when she was a teenager – an act that shattered Reese's family – and fears that her rival is plotting revenge for her youthful transgression.

Carly's guilt and her anxieties about her status as wife and mother are frighteningly rendered. During her breakdown, Carly wakes up screaming following a nightmare in which Reese and Sonny marry and Reese becomes 'mommy' to Carly's children. Like *The Bold and the Beautiful*'s Brooke, Carly regresses to a confused, infantile state, mixing up her partner Sonny with her father ('you're such a good dad. I wish I had a dad like you'). In many other scenes, Carly combines a wide-eyed, innocent appearance with childish emotional lability and high-pitched, quavering voice. Carly's behaviour becomes particularly troubling when she begins to experience hallucinations of the evil Faith Rosco, a character presumed dead by everybody else, but whom Carly imagines is plotting to steal her children. In an eerie night-time scene, she whispers to her psychiatrist that she possesses 'special powers' enabling her to detect threats to her children's safety, invoking the traditional association of femininity with the supernatural. Moreover, in contrast with more clearly feminist supernatural films such as *Gothika*, the heroine's supernatural claims are not vindicated in the diegesis and are quickly exposed by the psychiatrist as delusional.

Carly is also prone to violent outbursts. Over the course of two months, she tries to shoot Sonny and attacks Reese with, variously, a paper knife, a kitchen knife and a baseball bat as well as throwing her against a locker. In another scene, Carly imagines that another *General Hospital* character, Emily, is taking her children from her, and attacks her with a scythe. The effect of these images of violence is anticipated and supplemented by the on-screen captions which appear through these episodes, such as 'Next: Carly is more dangerous than Reese realises' and 'Next: Carly goes on a rampage!'. The unprovoked nature of Carly's attacks on 'innocent' characters, together with their sheer quantity and the drama's provocative captioning, together suggest an exploitative intent. Carly's mad behaviour is further spectacularised by the manner of its framing. During several of her manic peaks, Carly brandishes a weapon at her perceived adversary for several seconds leading up to the advertising break, resulting in a brief tableau vivant of violent madness (the same technique is used to shoot *The Bold and the Beautiful*'s Brook during her Barbados breakdown). Each time this happens, Carly is eventually disarmed and immediately reverts a vulnerable, quivering wreck, recalling Carol Spitzack's (1993: 2) remark that, repeatedly in media fictions, 'women are revealed as persons who cannot manage the body: women lose control, succumb to fleeting pleasures, make poor judgements'. One might well wonder whether the sexist presentation of Carly's breakdown might have alienated rather than attracted audiences; for whatever reason, the actress playing Carly, Jennifer Bransford, proved unpopular with audiences (although this may perhaps have had much to do with the popularity of the role's previous, longer-serving incumbent, Tamara Braun) and the role of Carly passed to Laura Wright when Carly's mental distress storyline ended.

Carly's unpredictable behaviour contrasts, markedly with *General Hospital*'s representation of *male* emotional distress. In a 1999 storyline, mobster Sonny Corinthos loses control of himself after his son is beaten up by a rival mafia boss. Sonny becomes distressed and verbally abusive, smashing up his penthouse. Drunk on whisky, he shouts at his friend Jason, 'I don't know how to fix it!'. Sonny's lament suggests that he is experiencing only a temporary malfunctioning of 'normal' masculine competence and typifies the instrumentalist approach towards emotional problems typically adopted by men and encouraged, as I suggest in Chapter 5, in men's magazines. However anguished he may be, Sonny, unlike Carly, remains active and assertive; his authority is conveyed through his voice, unlike the mute or whimpering madwomen of US soap operas.

The typical representation of psychiatric settings in US soap is also quite problematic. Fruth and Padderud (1985: 387) found in their study of soap opera that 'mentally ill characters are seldom shown in any type of therapeutic setting'. *General Hospital*'s take on incarceration is ambiguous. While Carly does spend time recuperating in the luxurious Roselawn retreat, she also often expresses her fear of being sent to Roselawn's diabolical institutional 'other', the ominously named Shadybrook. As Carly tearfully explains to Sonny, 'they'll lock me up

in Shadybrook. They'll put me in a little room, like a coffin in a grave.'
As so often in fantasy, science fiction and horror texts, the psychiatric
institution is here presented as a frightening and fatal place; yet while
in other texts the gothic asylum can at least fulfil a critical purpose as
an embodiment of psychiatric or patriarchal exploitation, Shadybrook
possesses no redeeming metaphorical or critical import.

The images of mental distress in *The Bold and the Beautiful* and *General
Hospital* matter because they appear in dramas with massive audience
reach. It would be wrong to imply that they are always wholly reac-
tionary. Elsewhere in *General Hospital* example, Emily's panic attacks
following her rape (March 2005) are both believable and harrowing. The
storyline concerning Sonny Corinthos' mental problems, meanwhile,
has been developed over several years, giving it a sense of verisimilitude. Finally, the actor playing Sonny, Maurice Bernard – who himself
was diagnosed with a mood disorder aged 22 – recorded a public service announcement on behalf of the Depression and Bipolar Support
Alliance which was aired after an episode of *General Hospital* in 2006.
Despite such worthy efforts, however, the US soap opera treatment of
mental distress seems sensationalising and misogynistic.

Perhaps mindful of their traditional public service obligations, British
soap operas have responded to the anti-stigma agenda far more boldly
than their US counterparts. *EastEnders*, for example, earned widespread
praise for its careful portrayal, in 1997, of Joe Wicks' schizophrenia,
which was developed in conjunction with the National Schizophrenia
Fellowship, if not always harmoniously. One of the script advisors for
the storyline, psychiatrist Adrianne Reveley (1997: 1560), notes:

> The basic story – Joe's initial diagnosis of psychotic depression and
> then the diagnosis of schizophrenia – remains true to life. I have
> begged for the storyline to include modern treatment with a limbic-
> selective antipsychotic, good response, return to normal life, followed
> by scenes in which Joe experiences stigma.

In more recent years, *EastEnders* has indeed incorporated the 'return
to normal life' and anti-stigma themes requested by Reveley, most
notably through the storyline following Jean Slater's bipolarity. Harrowing episodes of soap operas are also routinely followed by telephone
helpline numbers, which makes them potentially more helpful vehicles for public health information than narrative films. Furthermore,
as in the US, television portrayals of distress are often supported by
their actors' and actresses' involvement in mental health awareness

campaigns: for example, Lacey Turner, who plays the daughter of bipolar sufferer Jean Slater in *EastEnders*, publicly supported National Carers Week 2006.

Of all British soaps, the now discontinued Channel 4 soap opera *Brookside* has been the most self-conscious in its engagement with mental distress issues. True to Channel 4's founding remit to pursue social issues and to *Brookside* creator Phil Redmond's commitment to 'social drama' (Henderson, 2007: 34–6), *Brookside* explored the human impact of changes in mental health care provision through the character of Jimmy Corkhill. In an episode broadcast on 21 November 2001, Jimmy, a bipolar sufferer over a number of years, talks extensively about the stigma of his condition to his young neighbour, Nikki, as part of her university psychology course. This episode might be seen as *Brookside*'s response to previous criticism (Philo, McLaughlin and Henderson, 1996: 67) of the drama's violent characters in storylines in the early 1990s, such as the brutal rapist and wife-beater Trevor Jordache – who, although never clinically identified as 'mad' – was held to be so by other *Brookside* characters.

Later episodes follow Jimmy's attempts to self-regulate his antipsychotic medication. In an episode broadcast on 4 January 2002, Jimmy informs his GP of his intention to abandon his lithium tablets on the basis of information gleaned from the Internet, after claiming to have lost contact with his 'real' feelings. The scene is unusual in soap opera, in that we are taken into the doctor's consultation room – the sort of environment often deemed by television writers and producers as too boring to appeal to soap opera audiences (Henderson, 1996). The surgery scene illustrates *Brookside*'s high level of self-consciousness of about mental health issues. Jimmy's ill-fated attachment to advice derived from the Internet shows an awareness of the changing nature of mental health care, as psychiatric patients become increasingly responsible for their own treatment and well-being in the community – the much-vaunted 'patient power'. Jimmy's doctor, meanwhile, shows his awareness of the public perception and media presentation of mental distress, warning that if Jimmy stops taking his medication, he could cause harm 'to [himself] or others' and might end up either as a casualty or as 'a headline in some local newspaper'. Indeed, there is a remarkable self-reflexivity about this scene: it is a media discourse about madness that is consummately aware of the media's discourse about madness.

In a later scene, Jimmy talks animatedly to his young lodgers Emily and Tim, declaring his intention to lock himself inside a room in his house and to withdraw from his medication. In this comically overplayed scene, Jimmy runs through a list of possible side-effects of his going 'cold turkey', including becoming promiscuous ('so, lock up your daughters!'), which again makes for a highly self-conscious treatment of mental distress. Jimmy's lodgers, meanwhile, act as comic foils – and surrogate audience members – asking Jimmy the 'dumb' layperson's questions about mental distress. Emily is curious asks Jimmy to explain bipolar disorder, while Tim expresses alarm: 'This isn't going to be like the *American Werewolf in London* is it? He was dead violent'. Tim's comment indicates an intention of the part of *Brookside*'s producers to challenge widely perceived stereotypes of mental distress and the ultimate failure of Jimmy's scheme serves as a warning to audiences of the perils of ignoring medical counsel. Like the schizophrenic couple in *Angel Baby*, Jimmy enacts a cautionary tale about the dangers of pharmacological self-regulation. At the same time, the scene might be argued to sensationalise personal distress. Before the onset of his emotional problems, Jimmy was already a comic character with eccentric mannerisms. Jimmy's manic speech and physical gestures during the scene with Emily and Tim make him a laughing stock and seem to confirm the cultural equation between 'comic madness' and masculinity. Rather like the asylum-dwelling character 'Howling Mad' Murdoch in the 1980s US television drama *The A-Team*, Jimmy combines screwball eccentricity with medically diagnosed 'mental illness'. On television, as in cinema, comic madness seems to be reserved for male characters.

A more prosaic storyline following Garry Hobbs' psychological problems in *EastEnders* (19–26 July 2004) typifies the trend towards sympathetic representations of male, as well as female mental distress in British soap opera. Like Jimmy Corkhill's breakdown, Garry's depression and eventual suicide attempt comes as the culmination of a variety of personal problems, principally the breakdown of his relationship with his wife, Lynn. After his suicide attempt, Garry and his stepfather talk in the garden area of Albert Square – the irenic *locus amoenus* of *EastEnders*, where characters often reconcile with one another or simply take stock of their situation. When Garry reflects, 'perhaps I was covering up better than I thought', his stepfather reminds him of the importance of communicating his feelings, rather than 'making a joke of everything'.

Indeed, in contemporary Western societies, men are increasingly encouraged to communicate their emotions and to be alert to signs of mental distress among their friends and family, an injunction given particular urgency by the increasing suicide rates among young men in Western nations (Fortune et al., 2007). Since the Garry Hobbs storyline, *EastEnders* has continued to reinforce the importance of emotional communication to men's mental health. In an episode broadcast on 27 March 2006, for example, the notorious 'tough guy' Grant Mitchell, played by actor Ross Kemp, confides in his agitated brother Phil that he has received psychotherapy to treat his angry temperament, advising his brother to 'confront [his] demons' and then 'let them go'. Over many years, the character of Grant has been doubly coded as both physically brutal and emotionally vulnerable (Philo, McLaughlin and Henderson, 1996: 73). Ross Kemp's 'tough guy' credentials, established through his hosting of the testosterone-driven Special Air Service documentary *Ultimate Force* (ITV1, 2002–2006) and *Ross Kemp on Gangs* (Sky1, 2006–), reinforces the importance, even for 'hard men', of emotional expressiveness.

Other treatments of mental distress in *EastEnders*, notably Jean Slater's bipolarity, which has been portrayed in many episodes since 2005, have unfolded over several years. Like Jimmy Corkhill, Jean is subjected to stigmatisation (she is verbally abused by local youths) and her problems are circumscribed by a discourse of personal responsibility (her reliance on medication is often emphasised). Similarly, ITV1's soap opera *Emmerdale* charted the course of Zoe Tate's paranoid schizophrenia over several years. Zoe's problems begin when she shoots dead her vengeful half-brother and worsen after her rejection by her female lover. After burning down the local church and receiving a diagnosis of schizophrenia, Zoe faces the widespread public disapproval of the close-knit community. But although Zoe's distress has its origins in her unpleasant life experiences, it is ultimately medicalised. In one episode (5 August 2002), Zoe is desperate to understand her condition and turns to her friends for help; they insist that Zoe must accept her diagnosis of schizophrenia if she is ever to recover. Later, in 2004, Zoe's mental disturbance returns when, after drinking heavily, she neglects to take her medication. Indeed, while they commendably focus on the social origins and public stigmatisation of distress, the Jean Slater and Zoe Tate storylines both broadly endorse the biomedical model of mental distress – an extremely problematic implication for reasons discussed earlier.

Indeed, we must not paint too rosy a picture of British soap opera representations of madness. While soaps generally offer 'positive' representations of mental distress, especially in Britain, problems remain, particularly in relation to gender politics. For example, while male characters are increasingly seen as sensitive victims of distress, female distress is often associated with violence. In an *EastEnders* storyline from September 2004, an incidental character, Sarah, becomes obsessed by Martin Fowler, culminating in a fight in which Sarah stabs the object of her affection. The attack scene is underlit to create a chiaroscuro effect, emphasising Sarah's dark and dangerous nature (the same lighting technique was used in teaser trailers for the 2005 *Coronation Street* storyline in which 'Killer Katie', as the trailers dubbed the character Katy Harris, murdered her father). The Sarah/Martin storyline aired just a few months after *EastEnders'* Garry Hobbs storyline, yet seems to have been much less well researched: Alison Parteger, who played Sarah, admitted in an interview on the *EastEnders* website that she had undertaken no research for the role. The manner in which Sarah suddenly transforms from calculating psychopath to unhinged assailant recalls the distinctly unrealistic blending of psychopathy and psychosis in thriller films such as *Taking Lives*. Moreover, there is a rather lazy recourse here to the misogynistic stereotype of the unstable 'woman spurned' made familiar by films such as *Fatal Attraction* (Adrian Lyne, 1987).

Media stories about dangerous and unpredictable women are hardly a new phenomenon; indeed, sensational and moralising tales of homicidal women have always been popular in British popular culture; they were a veritable staple of early newspapers, for example. Nor is *EastEnders* the only soap opera regularly to feature such storylines. The Glasgow Media Group criticised a March 1993 *Coronation Street* storyline in which Carmel becomes romantically obsessed with Martin and eventually attacks Martin's wife Gail (Philo, 1993: 39). Yet such storylines remain common in *Coronation Street*. Across several episodes in 2007, for example, Casey Carswell 'stalks' Ashley Peacock and abducts Ashley's son. The 2004 storyline involving the obsessed Maya Sharma was even more spectacular. Spurned by her finacée Dev Alahan, Maya frames his new fiancée Sunita for a crime she did not commit, sets fire to Dev's shops, and holds both Dev and Sunita hostage. When Dev and Sunita escape, Maya drives her car at the pair but instead crashes into a shop. Just when everybody thinks Maya is dead, she raises her head, like any horror film monster, for one final assault. In one episode (29 October 2004), Maya is described variously as 'mad', 'evil' and 'nuts'. This overlexicalisation intersects with the misogynistic theme of the obsessed woman, a motif with cinematic parallels in films such as *Swimfan* (John Polson, 2002). Female erotomania seems particularly over-represented in film and television, since this kind of obsessive behaviour is more common among men than women, especially when it takes a violent form (Tallis, 2005). Moreover, erotomania is not presented convincingly either in the Maya storyline or on television in general, since the erotomaniac's 'target' is usually a subject with relatively high social status who is not known to the sufferer (Henderson, 1996: 23). Finally, some female soap erotomaniacs are othered through a variety of visual markers: the romantic obsessive Sketch in E4's teen drama *Skins* (2007–), for instance, is an unfashionable 'freak', a coding that aligns mental disturbance with a certain detachment from consumerist norms.

In the virtual absence of regulations for the television broadcasting of issues around mental distress (Morris, 2006: 167), television companies have an implicit duty to represent mental distress responsibly. This applies not just to the programmes they produce, but also to their promotional materials; yet the latter can be more problematic than the primary texts to which they refer. In relation to the Maya Sharma storyline, the *Coronation Street* web page offered a preview of 'Mad Maya Monday' – the day on which the character would exact her revenge on the lover who spurned her. The web page article, entitled 'The Alahan Effect' (2004), quotes a remark made by actress Shobna Gulati, who plays Sunita in the soap, that she did not believe Maya to be 'mad'. Yet the article emphasises Maya's madness in the most salacious tabloidese:

> Dev fell for loopy lawyer Maya Sharma – a woman madder than an island of hatters! [...] When she nicked a vase from a posh shop while they were out, he put it down to kookiness. But the reality was Maya was utterly mad. And when Sunita became a free woman again, Maya turned up the crazy dial to full!

The emotional lability of British female soap characters is also reinforced in press commentary. Claire Peacock's postnatal depression in *Coronation Street* in September 2006 was described on ITV's web site ('Push Off!', 2006) as follows: 'A worried Ashley's fretting over his wife's mental state – and with good reason, as she absolutely loses it tonight!'. In the episode, Claire, suffering from postnatal depression, pushes her son's pram into oncoming road traffic, requiring her husband Ashley to rescue the child. In a *Coronation Street* storyline earlier in 2004, Sally Webster becomes obsessed about her daughter's acceptance into an exclusive private school. The *Guardian* soap opera critic Grace Dent (2004: 13) informed readers that Sally was 'a very unwell lady indeed who shouldn't be placed in charge of a busy, dangerous environment like a car yard. Or, for that matter, allowed out of her house without the benefit of a snug, backwards-fitting, buckled pyjama jacket'. Dent's comment illustrates the continuing appeal of hackneyed images of mental distress as a comic device. The suggestion that no 'lady' should ever be allowed 'out of her house', especially into the masculine environment of a 'car yard', also shows the ease with which discourses about female madness shade into misogyny.

The problem with all of these images of deranged women is not simply that they depict violence towards others, but that this violence has no redeeming rationale and contrasts strikingly with the relative self-composure of distressed male characters. Indeed, the soap treatment of female erotomania surely qualifies Christine Geraghty's (1990) argument that soap operas present women as rational in a culture that often views them as irrational. Soap operas may be relatively progressive in their representation of gender, yet their treatment of mental distress too often draws on the patriarchal or sexist association of femininity with dangerous irrationality.

Freaks, geniuses or biological citizens?: Discourses of mental distress in television documentary

So far this book has had little to say about factual forms of media; yet television documentaries, in particular, increasingly focus on mental distress themes. In the US, public television productions often address issues of stigmatisation from an informational perspective. Detroit Public Television's documentary, *No Ordinary Joe: Erasing the Stigma of Mental Illness* (2004), explores the life of Joe Laurencelle, who was diagnosed with bipolar disorder at age 22 and committed suicide at 26; following the broadcast, a 30-minute town hall meeting was aired, allowing local participants to discuss the issues raised by the programme. The TPT Minnesota Channel and NAMI (National Alliance on Mental Illness) co-production, *Hope for Recovery: Understanding Mental Illness* (2005), meanwhile, combines interviews with mentally distressed adults and their families with medical testimony. Public service television in the UK is typically less meritorious, combining information with entertainment: Channel 4's *A–Z of Your Head* (22 September 2006) offers medical advice about mental distress to young adults and, through bright visuals and a pounding soundtrack, seeks to normalise psychological distress as part of teenage life. The focus of this section, however, is on British prime-time documentaries produced for mass audiences.

Frank Bruno: Gloves Off (ITV1, 2005), which was nominated for a Royal Television Society Award for Best Sports Programme in 2006, typifies the growing body of sympathetic mental distress documentaries, and functions as a counterweight to *The Sun*'s 'Bonkers Bruno' headline, published on the occasion of the former boxer's sectioning under the Mental Health Act in 2003. The documentary explores the reasons behind Bruno's bipolarity and breakdown, including his loss of the World Heavyweight Champion title to Mike Tyson in 1996, his marriage breakdown, the suicide of his long-time friend and trainer George Francis and his recreational drug use, while Bruno himself talks 'honestly and openly' as the continuity announcer put it, 'about his battle with mental illness'.

Gloves Off belongs to the subgenre of the 'comeback documentary' and provides an opportunity for maligned or stigmatised celebrities to 'set the record straight' about their breakdowns (another example is MTV's *Britney: For the Record*, broadcast in the UK by Sky1 on 22 December 2008, in which the singer, at the end of a tumultuous year, expresses her frustration at having been categorised as 'ill' and a 'victim' in the media). From the documentary's interviews with Bruno and some of his friends and family, two messages emerge. The first has to do with the importance of medication in Bruno's recovery: Bruno notes that he had initially neglected his medication and implies that his drug compliance played a major part in his recovery. The second message is the importance of communicating one's problems to others. As Bruno puts it: 'As a man, I thought I could do it by myself [...] I was taking it all in and absorbing it by myself, rather than talking it out'.

The restorative powers of medication and communication are staples of other British television documentaries that tackle celebrity mental distress. Channel 4's *The Madness of Prince Charming* (17 July 2003) sketched the life of Stuart Goddard, also known as the pop star Adam Ant, who has experienced bipolar disorder throughout his life. The documentary explores the relationship between Goddard's mental distress and his construction of his own self-image. Goddard is reported to have 'reinvented himself' after his treatment, using his 'music as medicine'. The psychiatrist interviewed for the documentary, Trevor Taylor, further suggests that Goddard's distress was intimately connected to his creative talent, drawing comparisons between Goddard and Van Gogh, Byron and Virginia Woolf. The programme repeatedly links Goddard's mental distress with his creative genius – an association with ancient origins as well as many cinematic parallels, as we have already seen. In fact, the stereotype of the tortured genius is widespread in contemporary non-fictional media discussions of mental distress; although the precise state of popular musician Michael Jackson's mental health has been a matter for debate, Jackson is frequently lauded as a genius in documentaries about his life (for example, Channel 4's *The Ultimate Pop Star*, 2005). *The Madness of Prince Charming* also reinforces the medical model of mental distress. The documentary covers Goddard's numerous personal difficulties – including a broken family leading to behavioural problems at school, a failed marriage, exam pressures and, later, stresses attending the decline of his fame and his experience of being stalked by a fan ('it drove me bonkers'). Yet the psychiatrists whose interviews punctuate the programme repeatedly stress that bipolar disorder is an 'illness', while the narrator asserts that bipolar disorder is 'often genetic' in origin.

In a two-part documentary, *Stephen Fry: The Secret Life of the Manic Depressive* (BBC2, 2006), the celebrated actor and comedian reflects in characteristically urbane fashion on his bipolarity and discusses the condition with other sufferers, including some high-profile celebrities such as singer Robbie Williams, television chef Rick Stein and actress Carrie Fisher. Produced and directed by Scott Wilson, the documentary is worthy of particular attention because of its range of interviewees (both celebrities and non-celebrities), its cultural prominence (the production won an Emmy award in 2007 for Best Documentary) and the scope of its enquiry into the symptoms and treatments of bipolarity. Like the documentaries noted above, *The Secret Life of the Manic Depressive* combines a commercial focus on celebrity with the BBC's public service remit to explore social issues – a remit whose continuance was very much in question in the run-up to 2006, when the BBC's ten-year Royal Charter was finally renewed after much critical discussion following the damning Hutton Report of 2004.

The journalistic reception of the documentary was overwhelmingly positive. 'This bold, touching, unsentimental film should help rid mental illness of some of its stigma', wrote Sam Wollaston (2006: 32) in *The Guardian*'s review of the programme; 'Fry does for manic depression what Pete [a *Big Brother* contestant] did for Tourette's'. Wollaston has a point. *The Secret Life of the Manic Depressive* depicts the plight of various groups of sufferers who are all but invisible in more glamorous cinematic representations of madness, such as older people and women suffering from postpartum depression. Its sympathetic treatment of celebrity mental distress, meanwhile, counteracts the widespread mockery of celebrity madness elsewhere in the media. While singer Robbie Williams was being treated for depression in February 2007, for example, the presenter of ITV1's Brit Awards, Russell Brand, joked that he possessed 'the keys to Robbie Williams's medicine cabinet'. A few days after the Brit Awards, the guest presenter of Channel 4's late-night entertainment show *The Friday Night Project*, actress Ashley Jensen, remarked that Williams's absence from the event was regrettable given that 'he'd already picked out his jacket'; Jensen's comment was accompanied by a visual image of a straightjacket, provoking laughter from the audience.

Fry spends some time addressing the life problems that may have contributed to the distress of the documentary's subjects and the documentary offers extensive evidence that psychiatric practices – such as the typical ages at which children are diagnosed as bipolar – vary between the UK and the US. This in turn implies that cultural factors play a large role in the construction of mental illness. Moreover, visiting London's Maudsley hospital, Fry is told that there is no 'brain test' that would indicate his bipolarity and at Cardiff University he discovers the inconclusiveness of research into the 'bipolar gene'. *The Secret Life of the Manic Depressive* also contains perspectives that counter biopsychiatric orthodoxy. Fry interviews an ex–Bethlem hospital patient – and high-profile ex-neurosurgeon – Liz Miller, who was sectioned three times, but who eventually stopped taking her medication and who has remained well for 15 years. Miller explains that 'medication is like the training wheels on a bicycle' – useful at first, but ultimately unnecessary.

Despite all of this, however, the documentary's dominant discourse is that of biopsychiatry, as Fry's voiceovers repeatedly stress that bipolarity must be understood as a hereditary illness ('it *is* an illness'; 'manic depression is an illness that's always handed down in families'; 'if you have it, the chances are that somebody else in your family had it too'; 'I have a disease of the brain that I share with four million others in the UK'). By presenting Fry's interviews with sufferers as intimate conversations between friends, *The Secret Life of the Manic Depressive* also constructs a community of celebrities who readily identify their conditions as biological and who make common cause with other sufferers. The sufferers' rapport, and in the case of Williams, close friendship with Fry constitutes a mediated version of what Paul Rabinow (1996) calls 'biosociality', or what Nikolas Rose (2007: 134) terms 'biological citizenship': 'collectivities formed around a biological conception of a shared identity'. The medical model of distress is also accented by a range of expert interviewees, such as Aberdeen University's Professor Ian Reid, who advocates pharmaceutical and ECTs.

The documentary's emphasis on madness as illness is hardly original. Writing about a psychiatrically themed episode of BBC2's *The Human Brain* in 1982, the *Times* television critic Peter Ackroyd (1982: 15) notes:

It has been characteristic of this series, of which last night's programme was the conclusion, that it has taken case histories both moving and dramatic and then proceeded to 'explain' them in terms which are not at all persuasive. In this episode we saw all the paraphernalia with which we have become so familiar – electrodes placed on the skull, computer screens tracing bright signals, and some horrifying experiments performed on rats in a Swedish laboratory. The brains of 'dead schizophrenics' were laid out on a slab like hamburgers waiting to be fried.

This disparity has been everywhere apparent – between the living sufferer, uncertain, anguished, complicated, and a somewhat mechanistic and behaviouristic account of that suffering.

The Secret Life perpetuates this sense of a 'disparity' between lay and professional discourses. Personal testimonies are framed by scientific explanations. An early scene in Part One combines Fry's voiceover, in which he asserts his intention to 'find out' about his and others' conditions, with images of computer screens showing the output of CT scans, creating the impression that medical science has the power to unravel the 'mysteries' of mental distress and in turn invoking the progressivism and positivism that have long characterised television science programming (Gardner and Young, 1981).

Like *The Madness of Prince Charming*, *The Secret Life* takes up the theme of madness and genius. Fry speculates that his mania has been largely responsible for his creativity and career success. 'It's tormented me all my life with the deepest of depressions', he notes at the start of the second episode, 'while giving me the energy and creativity that's perhaps made my career.' *The Secret Life* also links bipolarity to notions of genius and success through its selection of interviewees, many of whom either are, or had once been, professional 'high fliers'.

This linkage is also implicit in a BBC2 documentary written and presented by the ex-Labour party spin doctor Alastair Campbell, *Cracking Up* (2008), in which Campbell discusses how he paid for his high-flying journalistic career with alcoholism and subsequently psychotic depression. *Cracking Up* creates a sense of authenticity through its informal and frank mode of address. Campbell's voiceover is characterised by a breezy intimacy (on talking to his erstwhile GP, Campbell notes, 'bloody hell; this is weird') and the documentary is framed at the beginning and end by an address to camera in which Campbell calls for an end to the stigmatisation of mental distress. Unsurprisingly, the documentary makes no mention of Campbell's behaviour during the lead up to the suicide of David Kelly, the government weapons inspector whom many believe was hounded to his death in 2003 after Campbell's campaign to 'out' him as the source of BBC news reports criticising the adequacy of the government's military intelligence leading up to the allied invasion of Iraq. There is also a distinct irony in the fact that Campbell launched a sustained assault on the BBC over the standard of its reporting in 2003.

It is instructive to compare Fry's *Secret Life* and Campbell's *Cracking Up* with the portraits of mental distress presented in *My Crazy Parents*, an explicit and harrowing two-part documentary broadcast on Channel 4 in 2004, in which children and teenagers document their experiences of living with a distressed parent using a 'video diary' format to chronicle their lives from their own point of view. The first programme focused on the relationship between 15-year-old Lucy, a heavy drinker and self-harmer, and her mother Elaine, who has a 20-year history of mental health problems, including anorexia, alcoholism, voice-hearing, suicidal thoughts and self-harm. The same programme also follows the life of 17-year-old Martin. Seven years after the death of his mother, Martin tries to deal with the erratic and abusive behaviour of his self-harming alcoholic father, Graham, who suffers from severe depression after his younger son was taken into care. The second programme follows a Glaswegian self-harmer, Michelle, from the point of view of two of her three children. Michelle suffers from psychotic depression and has a long-standing addiction to numerous prescription drugs. She blames some of her problems on the side effects of these drugs; desperate to wean herself off her drugs, she checks herself into a psychiatric hospital while her younger children go into care.

My Crazy Parents divided critics, illustrating the difficulty of agreeing upon criteria for evaluating media representations of mental distress. Writing in *Community Care* magazine, the child protection officer Clea Barry (2004: 49) noted that the video diary format and the absence of interviews with professionals or other outsiders locks the audience into the isolated existence of the families concerned, producing a powerful if disconcerting effect on the viewer; moreover, 'there is no story of triumph over adversity'. Yet one can also partly agree with Nick Johnstone's (2004) excoriation of the programme, in *The Guardian*, as 'sensationalist', 'voyeuristic' and 'exploitative'. The programme is certainly hard-hitting; but this is not problematic in itself; it is only really possible to judge the adequacy and significance of the programme with reference to other documentary treatments of the same topic.

'Both instalments of *My Crazy Parents* contain scenes of self-harm'. The second programme, for example, graphically presents the effects of Michelle's cutting her arms with a razor as she breaks down in front of the camera and family members – a shocking image of abjection.

The mode of address here is quite different to that of *The Secret Life of the Manic Depressive* or Campbell's *Cracking Up*. Here the effects of serious mental distress are shown on camera, rather than described retrospectively. The framing of these images is also noteworthy. At the start of the second programme, a voiceover supplies some contextualising information about Michelle's condition, accompanied by shots showing scenes of working-class family life: Michelle's teenage son Tony is seen resting his arms on an upper story windowsill of the family's council house as he talks to friends outside; we also see him smoking, arguably another signifier of working-class status. The shaky camera and the blurred focus of many of these shots index a seemingly raw emotionality and authenticity, recalling Jon Dovey's (2000: 55) observation that 'the low grade video image has become *the* privileged form of TV "truth telling"'. This 'immediate', tabloid style contrasts with the more sedate look and pace of Fry's documentary. Focusing on dysfunctional working-class families rather than the troubled celebrities and professionals of Fry's documentary, *My Crazy Parents'* spectacularisation of working-class abjection contrasts starkly with *The Secret Life of the Manic Depressive*'s more measured reflection on the sufferings of the professional classes and its loftier speculations about 'creative genius' – a discourse seemingly reserved for middle-class or celebrity sufferers.

A sense of drama unfolding 'before our eyes' seems to be increasingly important in mental distress documentaries. Channel 4's *The Doctor Who Hears Voices* (26 April 2008) is a docudrama that combines real-life interview and testimony material with dramatisation. It tells the real-life story of the psychologist Rufus May, who plays himself in the docudrama, and a voice-hearing doctor, Ruth, played by Ruth Wilson. Much of the drama is based on the real-life transcripts of the conversations between May – a controversial psychologist who, we are told, 'does not believe' in mental illness – and his patient. As Ruth, unmedicated and with May's help, eventually finds a way to accommodate the voices she hears into her life, the docudrama hints at the limitations of the medical model and of pharmaceutical treatments of distress. Indeed, the docudrama contains an interview with a conventional psychiatrist, Trevor Turner, who, fittingly enough, contributed his medical expertise to Channel 4's earlier *The Madness of Prince Charming*. Turner's contributions provide a counterbalance to May's unorthodox views; but it is May's critical perspective on psychiatry that prevails. Clearly, within British documentary at least, the hegemony of biopsychiatric explanations of distress is not entirely secure.

For all their faults, indeed, British documentaries show a reasonably diverse range of perspectives on mental distress. As well as presenting stories about mental distress, however, documentaries also frequently address the importance of cultivating contentment. From a historical standpoint, this is arguably a fairly recent development. 'For most of human history', as Bauman (2002: 138) notes, 'happiness was not the self-evident purpose of life. If anything, the contrary assumption prevailed. Suffering and pain were seen as permanent companions of life.' Yet in the past few years, the publication of books such as Richard Layard's *Happiness: Lessons from a New Science* (2005), which argues that happiness can be taught, has signalled a renewed cultural focus on the cultivation of happiness. This discourse permeates lifestyle documentaries such as *The Happiness Formula* (BBC2, 2006), in which a variety of psychologists emphasise the importance of holidays and engagement in artistic endeavour and other unalienated labour in combating 'stress' and promoting happiness. The documentary ends with the narrator's claim that 'governments are now realising people need to be happy as well as wealthy and are now working out how to convince us to change our lives.' Leaving aside the implicit statism of this conclusion, it seems likely that in the UK and US, where most people are becoming poorer rather than wealthier – and where longer working hours and fewer holidays are increasingly required – such recommendations will be regarded with appropriate scepticism.

Airing dirty laundry: Daytime tabloid talk shows as 'Therapy TV'

Attracting very large audiences, daytime television talk shows are a cheaply produced, massively profitable and much derided media form that have become a leading source of information about mental heath issues for many people (Heaton and Wilson, 1995). Yet these programmes' treatment of issues surrounding psychological distress and of their mentally distressed participants are highly problematic.

Undoubtedly, many participants in tabloid talk shows 'get something out of' appearing on them. To discover why people go to the extraordinary lengths of confessing their problems on national television, Patricia Priest and Joseph Dominick (1994) conducted face-to-face interviews with participants on the original daytime television talk show, *The Phil Donahue Show* (1967–1996), showing that Donahue's guests were self-possessed manipulators of their situation whose public disclosures could have a purging, healing and stigma-challenging effects. Priest and

Dominick's respondents often represented 'out groups' such as homo-sexuals, transsexuals, intergenerational couples, people with AIDS, and swingers who all felt socially stigmatised and who did not normally appear in mainstream media. Their appearances on *Donahue* allowed them either to express their normality or to recruit others into their groups. In either case, guests were extremely pragmatic in their approach to their evangelical mission. Some of them omitted to mention infor-mation on the programme that they felt would be detrimental to their particular interest group; others dressed in ways which would present their group in the most effective manner. Some of Priest and Dominick's interviewees appeared on *Donahue* in order to represent their deviant behaviour, and thus win political gains; they saw their appearance on the show as a stage in their group's counter-hegemonic struggle and of visibilising their difference and many were 'evangelical' about their mis-sion to inform the public. In view of all this, Priest and Dominick took a positive view of the television talk show as a politically progressive cultural form.

Indeed, it is sometimes suggested that talk shows are more demo-cratic than many other television formats. After all, the audiences in the studio audience and the viewers at home are encouraged to form their own opinions about the issues discussed and to meditate self-reflexively on their applicability to their own lives. Sonia Livingstone and Peter Lunt (1994) have argued that talk shows permit the voice of 'ordinary' people to be heard, while other critics have discussed the lib-eratory potential of 'letting the freaks speak' (Fiske and Hartley, 1978; Gamson, 1998). Yet, as Mark Andrejevic (2004) notes in his work on voyeurism and reality television, perversion, far from being synony-mous with subversion, reinforces rather than transgresses the moral order. Moreover, in the case of mental distress, participants are not always able or encouraged to speak for themselves, typically being dis-missed as feckless and irresponsible, as I shall suggest in this section. In fact, in the US, tabloid talk shows, epitomised by *The Jerry Springer Show* (NBC, 1991–), frequently parade what their producers call 'freaks of the week' and 'nuts and sluts' (Kneale, 1988). This last phrase encapsulates the tendency of talk shows to bracket together distressed, usually working-class, individuals with sexual 'deviants', often female, within a moralistic framework; its flippancy, however, obscures the fact that guests are sometimes deeply emotionally distressed. While they tend to be less brash in style than their American counter-parts, British talk shows also regularly feature psychologically disturbed guests.

Talk shows have attracted strong criticism from professional psychologists and psychiatrists. Heaton and Wilson (1995), for example, argue that talk show hosts are expert in 'psycho-babble' and platitudes. While there is reason to doubt the impartiality of such concerns – after all, Heaton and Wilson advocate increasing the involvement of professional psychologists such as themselves in talk shows – there is no doubt that talk show discussions of personal problems tend to sacrifice analysis for populist moralism. Like Heaton and Wilson, Vicki Abt and Mel Seesholtz (1999) are vociferous critics of talk shows, arguing that they misappropriate and distort psychotherapy for their own nefarious purposes. Talk shows, they argue, lack traditional safeguards built into the therapist–patient relationship (such as confidentiality, case-by-case treatment, follow-up), while their narrative structures depend on guests being thrust into crisis without screening or evaluation and they often imply that hosts and 'expert' guests are acting in a professional capacity. Some hosts do have qualifications, of course: Trisha Goddard, for example, used to be a counsellor. But this is not always the case. Montel Williams, for instance, describes himself as a 'motivationist', but has no qualifications or training that might relate to this. Moreover, all talk show therapies, complain the critics, appear to be the same and seem to be uniformly successful. Also, self-esteem is seen as a panacea, while social factors such as educational inopportunity and economic deprivation are seen as but the slings and arrows in the path of the determined seeker after personal truth.

The therapies recommended on talk shows are, Abt and Seesholtz claim, trivialised, undermining professional credibility and audience's trust in therapy. Often this therapy is condensed (although shows like *Trisha* attempt to emphasise the presence of counsellors both during and after the show). Yet the therapies for mental distress most often recommended in talk shows – drug therapy and Cognitive Behaviour Therapy (CBT) – both deal primarily with the individual rather than the nature of his or her social relationships. As Godsi (2004: 53) writes:

> the form of therapy that has come to dominate the mental health world has been cognitive behaviour therapy, which emphasises the role of our individual thought processes in shaping our beliefs and our behaviour and in causing us to be distressed. These approaches all too often ignore the simple fact that we collectively make decisions, we remember together and we solve our problems largely with the assistance of other people.

The clinical psychologist and writer Oliver James (2008: 197–205), meanwhile, regards CBT as a 'sticking plaster' approach to mental distress that tends to overlook deep-seated issues such as childhood abuse and focus on symptoms rather than causes. James argues that the outcomes of CBT treatments are poor and that where the method is effective, its benefits are short-lived. Lisa Appignanesi also sounds a note of scepticism about CBT: 'With its supposedly limited term, its spoken therapeutic goals, its "proven" cost-benefits in relation to patients' lowered use of other parts of the health services, CBT seems to share a language of government targets and savings.' While outright rejection of CBT is unduly dismissive of a therapy that helps many people to live more happily and effectively, it also seems that in general terms, CBT offers only short-term and individualised solutions to psychological problems.

The most prominent and controversial British talk show in recent years has been *The Jeremy Kyle Show* (ITV1, 2005–), a programme that focuses on personal and relationship problems and which is widely regarded as the UK's equivalent to *The Jerry Springer Show*. A section of a 2006 episode of *Jeremy Kyle* – 'Lapdancing and binge boozing... make more of your life!' – shows a clear lack of concern for participants and is susceptible to many of the criticisms made by Abt and Seesholtz. A young woman, Anita, comes onto the stage to discuss her concerns about her friend, a lapdancer named Emilie, who, Anita feels, is drinking excessively. When Emilie finally appears, Kyle encourages her to 'sort her life out'. Several seemingly momentous issues are also touched upon but not explored, such as Emilie's feelings of social alienation, her troubled relationship with her boyfriend and her mother, a physical assault and a miscarriage as a result of excessive alcohol consumption. Kyle encourages Emilie to take responsibility for her present life; but the time restrictions and thematic priorities of the show preclude any discussion of the multiple and complex influences of Emilie's past upon her present predicament. Although Anita points out that working as a lapdancer often involves 'going into a fantasy world' to inure oneself to one's working environment, neither Emilie's numerous personal and social problems, nor the question of her working conditions as a lapdancer are discussed. On the contrary, the title of the section implicitly condemns lapdancing as immoral and this opprobrium is reinforced by cuts to audience members exchanging disapproving glances with one another. Although Emilie, like all troubled guests, is placed on a counselling programme, Kyle emphasises her personal responsibility with unprovoked aggression: '[If] you wanna crack, I won't be there to see it, that's fine, let's go, do it'. As this example suggests, tabloid talk show discourse tends to elide or reject social explanations of emotional distress in favour of populist moralism (see also Shattuc, 1997: 96). I therefore disagree with Heaton and Wilson's contention (1995: 136) that talk shows discourage guests from reflecting on their personal responsibility for their problems; on the contrary, it could be argued that talk shows focus almost exclusively on personal failings at the expense of political explanations.

The psychological consequences of participating in such talk shows also merit consideration. Journalist Carole Cadwalladr (2008) investigated the impact on vulnerable participants of appearing on *Jeremy Kyle*, tracking down Jamie, a man with diagnoses of bipolar disorder and paranoid schizophrenia, who was verbally abused by other participants, the audience and even Kyle himself during an episode of the programme, despite having informed the programme's researchers about his diagnoses. Jamie's stepmother tells Cadwalladr:

> 'It was so, so very wrong what they did. It was almost like ritual abuse. And I wasn't allowed to see him beforehand! They kept him from me [...] Afterwards, when I saw him, when I hugged him, and he was crying his eyes out, he was absolutely shattered by the experience'.

Cadwalladr also interviewed a former producer on the show, who expresses serious concerns about the exploitation of mentally distressed individuals on the show, the inexperience of producers and doubts about the level of aftercare (2008: 6).

It is impossible to dismiss entirely the therapeutic value of all tabloid talk shows. Whereas *The Jeremy Kyle Show* has been criticised for stoking tensions between participants and even plying some alcoholic guests with alcohol, *Trisha* has been praised for its relatively sensitive and humane approach to vulnerable guests (Smith, 2007: 26). Sherryl Wilson (2005) provides a nuanced account of *Trisha*, emphasising, for example, the difference between the relatively sedate presentational style of Trisha Goddard and the more sensationalist one of her predecessor, Vanessa Feltz. Wilson argues that talk shows such as *Trisha* enable the negotiation of personal difficulties within the only context available in a consumerist, neoliberal age, such that *Trisha* contributes to a redefinition, rather than outright rejection, of the values of public service television. Moreover, as Wilson argues, there is often a contrast between the tabloid framing of *Trisha*'s stories (achieved through shots of arguing guests and on-screen captions) and the actual unfolding of the stories.

Wilson (2005: 169) shows that *Trisha*, unlike many talk shows, does not go for the 'money shot' – 'the moment of emotional catharsis signalled by tears/anger/rage'. In this way, *Trisha* eschews the more exploitative aspects of the talk show. Yet even Wilson (2005: 167) is forced to concede the criticism of *Trisha* made by Women's Aid and Refuge that the show sensationalises complex issues around personal abuse.

Elements of the tabloid talk show discourse now appear in ostensibly more reputable, celebrity-based chat shows such as *Shrink Rap*. Broadcast on Channel 4's self-styled serious, adult-oriented channel More4, *Shrink Rap* remediates the celebrated Radio 4 talk show *In the Psychiatrist's Chair* and purports to offer insights into the emotional lives of celebrities through in-depth interviews. Sharon Osborne, Stephen Fry, David Blunkett, Robin Williams and Sarah Ferguson have all been 'analysed' by the show's host, therapist Pamela Connolly. In an interview, Connolly (Channel 4, 2006) describes the rationale for the programme in terms which stress its authenticity. While chat shows normally reveal only what their celebrity subjects choose to expose, Connolly argues that, through 'deep, psychologically-based conversation', *Shrink Rap* lays bare the guest's 'true self' and not just 'a chosen aspect of the individual'. While this may be true, it is difficult to see what guarantee the audience has of the guests' emotional honesty and several details – such as Connolly's insistence that Kiss lead singer Gene Simmons remove his sunglasses at a moment of emotional intensity so that his tears can be seen – suggest that the programme aims to capture moments of acute distress via the 'money shot'.

One may also question, of course, the purity of audiences' interests in celebrity disclosure. 'What most people are really enjoying is a quasi-tabloid revelation of the private life of a public figure', remarks psychologist Oliver James of *In the Psychiatrist's Chair*. 'That we are none the wiser at the end about why this person is like they are is not important; all that matters is that we have witnessed the simulacrum of intimacy and heard a few biographical anecdotes' (cited by McKie, 2001: 27). Given the high public profile of the interviewees selected to participate in *Shrink Rap*, suspicions of inauthenticity are certainly justified: such interviewees may well see their participation in such television programmes as a self-promotion opportunity. As Beverley Skeggs (2004: 184–5), drawing on the work of Wendy Brown, notes, painful experiences are increasingly seen as a resource by powerful individuals within Western society. Until recently, few politicians were likely to divulge their intimate sorrows on the public stage; now, however, they increasingly exploit emotional rhetoric (Marshall, 1997: 203–40) in a bid to appear 'authentic' or to 'connect' with an electorate often said to be apathetic towards traditional modes of democratic participation. The political spin doctor Alastair Campbell has talked about his depression on BBC1's *Breakfast* programme (10 October 2006) as well as in *Cracking Up* (2008) and in several other television interviews, while David Blunkett, a bluff, 'no-nonsense' politician who has emphasised his working-class origins throughout his career, has guested on *Shrink Rap*. Yet any celebration of 'emotional democracy' here must be tempered by the recognition that these celebrity analysands are able to draw upon far greater financial and cultural resources than most talk show guests, who are often educationally and financially disadvantaged (Wilson, 2005: 160).

Clearly, then, the opportunities for emotional catharsis offered by talk shows are distributed unevenly: although talk shows such as *Trisha* eschew the worst excesses of stigmatisation and abusiveness, tabloid talk shows tend to inveigh against the moral and emotional incompetence of the working class, while the more elevated cultural form of the celebrity chat show showcases and valorises the emotional candour of stars and politicians. While powerful or influential individuals who suffer mental distress, such as Princess Diana, can serve as role models for those trying to cope with the same conditions (Morris, 2006: 82), it is nonetheless concerning that 'positive' messages about mental distress are attached mainly to those possessing the requisite cultural capital.

More generally, the extension of therapeutic discourse into the talk show suggests that the public expression of personal emotion has become hegemonic in the Western media. Emotion, unlike 'affect', is always already individualised; it is 'intensity owned and recognized' (Massumi, 1996: 221); hence the expression of emotion in talk shows tends to elide the social. As Dovey (2000: 121) provocatively asserts,

> there is an astonishing concurrence between dominant ideologies of late twentieth-century capitalism and narratives of personal recovery and growth. Is it any surprise that an economic system that offers us personal power only through consumer choice should also offer the often unattainable goal of personal liberation through 'quick fix' psychic solutions, rather than through a therapeutic process or sense of socially situated action? Narratives of personal change are the *only* narratives of change that the television of neo-liberalism can offer.

Dovey's invocation of neoliberalism here is intriguing, since the proliferation of the television of personal trauma since the 1990s noticeably parallels and arguably compensates for the recession of the welfare state in the same period (Elsaesser, 2001). However that may be, the individualistic framing of talk show discourse seems to compromise its potential to constitute a democratic space for the discussion and resolution of psychological problems.

Stigmatising or satirising?: Mental distress in television comedy

A perennial concern of anti-stigma critics has been the tendency to use comic images of mental distress as an attention-grabbing gimmick, especially in advertising (Wahl, 1995: 22–8). In the US, to take a particularly dismal example, the presenter of the CNBC programme *Mad Money*, Jim Cramer – a well-known financial pundit and presenter – rants and raves about share values as he dispenses stock market advice. Such treatments of mental distress seem intended to exploit mental distress as a laughing matter.

The popular British sketch show *Little Britain* also ridicules mental distress without any redeeming rationale. In one sketch, comedian David Walliams plays a dowdy middle-aged woman called Anne, a Monty Python-derived stereotype who disrupts a variety of more or less formal situations by making a series of inarticulate animal noises to the horror of those around her. Writing in *The Guardian*, former depression sufferer Tim Lott (2006: 25) enthuses that 'the comedy mocks the sanitisation and political correctness of the mental health industry – and it also reinforces every imaginable stereotype.' Yet while Lott's second observation is true, there is scant textual support for a progressive reading of Anne's behaviour. Lott goes on to endorse stereotypes of madness on the grounds that we live in a 'post-PC' culture which 'would be immeasurably poorer if it censored its own fascination with mental illness on the grounds of taste and an unwillingness to cause offence'. The validity of this defence of comic license, however, surely depends upon *whose* tastes are scandalised and *whose* sensibilities are offended. The problem with the character of Anne in *Little Britain* is that we are encouraged to laugh at a stereotypical representative of a relatively powerless group who has no redeeming features and serves no obvious progressive or satirical function.

Similar accusations might be levelled at an episode of another cult British comedy, Channel 4's *Peep Show*. One episode (18 November 2005) centres on the reactions of the sitcom's two male protagonists, the ultra-conservative Mark and his spineless housemate Jeremy, to the mental breakdown of their Canadian friend Merry. Merry begins to stare wildly and to talk nonsensically and eventually appears before her friends with shaving foam on her face and a razor in her hand, recalling Jane Ussher's argument (1991) that gender role reversal is one of the definitive cultural signifiers of madness in both sexes. Mark telephones NHS Direct to have Merry sectioned, coolly assuring the operator that 'she's completely mental' and enquiring whether he would need to be 'involved' in the sectioning process. Later in the episode, Mark reflects on the possibility of embarking on a romantic relationship with Merry, calculating that 'it would kind of suit [him] to have a girlfriend in an institution', as it would guarantee 'regular meeting times'; 'I might even have a say in her medication', he muses. As the episode continues, the farce intensifies, and Mark, Jeremy and their mutual friend Super Hans all end up attempting to section each other.

All of these scenes expose Mark's creepy neuroticism and Jeremy's pseudo-radicalism (attempting to liberate Merry from the hospital, for example, Jeremy launches a self-righteous tirade against the readiness of psychiatrists to wield the 'chemical cosh' to subdue its charges). Clearly, the episode's psychiatric farce primarily underscores the idiocy of the male protagonists; yet the representation, or rather non-representation of Merry remains a problem. Merry, who never reappears from the hospital in subsequent episodes, is a comic foil, rather than a rounded character with whom the audience is invited to sympathise. Conversely, the audience is enjoined to sympathise with Mark when, in an earlier episode, he cuts his arm with a knife in a bid to win back his girlfriend, arguing that 'self-harm might be very appealing. She'll want to take care of me'. Here again, it is apparent that only male characters are permitted to be both funny and mad.

Although it was not shown in the UK, the short-lived odd couple comedy drama *Head Cases*, broadcast in the US on the Fox network in 2005, offers a more ambiguous rendering of 'comic' madness. Here Jason Payne is a lawyer whose marital problems have caused him to have a breakdown. After recovering from his anxiety disorder, he is paired as part of his therapist's buddying scheme with another lawyer, Intermittent Explosive Disorder sufferer Russell Schultz. The two men establish an unorthodox law practice together, taking on a range of bizarre cases *à la* Fox's earlier legal drama *Ally McBeal* (1997–2002). Significantly, *Head Cases* was approved in the wake of the USA Network's success with *Monk*, a quirky crime show about a detective with OCD. Yet unlike *Monk*, *Head Cases* suffered falling ratings and the drama was pulled by Fox after just three episodes.

Head Cases depicts the trauma of stigmatisation. In the pilot episode, Payne, suffering from depression, is sacked for projecting the 'wrong image' for his law firm. He is kicked out of his home by his wife after struggling to find another job; yet Payne does not even discuss the possibility of suing for wrongful dismissal, compromising the verisimilitude of the drama. The presentation of Russell Schultz is even more problematic. Schultz's unorthodox professional methods include gagging and kidnapping a potential witness and violently attacking an opposing counsel with a legal tome, both with seemingly little consequence. Shultz's lack of concern for others after his outbursts make him seem childish and amoral and raise suspicions that his Explosive Disorder – at the time of writing a recognised psychiatric disorder in the US, but not in the UK – is merely an exploitative device. The condition is certainly handled more dextrously in other texts. In Paul Thomas Anderson's darkly comic film *Punch-Drunk Love* (2002), for example, we are made to share the pain and confusion of the protagonist Barry Egan through a combination of disorientating visual effects, as well as intrusive, sometimes discordant non-diegetic music and several scenes which symbolically frame Barry as 'trapped' behind or within glass structures. Moreover, Barry's outbursts in *Punch-Drunk Love* clearly occur in response to his frustration at being constantly mocked by his shrewish sisters, while Schultz's rages in *Head Cases* seem to come from nowhere.

Head Cases, then, presents two contradictory perspectives on mental distress. Payne's plight documents the effects of stigmatisation, while Schultz's antics provide the light relief of madcap comedy. This combination approach, in which potentially offensive comedy is mitigated with worthier representational correctness, could be seen as a rather cynical attempt by the drama's producers to 'have it both ways'.

Many comic representations of distress are defensible, however; some even embrace a destigmatisation agenda. In an episode of the BBC3 drama *Ideal* (8 February 2005), Moz, a drugs dealer played by comedian Johnny Vega, speaks to his policeman friend about a young man who has just thrown a tin can through his window: 'What kind of world are we living in', he asks, 'when drug dealers are persecuted, and the mentally ill aren't kept in cages?' Moz's quip shows a reflexive awareness of contemporary stereotypes around mental distress and playfully subverts them. More politically charged is the inaugural episode of Chris Morris's Channel 4 comedy series *Jam* (23 March 2000), which contains a sketch entitled 'The Day Kilroy Lost His Mind'. In the sketch, a lookalike of the British television talk show host and politician Robert Kilroy-Silk, runs naked around a shopping mall in fast motion, attacking a mother with a pram and urinating over his own television image in an electrical store. Described thus, the sketch seems outrageously sensationalising; nevertheless, it acquires satirical force in the context of 'anti-schizophrenic' comments Kilroy-Silk made earlier in a *Sunday Express* article (Kilroy-Silk's erstwhile political party, the UK Independence Party, notoriously placed a bar on candidates diagnosed as schizophrenic). The sketch ends with a looped video clip – extracted from an episode of Kilroy-Silk's television talk show – in which Kilroy-Silk winks to the camera and sententiously advises his audience to 'take care of each other'. To a media-savvy audience, the sketch exposes the inconsistency between Kilroy-Silk's homespun advice to care for one another and his prejudicial comments elsewhere in the media. This contextualisation of the sketch partially, if not wholly exonerates an otherwise demeaning depiction of a psychotic episode. Unlike *Little Britain*'s Anne or *Peep Show*'s Merry, *Jam*'s Kilroy-Silk packs a satirical punch, poking fun at a representative of social and political conservatism.

Psychiatrists, as well as sufferers, often receive comic treatment in television drama. Male psychiatrists tend to be coded as wacky or 'New Age' – like the hippie Dr Jacobi in *Twin Peaks* (ABC, 1990–1991) – or as hapless yet likeable clowns, like the Chicago psychologist in the 1970s comedy *The Bob Newhart Show* (CBS, 1972–1978), who battles with his own neuroses and whose wife and family are eminently more equable than himself. NBC's *Frasier* (1993–2004), which has enjoyed enormous popularity in Britain on Channel 4, offers the same wry take on the theme of the 'troubled psychiatrist'. *Frasier* portrays the snobbish and neurotic psychiatrists Frasier and Niles Crane, consolidating the stereotype of the 'psychiatrist as buffoon' (Pies, 2001). Frasier himself is almost certainly television's longest-running television psychiatrist, carrying over his pompous character wholesale from NBC's earlier comedy *Cheers* (1982–1993). Much of the comedy's humour derives from the puncturing of Frasier's vanity as a pompous radio celebrity, which in turn gently mocks the bourgeois pretensions of the psychiatric milieu. This mildly satirical representation, however, is nonetheless grounded in androcentric assumptions about the incompatibility of femininity and comedy. As in cinema, television's female mental health professionals, such as *The Sopranos*' Jennifer Melfi or *Ally McBeal*'s Tracy Clark, are competent and amiable, but seldom funny.

Conclusions

According to John Ellis (2000: 80), television, taken as a whole, is a profoundly anti-didactic medium, such that 'television itself, just like its soap operas, comes to no conclusions [...] It exhausts an area of concern, smothering it in explanations from almost all and every angle.' Television's generic and formal diversity makes the representation of mental distress on contemporary television difficult to characterise briefly; yet Ellis's assertion of television's perspectival pluralism may be overstated. It is certainly clear from the foregoing discussion that television images of mental distress, like all media representations, are thoroughly 'structured in dominance', rooted as they are in capitalist, patriarchal and racist discourses.

In the mid-1990s, Greg Philo (1997) observed that there had been no improvement in the acceptability of television images of mental distress in the previous few years, despite the work of the Glasgow Media Group in highlighting media stigmatisation. Yet it is impossible to argue that mental distress is generally presented in hostile or stigmatising ways today. If anything, television does an even better job of presenting mental distress as part of everyday life than film. Soap operas, especially in the UK, often treat mental distress themes sincerely and frequently portray the stigma faced by sufferers. Increasingly, too, British soap opera storylines implicitly endorse the medical model of mental distress. As Pirkis et al. (2006: 536) put it, '*EastEnders* [...] exposed 10 million people to the idea that schizophrenia is a treatable illness that affects ordinary people'. Moreover, soap opera in Britain more and more focuses on male mental distress as a respectable subject of concern.

There are more radical television treatments of distress, too. In the UK, there is a modest historical tradition of 'authored' television drama that tackles mental health issues from a leftist or reformist perspective, critiquing social structures and psychiatric hegemony. For example, David Mercer's *In Two Minds* (1967), which was produced by Tony Garnett and directed by Ken Loach, presents a distinctly Laingian narrative of young woman diagnosed as schizophrenic as a result of suffocating family pressures. In Dennis Potter's later, highly prescient futuristic television satire *Cold Lazarus* (Channel 4, 1993), the president of a pharmaceutical company seeks to exploit the media to broadcast an anxiety-inducing show in order to create a market for her organisation's tranquillising drugs. While few contemporary television dramas are as directly political as these, they sometimes filter criticisms of gender, racial and class inequalities through the theme of mental distress. Television dramas also tend to eschew the cinematic commonplace of the heroic genius and instead often focus on the everyday problems of working-class characters.

Television dramas, like the films discussed in Chapter 3, often gently undermine masculinist psychiatry while presenting female therapists as positive and nurturing. Adrianne Reveley (1997: 1560), an *EastEnders* script advisor in 1997, complains that Joe Wicks' male psychiatrist was presented as aloof and uncaring:

> Some of the draft scripts offered a stage version of psychiatry. The psychiatrist initially came across as a self important, prejudiced neo-Nazi who seemed keen to punish Lorraine (Joe's mother) for her son's problems. I tried to change it, tried to make him more informed, but in the finished version the psychiatrist still comes across as patrician, aloof, and oleaginous.

On the other hand, *EastEnders'* presentation of male psychiatrists may have improved in recent years – Garry Hobbs' psychiatrist, for example, is considerate and broad-minded. However that may be, television drama, like narrative cinema, often counterposes buffoonish male psychiatrists to sympathetic female therapists. This certainly constitutes an advance on television's presentation of *non*-psychiatric doctors, whose male representatives are competent, but whose female counterparts are likely to be 'literally or metaphorically incapacitated' (Philips, 2000: 59).

Some television channels are especially progressive in their handling of distress themes. Since its screening of Stephen Frears' film about mental retardation, *Loving Walter*, on its opening night in 1982, Channel 4 has consistently produced a range of factual and fictional work dealing with the subjects of mental and physical illness, in keeping with its public service remit to represent minority groups. Programmes as diverse as *The Madness of Prince Charming*, *The Illustrated Mum* and *Brookside*, young adult dramas such as *Losing It* and innovative docudramas such as *The Doctor Who Hears Voices* demonstrate Channel 4's dedication to the broadcasting of informative, non-stigmatising and sometimes even dissenting programmes about mental distress. It remains to be seen, however, if British television's distinctive public service culture will survive as the ecology and delivery of British television undergoes massive shifts in the process of digital switchover. The ongoing balkanisation of television, expressing itself in more channels with smaller audiences, may seriously threaten Channel 4's ability to finance and deliver high-quality public service content to large audiences. Similarly, the BBC has in recent years offered a rich array of public service television programming, much of it centring on mental distress; yet the organisation's future as a public service broadcaster is in question in the post-Hutton period, as the organisation weathers regular calls for privatisation and frequent criticisms of its programming quality, sometimes from its own employees.

On the representational level, moreover, many problems persist. Television comedies sometimes present mentally distressed people as amusing spectacles, while soap operas, particularly in the US, often present women as emotionally fragile or labile. Even the less sensationalist British soap operas have a fondness for spectacular images of dangerously deluded female erotomaniacs. These images of female violence in soap operas contrast with the typical representations of male mental distress, which often emphasise the fundamentally active nature of male sufferers. Moreover, the distressed characters and individuals seen on television are overwhelmingly white. The long-standing Western association of blackness with madness (Gilman, 1985: 131–49) certainly has been mobilised in public discourse, notably in newspaper reports of the 1992 case of the murder of Jonathan Zito by a black man with a diagnosis of schizophrenia (Neal, 1998). Yet images of visible minority sufferers are almost as rare on television as they are in film. The guests on television talk shows are predominantly white and working class. And while the few television representations of black mental distress that exist are broadly sympathetic, they pose problems in other ways. *Shoot the Messenger*, for instance, seems to translate the social and economic oppressions that may lead to mental distress among black people into problems of black 'attitude' and culture.

Like television drama, non-fictional television handles mental distress themes in diverse ways. Documentary films sometimes represent groups of sufferers whose mental health needs are often neglected in society, such as older people (Lishman, 2007: 4). On the other hand, many documentaries – particularly those based around the experiences of celebrity sufferers, such as *Frank Bruno: Gloves Off* and *The Madness of Prince Charming* – invoke the dubious stereotype of the 'mad genius'. Moreover, as psychiatric perspectives on mental distress become increasingly dominant on television, productions such as *The Secret Life of the Manic Depressive* seem wedded to the medical model of mental illness. And while all of these documentaries lionise their celebrity or middle-class sufferers, *My Crazy Parents* seems to spectacularise working-class mental distress.

Similar representational patterns are discernible in talk and chat shows, which tend to dismiss or even vilify working-class suffering, exalt celebrity distress and frame psychological issues individualistically. Factual television, indeed, seems to contribute to Western culture's general distrust and rejection of social explanations of distress in favour of medical, personal ones, while documentaries such as *The Happiness Formula* advocate as the solution to mental distress the management of emotions and lifestyle within the precincts of consumer capitalism. In summary, then, while British television undoubtedly now offers many 'positive', 'accurate' and destigmatising images of madness, it also continues to reflect and reproduce unequal social relations of class, gender and race – and all too readily reassures audiences that psychological equilibrium can be achieved while such relations obtain.

5
A New Leaf?: Changing Representations of Mental Distress in Print Media

This chapter discusses some recent trends in the representation of mental distress in popular print media, focusing on how language and images construct mental distress through distinctions of social class, race and, in particular, gender. The chapter will also discuss images of distress in relation to the increasingly prevalent discourse of celebrity in newspapers and magazines. After all, while it has long been recognised that we live in a society in which 'reference to elite persons' (Galtung and Ruge, 1965) is an important news value and in which people increasingly define their salient relationships in terms of media 'personalities' (Meyrowitz, 1985), many of the pioneering early studies of the print media's representations of mental distress (e.g. Nunnally, 1961) pre-date the explosion of celebrity discourse in the capitalist media. The chapter also suggests that print media representations of mental distress are often embedded within discourses of consumerism, biopsychiatry and individualism, such that, while they are generally 'positive' and sympathetic, they also reinforce many elements of the dominant ideology.

The range and variety of texts evoked by the phrase 'print media' is, of course, vast; this chapter is therefore highly selective in its coverage. Rather than attempting to locate and discuss every single print media discussion about mental distress across newspapers and magazines, I have selected some only a few indicative examples to illustrate my general themes. Finally, as in Chapters 3 and 4, the focus here is upon the UK context, although many print media stories about mental distress, especially those relating to celebrities, reference North American people and events known widely in the UK.

Not quite the same old story: The changing newspaper coverage of mental health

The output of newspaper stories, feature articles and advice columns about all forms of mental distress, ranging from stigmatising stories of violent killers to sympathetic treatments of recovery to gossip column stories of celebrity breakdown, has grown significantly in recent decades. Focusing mostly on national newspapers, the following section briefly identifies some of the key concerns of this journalistic discourse and identifies some of the ideological presuppositions governing it. Some of the themes covered here – for instance, the concern over the link between mental distress and violence in news reporting and the misuse of psychiatric terminology – have been treated at some length earlier in the book. Where this is the case, I have kept further discussion to a minimum in order to devote greater attention to issues more relevant to the focus of this book: the intersection of mental distress with discourses of race, class, gender and political ideology.

As we noted in relation to television, the debate about the acceptability of representations of distress is no longer restricted to commentators located outside the media industries. More and more, journalists themselves express concerns about the media's responsibility for stigmatisation, albeit often in ways that conveniently vouchsafe the ethical irreproachability of the publication for which they write. For example, in the light of the tabloid media's obsession with the deteriorating psychological state of the singer Britney Spears, Peter Preston (2008), writing in the British liberal broadsheet newspaper *The Guardian*, argues that, since newspapers merely respond to public demand, 'we are all to blame' for the singer's hounding by the paparazzi. Similarly critical pieces have appeared subsequently in the same newspaper. Theresa Rebeck (2008), for example, challenges the sexist double standards at play in the coverage of celebrity distress in gossip magazines and blames the readers of those publications for encouraging the intrusions of the paparazzi; yet Rebeck's article arguably participates in the representational strategies it critiques, since it is illustrated by photographs of Lindsay Lohan's arrest for driving 'under the influence' and of Britney Spears apparently hiding from the paparazzi's cameras. It could also be noted that *The Guardian* itself closely followed the story of Britney Spears's breakdown – a point not lost on the contributors to the web page on which the online version of Preston's article appeared. Some of these contributors argued that newspaper journalists cannot so easily devolve responsibility for either the paparazzi harassment of Spears or the widespread coverage of her breakdown. Whether or not it is seen as hypocritical, Preston's piece attests to an increasing self-consciousness about mental health issues among journalists, who are now incentivised to take greater care over their reporting of the topic than they have traditionally done. The mental health charity Mind, for example, runs a Journalist of the Year award to promote sensitive and detailed reporting of mental health stories.

In fact, broadly sympathetic coverage of mental distress is widespread. The so-called broadsheet newspapers, in particular, often print autobiographical accounts of mental distress. In 2006, for instance, *The Observer* serialised journalist Stephanie Merritt's account of her depression, which was later published in book form. Another feature in *The Times* (O'Brien, 2007) describes advertising executive Matthew Johnstone's experience of depression, which was also turned into a book (both writers claim to have used their writing as therapy). The indie rock star Juliana Hatfield (2008) has also written unflinchingly about her anorexia and her daily life in an American treatment clinic. Other feature articles even suggest that mental distress can bring unexpected benefits to sufferers. Beth Pearson's (2006) phlegmatically titled *Herald* article 'Get it under control and your life can be okay' and Magnus Linklater's (2006) 'Let's put an optimistic spin on depression' in *The Times* both end with a roll call of celebrity bipolar sufferers – including, pre-eminently, Winston Churchill – who are all claimed to have possessed remarkable talents. If there ever was a taboo of silence surrounding mental distress, it has certainly been shattered in recent years. Yet newspaper coverage of mental distress – even where it is ostensibly 'positive' in nature – remains problematic in many ways.

The typical objections of anti-stigma critics to film and television images of madness can certainly be extended to print media representations. Critics have expressed concern, for example, about the journalistic misappropriation of psychiatric terminology. Chopra and Doody (2007) note that the adjective 'schizophrenic' is still widely used in a metaphorical sense in newspaper references to people who simply hold multiple or conflicting roles or opinions. Yet leaving aside the problematic nature of schizophrenia as a diagnosis, this concern for terminological 'accuracy' sails close to linguistic essentialism: the word 'schizophrenic' long ago slipped its moorings in psychiatric discourse and it now seems foolhardy to advocate restricting its use to psychiatric contexts.

Other commentators note that newspaper stories about mental distress routinely link mental distress with physical violence in the most lurid terms: the *Mirror* headline 'Maniac freed to stab dad 82 times in front of kids' (Gregory, 2008) encapsulates the tendency. On the other hand, it is not at all clear that newspapers present mentally distressed people as uniquely violent. As argued in Chapter 2, moreover, there is a range of problems with anti-stigma arguments that focus solely on the presence or absence of interpersonal physical violence in stories about mental distress without considering the social or political contexts of that violence. Finally, there is some evidence that the increasingly sympathetic tone of many portrayals of mental distress in film and television is paralleled in newspaper reporting: quantitative analyses of news coverage in Australia shows that print news media discussions of mental distress are generally of 'good quality' and less focused on crime and violence than might be expected (Frances et al., 2004). For these reasons, I am not primarily concerned with stories about violence here.

The *style* as well as the content of newspaper reporting of mental distress themes has also attracted critical censure and critics have concentrated on the disrespectful and insulting vocabulary that typifies tabloid journalism, in particular. There is no doubting the power of tabloid newspapers to influence public discourse about mental disturbance; to take a well-known example, tabloid descriptions of the obsessive lover in Adrian Lyne's 1987 film *Fatal Attraction* brought the term 'bunny boiler' into general parlance as a sexist synonym for a psychologically disturbed woman. Similar alliterative abuses remain common in tabloid journalism, among which *The Sun*'s 'Bonkers Bruno' headline, discussed below, is most notorious. Moreover, the list of insulting synonyms for mental distress in contemporary English – 'nuts', 'wacko', 'loony', 'psycho', 'basket case', and so on – is lengthy, recalling the litany of pejorative terms for drug use ('druggie', 'smackhead', 'stoner', etc.). In linguistics, this phenomenon is known as over-lexicalisation: the proliferation of quasi-synonyms to denote a single phenomenon, the presence of which often indicates the morally problematic or contentious nature of that phenomenon (Halliday, 1978: 165).

While legislation and guidelines designed to combat abusive language in newspapers exist, they are usually unenforced. The British Press Complaints Commission drew up a code of conduct over the reporting of mental distress themes, which was agreed to by newspaper editors, in 1997. The code stipulates that: 'the press must avoid prejudicial or pejorative reference to [...] any mental or physical illness' and that 'whenever it is recognised that a significant inaccuracy, misleading statement or distorted report has been published, it must be corrected with due prominence.' Yet many newspapers consistently violate the PCC guidelines, raising concerns over the usefulness and effectiveness of the code itself. Famously, on 23 September 2003, *The Sun*, a newspaper that had once hailed boxer Frank Bruno's greatest sporting triumph with the phrase 'Arise, Sir Bruno!', reported on Bruno's mental breakdown with the headline 'Bonkers Bruno Locked Up', although after a public outcry this headline was amended, in the newspaper's later editions, to 'Sad Bruno in Home'. The response to *The Sun*'s initial headline was swift and furious. Copies of *The Sun* were reportedly destroyed in their newspaper stands, while angry radio listeners called in to BBC's Radio 5 warning that the gaffe might prove to be 'another Hillsborough' for the newspaper (*The Sun* is still widely boycotted in Liverpool by the public – and even some newsagents – following its false attribution of the Hillsborough football stadium tragedy in 1989 to the criminal and loutish behaviour of Liverpool fans). In one sense, it is troublesome to compare the reporting of Frank Bruno's private troubles with that of the Hillsborough disaster – an appalling public tragedy in which 95 football supporters died. Nevertheless, just as *The Sun*'s Hillsborough smear backfired spectacularly, showing a disregard for (amongst other things) its readership's sensitivities, so too the newspaper appeared to underestimate the strength of public affection for Bruno and, arguably, to misjudge public attitudes towards mental distress. While it is conceivable that a story about a less popular sportsperson might not have attracted so many complaints, the public reaction to the story suggests that British newspaper readers might be more aware than tabloid journalists of the need to discuss mental health issues sensitively. On a more theoretical note, the Bruno incident demonstrates that newspaper readers, like all audiences, cannot simply be conceived as the passive dupes of the media's construction of mental distress. Some research suggests that the effects of media representation on public awareness of mental distress are very strong. The Glasgow Media Group, for example, argue that whereas people's everyday experiences usually mitigate and even override media influence, this situation is dramatically reversed when audiences encounter stereotypes of mental distress: in these cases, audiences seem to reject their experience in favour of media (mis)representations (Philo, 1996, 82–104). The public reaction to *The Sun*'s Bruno slur shows that this need not always happen, however, and that audiences can sometimes resist media distortion or stigmatisation.

The public outcry around the *Sun*'s headline prompted the newspaper's editor Rebekah Wade to launch an appeal on behalf of the mental health group Sane, with *The Sun* itself donating £10,000 to the organisation. In return, Sane produced a style sheet to help *The Sun* in its future reporting of mental health stories. Marjorie Wallace, the founder and chief executive of Sane, was impressed with the newspaper's editor, claiming of Wade: 'It's quite extraordinary the level of interest she has. I do believe it is genuine' (cited by Mitchell, 2004: 25). Nevertheless, despite the editor's display of largesse, *The Sun* has continued to use derogatory terms in other reports involving mental distress. In a story about an incident outside the UK residence of David and Victoria Beckham on 20 July 2004, for example, *The Sun* printed two headlines: 'Nut's bid to torch Beckhams: intruder at Beckingham palace' and 'Posh's terror over ranting petrol nut'. The problem here does not simply inhere in the use of stigmatising language, but in the use of such a dismissive term in the absence of any explanation of the background, experiences or motivation of the 'nut'. Clearly, then, *The Sun*'s post-Bruno commitment to a more sensitive treatment of mental distress cannot necessarily be taken at face value.

The Sun's continued use of dismissive or abusive language to refer to certain distressed individuals also raises the question of precisely which social groups are accorded sympathetic press treatment and which are subjected to opprobrium. Tabloid journalism, like the television talk shows and documentaries discussed in Chapter 4, seems to reserve its most vituperative language for working-class individuals; the more 'respectable', broadsheet newspapers, meanwhile, tend to carry more flattering and even heroic stories about middle-class sufferers. However, as *l'affair* Bruno shows, attaining respect as a mentally distressed individual is not necessarily easy, even for a national sporting hero. In fact, in cases of depression involving sporting celebrities, newspaper discourse often elides the notion of mental distress altogether, as Stephen Wagg (2000) notes in his analysis of newspaper coverage of the English footballer Stan Collymore's depression and anti-social behaviour. Collymore has at various times been accused of physically abusing girlfriends and of engaging in the form of sexual exhibitionism known as 'dogging'; yet Wagg notes a journalistic reluctance to invoke psychological disturbance as an explanation for Collymore's aberrant behaviour and an unwillingness to investigate the possible social pressures – including, in Collymore's case, the experience of racism – that may have contributed to it. According to Wagg, sports journalism in tabloid, and increasingly in broadsheet newspapers increasingly unfolds within a neoliberal discourse in which highly paid yet emotionally disturbed footballers are cast as indolent or self-indulgent failures in the football market place rather than suffering subjects. Without doubt, this reluctance to acknowledge mental distress among footballers intersects with the wider cultural prohibition against

male displays of vulnerability or weakness; Western societies traditionally have valued the 'strong silent type' as the model of masculinity,
a cultural desideratum that may be particularly entrenched in Britain
(Busfield, 1996: 94).

Indeed, newspaper reports and features about mental distress are
distinctly gendered. In 2007, the Liverpudlian medical doctor Kate
McCann became a reluctant media celebrity after the abduction of her
three-year-old daughter Madeleine from the Portuguese resort at which
the McCann family were holidaying. As the British media went into
overdrive in its coverage of the case, all of the leading British tabloid
newspapers published photographs of McCann breaking down during
an interview on Spanish television. On 25 October 2007, *The Daily
Mirror*, for example, published a two-page feature entitled 'Tears of Kate –
After six months of holding her heartbreak in check...Madeleine's
mum breaks down on TV'. The article was accompanied by three pictures of Kate McCann, each with its own subtitle: 'SO EMPTY: Kate
tries to explain her loss on TV'; 'TOO MUCH: She can't hold back the
tears'; 'SOBBING: Kate and Gerry on TV'. The use of multiple images of
abjection – a feature also common, as we will see, in magazine framings of female celebrity distress – invokes the traditional iconographical
grammar of the *mater dolorosa*.

This religiose construction of Kate McCann is not straightforwardly
sympathetic, however; it can equally well be argued to reflect the misogynistic moralism that has characterised journalistic writing about the
doctor's public image since Madeleine's disappearance. As some newspapers – such as the *Daily Express* and the *Daily Star* (which later
apologised to the McCanns for their misleading coverage) – mooted
the possibility that the McCanns might somehow have been responsible for Madeleine's abduction, several journalists began to focus on
Kate McCann's worthiness as a mother. Writing in *The Times*, Andrew
Pierce (2007: 26) attempted to encapsulate public sentiment towards
Kate McCann:

We're filled with a mixture of admiration and disbelief at the way
Kate McCann always appeared so immaculate in public, when most
mums would have broken down long ago. We so want to admire her.
I hope at the end of this we still do.

As well as mentioning Kate McCann's well-kept appearance, which
many journalists felt did not befit a grieving mother, Pierce's comment burdens Kate McCann, rather than her husband Gerry, with a

responsibility for publicly regulating her emotions. Indeed, the intense scrutiny to which Kate McCann was subjected by journalists in 2007 far outweighed the attention devoted to Gerry. Journalists covering the McCann case seem to have been simultaneously fascinated by the abjection of a distraught mother and outraged by the too-perfect image of a woman who, it was suggested, may not care *enough*. Thus, the reporting of Kate McCann's very public distress was subsumed within wider discourses regulating female emotional display. In particular, the intense scrutiny of McCann's maternal competence intersects with the tabloid media's increasing insistence on the discourse of the 'bad mother' (Cobb, 2008).

As the treatment of Kate McCann indicates, newspaper journalists are fond of images of female emotional distress, even when the rationale for their inclusion in a story is unclear or questionable. A brief review of Lisa Appignanesi's (2008) book on the history of female mental distress in London's free *Metro* newspaper (Allfree, 2008), for example, is accompanied by a photograph of an open-mouthed, barefooted and seemingly intoxicated Britney Spears sitting on the pavement outside her house. This photograph of Spears had already acquired a certain public currency, having been much-circulated in celebrity gossip magazines; indeed, the inclusion of a photograph of an off-guard celebrity in a book review indicates the increasing cultural influence of these magazines. Yet the photograph is also curiously gratuitous. This choice of illustration would seem perfectly appropriate if Appignanesi's book were centrally, or even tangentially concerned with Spears. Yet apart from a chapter on Marilyn Monroe, the book under review does not discuss celebrity breakdowns and does not mention Spears, leading one to conclude that the image is there mainly as an instantly recognisable 'hook' to capture the casual reader. More importantly, the proliferation of such images of female celebrity distress in newspapers – particularly, in recent years, of Britney Spears and the troubled singer Amy Winehouse – suggests that female mental distress, more insistently than its male equivalent, is mediated through the rhetoric of the image. Like the crazed, wide-eyed heroines of US television soap operas, tabloid photographs of distressed female celebrities together constitute a grotesque tableau vivant in which femininity is associated with madness through tears and melodramatic gestures.

Newspaper coverage of mental distress, then, often appears to be exploitative and misogynistic. On the other hand, as I have suggested above, many newspaper stories about mental distress offer information and encouragement to sufferers. Even in such cases, however, it is possible to question the political uses to which newspaper journalists sometimes put 'positive' stories and images of distress. Although many feature articles about mental distress are written in a supportive tone, they often simultaneously reveal a commitment to particular political ideologies. Yvonne Roberts (2007: 29), in a *Sunday Times Magazine* article on Narcissistic Personality Disorder, for example, explains that, 'in its most extreme form, known as malignant narcissism, paranoia and physical aggression may also be displayed: Stalin, Hitler and Saddam Hussein spring to mind.' It might be suspected that the reason why these three official bogeymen – as opposed to other murderous, but putatively democratic world leaders – 'spring to mind' has as much to do with Roberts' ideological attachments as with any concern for diagnostic accuracy. Constructing the official enemies and folk devils of liberal democracy as mad serves to sanction the rationality of contemporary Western capitalist leaders, many of whom are responsible – directly or indirectly – for comparable or even greater atrocities.

The journalistic manipulation of mental distress for ideological ends is very apparent in the lionisation of Saddam Hussein's predecessor as a slayer of Kurds, Winston Churchill. Churchill famously suffered from bouts of depression, which he called his 'black dog', and is often invoked by journalists as an exemplary sufferer of mental distress. An *Observer* book review entitled 'How depression makes you stronger' (Revill, 2008: 19) is dominated by a central photograph of Churchill which is sub-captioned: 'dark periods fed Churchill's creativity'. Another article in *The Mirror* (Sayid and Smith, 2002) discusses numerous artists, musicians, intellectuals and politicians, including Churchill, under the headline 'No pain, no gain: the geniuses tormented by ill health'. As suggested earlier, the existence of any systematic link between madness and creativity is highly doubtful; yet the attempt to enlist Churchill to the anti-stigma agenda is also highly problematic on political grounds. Over his lifetime Churchill supported, *inter alia*, the slaughter of 'uncivilised' Kurds, organising troops to put down striking Welsh miners in 1910 and the forced sterilisation of so-called mental defectives. Churchill's government, it has also been argued, was complicit with the Nazi genocide, refused to accept displaced Jews into the UK, ordered hunger blockades and the 'terror bombing' of the civilian population of Germany, abandoned the Italian revolutionaries of 1943 to the Axis powers, starved the Indian population during the Second World War and supported the nuclear bombing of Japan (Glancey, 2003; Corrigan, 2006; Baker, 2008). One would certainly have to be very patriotic indeed, therefore, to regard Churchill as anything other than a brutal, racist despot.

Nonetheless, in 2006, the mental health charity Rethink commissioned a sculpture of Churchill in a straightjacket in order to portray a more 'positive' image of people with mental distress. John Leighton, of Rethink East Anglia, claimed: 'We all know that Churchill was a great leader and this statue is an illustration of what people with mental illness can achieve' (cited by Quinn, 2006: 33). Another spokesperson for the charity claimed that 'people have negative perceptions of those with mental health problems. But by showing them that Churchill suffered from depression we are challenging that notion' (cited by Parkinson, 2006: 13). However, after an outcry from the Churchill family and various establishment sources that was reported widely in the conservative newspapers *The Daily Mail* and *The Express*, the statue was later removed amid fears that it impugned the good reputation, not of mentally distressed people, but of Churchill himself.

The journalistic framing of Hitler as a 'malignant narcissist' and of Churchill as a noble sufferer is, of course, ideologically loaded. Given the centrality of the historical myth of Churchillian greatness to capitalist democracy, the establishment of Churchill as an anti-stigma figurehead can be seen to bolster the dominant ideology rather than destigmatise mental distress. However well-intentioned they may be, journalistic attempts to raise public awareness of mental health issues through the celebration of national heroes such as Churchill are not only undemocratic, but also serve to legitimise ruling-class ideology.

Indeed, although the point is seldom raised in anti-stigma literature, newspaper reporting of mental distress is strikingly classed. Middle-class sufferers, who are often highly literate and articulate professionals, are more likely to have their experiences serialised in newspaper features and magazine supplements, which in turn often follow, or function as a prelude to, the publication of book-length autobiographical memoirs. Working-class people, meanwhile, tend to feature more often in mental health stories as violent 'nuts'. Unlike their high-flying counterparts, most working-class sufferers lack the cultural capital required to have their stories told. On a more immediate and practical level, meanwhile, working-class individuals seldom have access to therapy or private clinics, as Wagg (2000: 69) points out:

> social class has become a greater factor in the addressing of mental distress, with better off patients often seeking help from among a growing diversity of treatments and receiving it on a private, fee-for-service basis. For the poorer sections of society, professional and institutional help has become sparse.

When the voices of working-class sufferers are heard in the newspapers, they often forcefully assert the disjunction between middle-class and working-class experiences of distress. A mental health service user, Sarah Carr (2008: 36), in a letter to *The Observer*, writes:

> I feel I need to offer a reality check to Emma Forest whose article on her own and Britney Spears's mental health problems [...] did not acknowledge the fact that most of us who are not fortunate enough to have access to private psychiatric care can feel damaged by a system that is meant to support us through acute periods of mental distress. Forest 'checked into the priory' which gave her 'pause to catch [her] breath and start from scratch' [...] But for every Emma Forest who can afford private care, there are thousands who call ourselves 'survivors' because not only do we survive the ravages of mental distress, but also the state psychiatric system.

Carr goes on to relate her own 'frightening, confusing and dehumanising' experiences of psychiatric care. As her letter implies, newspaper journalists are often guilty of reproducing, perhaps unwittingly, the implicit class distinctions characteristic of film and television treatments of mental distress.

Finally, it might be noted that newspapers, like film and television, increasingly tend to frame mental distress in biomedical terms. Nicole Hurt's (2007) discourse analysis of US newspaper articles about depression shows that while journalists often flirt with societal explanations for the prevalence of depression among women, it is common for these explanations eventually to be rejected in favour of biological ones. It is hardly surprising that newspapers elaborate a stereotype of women as 'biologically depressed' in the US, since this construction of female depression is also characteristic of direct-to-consumer drug advertising in that country (Grow, Park and Han, 2006). Yet in Britain, too, the need for pharmaceutical companies to disseminate information about treatments for mental distress ensures that newspapers often contain optimistic messages about pharmaceutical treatments. To take just one example, a 2005 *Daily Mail* article entitled 'First drug to tame manic depression' uses a human interest story with a happy ending to advertise the benefits of Seroquel as a treatment for bipolar disorder (Hagan, 2005). The medicalisation of mental distress in newspapers is only a tendency, however, and in newspapers such as the *Daily Mail* it is contradicted by other, often conservative concerns about the erosion of moral responsibility in the face of medicalisation. There is thus often an ideological tension between the *Daily Mail's* conservative editorial line and the newspaper's laudatory reporting of pharmaceutical breakthroughs, which is driven by the economic imperatives of liberal capitalism.

Tears, tragedy and celebrity: Mental distress in women's magazines

Many women continue to perform the traditionally female role of 'health gatekeeper' within families and relationships and magazine stories and features about mental health issues are often addressed to women rather than men. In the second half of the twentieth century, health became an increasingly prevalent concern of women's magazines. Gillian Dyer (1982: 16) notes that although discourses of health, illness and medicine have always been highly visible in women's magazine advertising, health issues constituted an increasingly prominent topic for feature articles across a wide range of titles throughout the twentieth century. Robin Bunton's (1997: 242) longitudinal study of *Good Housekeeping* concludes that 'health and well-being have become of increasing concern since the 1950s and perhaps indicative of increased individualised concern with health and the body.' In relation to mental health, at least, this individualisation has been accompanied by a certain democratisation of psychiatric discourse. In the post-war period, psychiatric discourse was in the ascendancy in magazines, as elsewhere in the media. In 1955, the cover page of a short-lived US magazine entitled *Psychoanalysis* offered thrilling 'stories of people searching for peace of mind through the modern science of psychoanalysis' and featured lurid images of distressed women disclosing their neuroses to earnest, besuited psychiatrists. By the 1960s, psychiatric discourse had become popularised, infiltrating even the letters pages of newspapers and magazines (Szasz, 1970: 73). Today, popular psychotherapy has become the pre-eminent explanatory paradigm in women's magazines; *Marie Claire*, for example, offers a 'Real Life Therapy' column each month. In this section, I shall discuss some of the features of this proliferating discourse and, more particularly, explore how stories about mental distress overlap with discourses of class, race and gender.

Before engaging in our own textual analysis, however, it is worth considering briefly *how* women read magazines, a question that has provoked much critical discussion. Joke Hermes famously found that much magazine consumption seems to involve relatively uncommitted reading; magazine reading, she notes, seems to happen in a context of 'everyday meaninglessness' and readers are not always able to recall details of articles which they had read (1995: 11–2). As Shaun Moores (2005: 134–5) observes, this points media researchers away from the text and towards the ritualistic uses of magazines within the context of everyday routines. Yet while women's magazines may generally be consumed distractedly, stories and articles about mental distress may demand deeper levels of engagement, concentration and self-reflection from their readers. Christy Newman's (2007) work on readers' letters to women's health magazines suggests that reflexivity is a key feature of the format and it is common for contemporary magazine articles to contain letters from readers eager to share their experiences of mental distress. To take just one example, an article on postnatal depression by *Observer Magazine* journalist Harriet Lane (2006) was followed up a month later by a selection of readers' letters on the same subject. Elsewhere, readers are encouraged to participate in surveys; a survey of 1000 women aged 20–35 published in the September 2002 edition of *Cosmopolitan*, for example, disturbingly revealed high levels of 'extreme sadness' among its readers. It therefore seems difficult to argue that magazine stories about mental distress are always treated lightly either by journalists or readers; rather, women's magazines offer sympathy and advice to distressed readers and may even solicit feedback about experiences and therapies. In this respect, women's magazines, like television soap operas, aim to encourage active participation rather than passive consumption and to foster in their readers a 'will to health'.

Women's magazine journalists treat mental health issues with a high level of sensitivity and reflexivity. *Marie Claire*, for example – certainly the most liberal of mass circulation women's magazines with its focus on world news and political events – has militantly pursued an anti-stigma agenda. Often the magazine's articles on the topic are underpinned by research findings; for example, a 2008 story on what 'stresses out' women is based on findings of a survey conducted by the American Psychological Association ('I'm so stressed out!', 2008). Role models are also extensively invoked. Thus *Marie Claire* journalist Emma Elms (2003: 96), who was shortlisted for Mind's Journalist of the Year award in 2004 for her reporting of mental health issues, begins an article about the experiences of two schizophrenic women as follows:

> Think of Jane Horrocks, Ruby Wax and Karen Mulder, and phrases like 'creative genius', 'brilliantly funny' and 'glamorous supermodel' probably come to mind. But these women have all been mentally ill. Surprising news, perhaps, in a climate where people with mental

health problems are often regarded with fear as 'axe-wielding psychos'. Yet Horrocks, who has obsessive compulsive disorder (OCD), Wax, who is a manic depressive, and Mulder, a chronic depressive, are not exceptions. In Britain, thousands of women with mental-health problems are battling daily to form successful careers and happy relationships.

Elms's article typifies magazine journalism's growing sensitivity towards issues of mental distress and implicitly critiques stigmatising representations of distress in other media forms. As I suggested in relation to newspaper journalism, there is a growing self-consciousness – in the more socially progressive print media, at least – about the media's own ethical responsibilities.

Elms's article goes on to discuss some of the precipitating factors for mental distress, broaching some topics not often covered in film and television treatments of mental distress. Commenting on the significantly elevated incidence of schizophrenia among African-Caribbean people in the UK, for example, the article quotes the psychiatrist Kwame McKenzie's list of risk factors, which include 'city life, thwarted aspirations, financial strain, low autonomy in employment and uncertainty about the future'. 'Afro-Carribeans in the UK', adds McKenzie, 'are more likely to be susceptible to these risk factors' (cited by Elms, 2003: 98). As we have already seen, the intersection of race and mental distress is seldom discussed in the media; nor is the possibility of a link between the structural oppressions of capitalism and personal psychology often broached, as it is here. *Marie Claire* therefore deserves credit for publishing articles that articulate, however cursorily, some of the structural dimensions of personal distress.

Insofar as it engages in discussion around class and race, Elms's article provides a socially contextualised understanding of mental distress; this is, however, counteracted by other elements within Elms's piece. Even those women's magazines at the liberal end of the ideological spectrum – such as *Marie Claire* – typically frame their understanding both mental distress and femininity within a middle class, neoliberal discourse of individualism. The notion that psychic health is achieved through the 'battle' for a 'relationship' and a 'career' (as opposed to decent social and working conditions for all), casts the problems of life – and the causes of mental distress – as so many barriers to personal fulfilment; as such, the article sails very close to the self-centred ethos of self-help literature. Elms's 'battle' metaphor, meanwhile, recalls Susan Sontag's (1991) critique of the metaphorical language of warfare that characterises media discussion of cancer. While the notion that women must battle for mental health usefully undermines the widespread conservative stereotype of women as helpless, childish victims of psychic circumstance, it is nonetheless clear that the envisaged struggle does not extend beyond the immediate concerns of the professional, cosmopolitan woman.

The individualistic approach to mental distress in women's lifestyle magazine finds its most direct expression in its articulation with discourses of consumerism. 'Retail therapy' is frequently posited as a cure for mild forms of distress. Thus a feature in *Glamour* ('New Season, New You', 2001: 50) offers suggestions on how to 'energise your brain' through shopping. A new pair of boots, the article claims, will allow the depressed reader to 're-evaluate [her] roots', while a new hat will provide 'peace of mind'. The chirpy tone of such features suggests a certain playfulness, perhaps even irony; yet this in itself does not subvert or vitiate the implied connection between consumption and psychic well-being. Even the newspaper advertising slogans for the more therapeutically oriented magazine *Psychologies* – 'If you want it, go and get it' and 'Get what you want and love what you've got' – co-opt self-help discourse and interpellate the reader as an acquisitive subject. Here again, such injunctions might be empowering from a liberal feminist perspective insofar as they contest those patriarchal discourses which make women feel guilty about 'what [they've] got', or indeed what they have not got. Yet they also frame mental health in voluntaristic terms, ignoring the social structures that contribute to women's psychological suffering and reassuring the reader that mental equilibrium can be achieved with a strong enough will and deep enough pockets.

In what seems like a contradiction of this message, another common argument in contemporary women's magazines holds that 'we' are more prone to depression despite supposed increases in our wealth – a staple argument of liberal writers about depression such as Richard Layard (2005). For example, the American version of *Cosmopolitan* magazine argues that 'even though people are wealthier and have more choices than ever, studies find they're also more unsatisfied and depressed. The remedy? Realising that, when it comes to what brings happiness, less is more' (Neumann, 2006: 183). In another article about depression in *Healthy* – a magazine published by the UK health food shop Holland and Barrett – a 'clinical researcher' asserts that 'the modern condition is doing little to ease depression numbers in the Western world, despite our ever-burgeoning levels of wealth' (Starling, 2004: 117). In fact, as I argued in Chapter 1, the assumption that the majority of working people in the Western world are increasingly wealthy is less tenable than it has been for several decades. In Europe and the US, working hours and the pensionable age have been increasing, especially since the 1980s, causing a steady fall in average real-terms wages. Job security and social welfare are being steadily eroded and levels of personal debt have increased dramatically. In consequence, a double income is required to provide the kind of lifestyle that 30 years ago one income used to support (Warren and Warren Tyagi, 2003). More generally, an intensifying economic crisis is now exposing the myth of Western wealthiness, making 'downsizing' a matter economic necessity rather than a therapeutic choice for the majority of the world's population. In the context of worsening material conditions for working-class people, the time-honoured adage that money does not bring happiness is highly serviceable to capitalism's ruling class: as well as obscuring an objective decline in living standards, it detaches issues of emotional health from considerations of material wealth. *Glamour* magazine thus assures its readers that it is 'normal' to be 'happier without that big pay rise. Research has found that big earners spend less time enjoying themselves than those on less money' ('How Normal Are Your Moods?', 2008: 52). This seems a disingenuous conclusion when, as psychiatrist Simon Wessely (1998: 83) argues, 'across the globe it is absence of wealth, rather than the side effects of affluence, that makes us miserable' and when women's pay is consistently lower than that of their male colleagues, especially in the UK and US (Gosling and Lemieux, 2004: 275).

Clearly, then, women's magazines offer mixed messages about the relationship between consumerism and mental well-being. Wealthy women must learn to manage the prosperity and wealth of options that capitalism delivers to them and spend their way out of their problems, while poor women should realise that money does not bring psychological equanimity. In other words, one of the central therapeutic morals of women's lifestyle magazines – that psychic well-being comes from contentment with one's lot – is strikingly at odds with these magazines' consumerist ethos.

The contradiction between the restless imperatives of consumerism and the need for psychological stability also informs the magazine treatment of the eating disorders anorexia and bulimia, conditions that exist at the intersection between physical illness and mental distress and which are correlated with depression and low self-esteem (Grogan, 1999: 171–2). Far from ignoring anorexia and bulimia, women's magazines often present articles and first-person accounts that discuss the dangers of developing of eating disorders. To the chagrin of many feminists, however, they do so alongside advertising that features extremely thin models – and that might therefore be argued to contribute to the onset of such disorders in readers (Wolf, 1991). It is the most liberal and therapeutically oriented magazines that encapsulate this contradiction most clearly. In June 2000, *Marie Claire*'s editor, Liz Jones – herself an ex-anorexic and a confessed magazine addict – launched a special edition of the title aimed at exploring issues around eating disorders and body image and the ethical responsibilities of the media and advertising industries. This was undoubtedly a bold move; indeed, many industry observers blamed *Marie Claire*'s 'worthiness' under Jones's stewardship for the subsequent sharp decline in the magazine's circulation. Nevertheless, the ideological progressiveness of Jones's initiative is hardly unambiguous.

Describing her inspiration for the special edition in her editorial column, Jones claims to have been depressed by encountering extremely thin models at a Paris fashion show. After the show, she vowed to devote an edition of her magazine to exploring the issues around body image and the pressures magazine images exert upon their readers. Writing in the special edition, television presenter Kate Thornton (2000: 129) applauds Jones's decision, while lending anecdotal support to the theory that media images contribute to the development of eating disorders:

> When Liz Jones, *Marie Claire*'s editor, told me about the magazine's pledge to provide healthier and more realistic role models for its readers, I applauded her, because I know that the paper-thin models who adorn the pages of fashion magazines played a big part in my illness. Like many women, I was very body-conscious throughout my teens and used these models as a blueprint for 'perfection'. Then I set about trying to emulate that look with as little food and as much vomiting as I could fit into my days.

Despite the discussion of eating disorders in the articles by Thornton and others, however, the special June edition of *Marie Claire* contains numerous advertisements featuring models who might reasonably be described as 'paper thin'. There is social scientific and cross-cultural evidence supporting a link between the development of eating disorders and exposure to media images of slenderness (Grogan, 1999: 94–116; Becker et al., 2002; Frith, 2004). Nevertheless, even if women's magazines do *not* play a causative role in the onset of anorexia or bulimia, there is a striking inconsistency between the June edition's editorial perspective and its advertising content. This contradiction is embodied in the cover story of the edition, which asks the question: 'Is this the ideal body shape?: Impossibly perfect Pamela Anderson versus realistically curvy Sophie Dahl?'. In order to draw attention to this question, half of the front covers of the edition sported fashion model Sophie Dahl's supposedly 'curvier' image, while the others featured actress Anderson's slimmer frame. Yet while this representational bifurcation achieves the laudable aim of presenting a marginally wider range of body types than is normally seen on magazine front covers, the description of Pamela Anderson's body as 'impossibly perfect' clearly implies that there *is* such a thing as an ideal body shape and that Anderson embodies it. Whatever its intentions, therefore, this edition of *Marie Claire* seems to reinforce the 'beauty myth' that Naomi Wolf (1991) and many other critics see as damaging to women's physical and psychological well-being.

In marketing terms, however, Liz Jones's concept for the special edition was shrewd. The edition's discussion of body image appeals to two constituencies of readers – or perhaps to two impulses within an individual reader. On the one hand, the magazine appeals to readers devoted to the construction of the 'perfect' body. Yet the edition's implied challenge to normative 'body ideals' also addresses the more progressive sentiments to which *Marie Claire* lays claim and to which many of its readers may be presumed to subscribe (the magazine's central concept is 'More than a Pretty Face'). Thus the magazine partakes in a typically postmodern form of 'complicit critique' (Arthurs, 2003), featuring images of alarmingly thin models while simultaneously laying claim to a more progressive agenda around issues relating to body image. The treatment of eating disorders in the June 2000 *Marie Claire* thus illustrates the contradictoriness of women's magazines as a therapeutic resource.

As is clear from the foregoing discussion, celebrities play an increasingly central role in the women's magazine discourse of mental distress. Zygmunt Bauman (2000: 70) notes that 'what are commonly and ever more perceived as public issues are private problems of public figures'. In the contemporary media landscape, the ancient figure of the mad genius has given way to the 'troubled' celebrity as the focus of intense public interest. As the explosion of tabloid or gossip magazine stories about Britney Spears's 2008 breakdown attests, journalists increasingly attempt to take their audiences 'behind the mask' to expose what celebrities are 'really' like (Littler, 2003: 11) via stories about the traumas and anxieties of the rich and famous. In recent years titles such as *OK!*, *Hello!* and *heat* have all extensively covered the mental breakdowns of female celebrities – although, like newspaper and magazine journalists, these magazines carefully 'absent [themselves] from the concept of media intrusion' (Holmes, 2005: 29). And as we have seen in the previous section, tabloid magazine framings of female distress more and more govern the style of newspaper reports on the subject.

Indeed, as Su Holmes (2005: 21) points out, celebrity magazines exert an increasing influence on other media forms. Even health-promotion magazines, for example, mediate mental health issues through discourses of celebrity. This strategy is central to *there there* magazine, which was launched in 2004 to increase public understanding of issues such as anger management, stress and addiction problems. Combining celebrity gossip with mental health reportage, *there there*, although short-lived, warrants close analysis as an example of 'zeitgeist publishing' that embodies the populist spirit of tabloidised anti-stigma discourse.

Written by health care and media professionals, *there there* was distributed in 6000 doctors' surgeries in the UK and its launch was supported by prominent figures in psychiatry as well as mental health charities. A distinguishing feature of the magazine is that mental health issues are discussed in relation to their representation in popular culture (a story about anger management, for example, is framed by references to the popular US television series *The Incredible Hulk*) or alludes to an exemplary story about a celebrity sufferer. Implicitly addressing a female readership, headlines include 'Tears in Tinsletown: even Marilyn got the blues' and 'Britney Returns: but is she really OK?'. The magazine affirms the liberal psychiatric nostrum that mental distress is ubiquitous and can strike anybody – even a celebrity – at any time. As an editorial puts it:

> In an age when our quality of life is continually under threat, *there there* will be on your side. We'll deal head-on with issues like anxiety, stress, depression and anger. And because we address life in all its colours, you'll also find celebrity interviews and profiles, provocative quizzes, as well as more esoteric features on, say, the effect of colour on mood. (It'll give us an excuse to discuss Carrie's wardrobe on *Sex & the City*). *there there* is passionate about life and how it can be lived better. We'll do it all: genes to jeans, outcasts to Outkast and more. Everything to make *there there* the essential manual for 21st century living.
>
> (*there there*, 2004)

The mode of address here is identical to that of women's magazines, namely 'one of allegiance to the reader, of being on your side with superior know-how and resources' (Wolf, 1991: 74). Moreover, *there there* articulates its coverage of health and lifestyle issues with the staple women's magazine emphasis on glamour, consumption and celebrity, simulating in particular the style of the more 'trendy' and fashion-consciousness celebrity magazine *heat* (Holmes, 2005: 23).

Like Emma Elms's *Marie Claire* article, *there there* purports to delve behind the glamorous image of celebrities, using a variety of presentational devices to create a reality effect. Jo Littler (2003) argues that audiences are increasingly responsive to presentations of celebrity that deploy the tabloid tropes of intimacy, reflexivity and 'keeping it real'. All of these tropes are carefully contrived in *there there*. The article on Britney Spears in the first issue, for example, is accompanied by a series of five close-up images of the singer crying with her hands over her face – a pose that has become familiar to audiences in recent years as Spears's psychological state has deteriorated. Although these images are actually stills from one of Spears's television appearances, they are self-consciously presented as a series of instant photographs taken in quick succession (a similar arrangement of several adjacent near-identical television interview stills – a presentation that mimics Andy Warhol's famous Marilyn Monroe prints – is used in the December 2008 *Skymag* interview with the singer). The 'multiple Polaroids' device posits Spears's breakdown as a spectacle to which we have privileged access via a series of stolen photographs. The self-referential character of these images, their insistence on their own status as photography, invokes Barthes's (1977: 17) notion of the photographic analogue – the 'message without a code' that creates an impression of immediate/unmediated recording of reality. It also invites the audience, primed by similar paparazzi-style photographs in celebrity gossip magazines such as *Hello!*, to invest the images with the apparent authenticity of the snapshot. The audience is thus encouraged to believe that it is privy to a shocking truth about Spears.

Writing about contemporary television, Charlotte Brunsdon et al. (2001: 55) write that the emphasis of contemporary lifestyle television is on 'what producers call "the reveal"'; a moment of revelation almost always coded as 'emotional' and 'melodramatic' through the use of the extreme close-up and the reaction shot. Such techniques are clearly at play in these magazine images. Moreover, since they are apparently 'stolen', *there there*'s images of Spears seem to bear witness to a 'higher truth' and to promise access to their subject's 'inner being' (Sekula, 1984: 29). This weight of mythology enables *there there*'s images to perform a double function. On the one hand, through their seemingly verisimilitudinous mode of address, such seemingly candid images of celebrity suffering promise to fulfil the demands of anti-stigma campaigners for more 'realistic' representations of mental distress. Yet they also satisfy the seemingly insatiable public demand for images of what celebrities are 'really' like. Indeed, a sense of the authentic would seem to be an important part of the pleasure that audiences derive from discourses of celebrity gossip and celebrity magazines could be argued to offer their readers resources for discerning the authentic from the manufactured (Holmes, 2005). Photographs of celebrities in distress therefore permit readers to apprehend the 'real' celebrity behind the innumerable 'fabricated' images spawned elsewhere in the media or perhaps even within the same magazine title. In this context, images of celebrities in distress seem to be indisputably genuine: after all, however much the sense of authenticity is understood by readers as having been contrived by the magazine apparatus, nobody believes that a celebrity would go so far as to *feign* a breakdown. Thus suffering becomes a guarantee of 'truth'.

Readers may derive other kinds of pleasures, however, from looking at photographs of distressed celebrities. The assertion in *there there* that our 'quality of life is constantly under threat' alludes to the sense of risk and fear that some critics believe to be pervasive in contemporary capitalist societies, raising the possibility that readers might derive comfort from the knowledge that even the rich and famous suffer. In her study of the role of celebrity stories in identity formation, Joke Hermes (1999: 80) reports that many female magazine readers admit that 'the misery of others made them feel better about their own lives' or helped them to deal with their own frustrations or sorrows. Such feelings of consolation or *Schadenfreude* may even make life more bearable for journalists: Mark Deuze's (2005) interviews with tabloid journalists and editors writing about celebrity misfortune suggest that *Schadenfreude* is a widespread sentiment amongst them.

Yet any such analysis must also be gendered. Magazine images of Spears or Monroe crying, like the representations of the distressed heroines of television soap opera, mediate mental distress through the 'hysterical' form of melodrama (Copjec, 1998) and seem to express something like Ang's (1985) 'tragic structure of feeling': a melodramatic affect correlating to a particularly female experience of frustration and disempowerment. Images of tearful celebrities contribute to what Hermes (1999: 80) calls a 'repertoire of melodrama', which

> can be recognised in references to misery, drama and by its sentimentalism and sensationalism, but also by its moral undertone. Life in the repertoire of melodrama becomes grotesquely magnified. In the vale

of tears that it is, celebrities play crucial and highly stereotyped roles, reminiscent of folk and oral culture.

While aiming to present mental health difficulties in a sympathetic light, then, *there there* also reinforces stereotypical constructions of hysterical femininity in a way that parallels melodramatic soap opera constructions of female emotional distress.

The representation of Spears in *there there* also resonates with images of tearful women in other print media stories, such as those accompanying newspaper stories about Kate McCann. Clearly, the media industries are increasingly interested in the public tears of culturally visible individuals. A recent biography of George Bush, for instance, describes the tears the ex-US president shed over the momentous public decisions made during his presidency (Draper, 2007), while Hillary Clinton has 'welled up' on many occasions, most recently on ABC's television news during a press conference as her challenge for the leadership of the US Democratic Party candidacy faded. But both the act of crying and the manner in which one cries are distinctly gendered. Eric Hayot (2008) notes that images of female crying often invoke feminine abjection:

> As Roland Barthes points out in his reading of Balzac's 'Sarassine', the 'male' tear is single (or double, but only one per eye), and therefore phallic: a hard condensation of emotional force, a pseudo-diamond. 'Female' tears, by contrast, flow, violate the boundaries of inside and outside, of control and loss of control; like the tears of children, which they resemble (and in which resemblance they document the Western habit of identifying femininity with childishness theorised by Ashis Nandy in *The Intimate Enemy*), they represent a failure of accommodation to the reality principle, which in adults denotes abjection and calls forth both pity and disgust.

'Male' tears are not the exclusive preserve of men; within Barthes's framework, Hillary Clinton's crying – a controlled 'welling up' – can be read as 'male'. Like the frequent emotional outpourings of her husband Bill, Hillary's restrained lachrymosity might be easily seen as the cynical manipulation of hegemonic emotionalism. If Barthes is correct, however, the images of Spears's uncontrolled crying in magazines such as *there there* seem more likely to invite the readers' pity and disgust.

Spears is not the only female celebrity, of course, whose mental distress has been circulated and reported in ways that undermine her credibility. Emma Bell (2008) has shown how three female British celebrities once known as 'bad girls' – Geri Halliwell, Gail Porter and Kerry Katona – have sought to recast themselves as 'mad girls', perhaps to boost their careers but also with the avowed purpose of using their biographies to raise awareness of mental distress issues. Yet, as Bell shows, journalists often subvert this attempt, undermining and pathologising their celebrity subjects. Indeed, the cultural denigration of distressed female celebrities is widespread. In a telling survey conducted by the UK's *Marketing* magazine published in May 2008, the respondents' top five 'most-loved' celebrities were men: Paul McCartney, Lewis Hamilton, Gary Lineker, Simon Cowell and David Beckham. The four 'most-hated' public figures were women, three of whom have suffered mental breakdowns of varying severity: Heather Mills, Amy Winehouse, Victoria Beckham and Kerry Katona.

Even where journalistic treatments of Britney Spears are sympathetic, they often reinforce patriarchal constructions of femininity. In an open letter to Britney Spears in the *Daily Mail*, for example, agony aunt Irma Kurtz (2008: 36) advocates crying as the first stage in the healing process:

> If I were your friend now, Britney, or better yet your auntie, the first thing I would do would be to hug you and stroke your hair and let you cry in a protective embrace. Tears would start to ease the burning humiliation and dry, hard pain we can all see on your face.

Thus the older woman calls on the younger one to acknowledge and visibilise her abjection. While Kurtz's sentiments here are benevolent and no doubt sincere, her advice nonetheless constructs Spears as a pitiful spectacle ('we can all see'): fragile, passive, infantile and not-responsible. These abject qualities are seldom attributed to male celebrities, even in their deepest distress. In Barthes's terms, Kurtz implores Britney to allow her 'dry, hard' and by implication masculine pain to yield to 'female tears'. Indeed, the injunction to shed tears is common in women's magazines. *Glamour* ('How Normal Are Your Moods?', 2008: 52), for example, notes that 'crying often' is one of '8 weird things that are very, very normal'. This is clearly gendered advice. It is true, of course, that crying is a valuable means of coping with emotional difficulties. 'Having a good cry' may even be in need of cultural revalorisation (Warhol, 2003); yet the advice to do so is unlikely to be proffered in men's magazines. The normalisation of female crying – even in a magazine that purports to destigmatise mental distress through stories of celebrity suffering, such as *there there* – reproduces long-standing stereotypes of feminine helplessness.

The liberal impulse to destigmatise mental distress through stories about female celebrity breakdown seems quite problematic, then. Moreover, recent psychological research suggests that an intense interest in celebrities may in itself have deleterious consequences for the mental health of certain sections of the population; as John Maltby et al. (2004) suggest, those who worship celebrities for 'intense-personal' reasons may be particularly 'at risk' of developing mental distress. Such conclusions clearly problematise the use of celebrities to raise public awareness of mental health issues in publications like *there there*. It would be wrong to assume, however, that magazine journalists are unaware of the ethical concerns around celebrity distress stories. Perhaps following the lead of several *Guardian* journalists, magazine journalists have begun to question the ethical propriety of reproducing stories of celebrity distress as entertainment. Writing in *Marie Claire*, Zoe Williams (2009: 28) – also a regular *Guardian* columnist – writes, 'when realities like cancer and mental illness crash into what was meant as a diversion, a game, you realise that you just don't feel like playing any more.' Williams goes on to question the appropriateness of passing health stories through the filter of celebrity – even though, as we have already seen, precisely this process occurs elsewhere in *Marie Claire*. In a distinctly self-reflexive, even postmodern twist, the public fascination with celebrity mental distress is exploited not only by tabloid celebrity magazines, but also by journalists eager to distance themselves from the messy and ignoble business of reporting the celebrity 'train wreck'. Commenting on media coverage of mental distress stories allows elite journalists to become 'moral entrepreneurs' (Becker, 1963), differentiating themselves and the titles for which they write from their supposedly less compassionate competitors. In general terms, then, the coverage of celebrity mental distress, like the reporting of stories about eating disorders, is characterised by an uneasy mixture of sensationalism and sensitivity.

Over the past 50 years, mental health policy has increasingly concentrated on mental health as well as mental distress (Rogers and Pilgrim, 2001: 207). The changing style and contents of women's magazines clearly reflect this shift in emphasis. Magazines more and more interpellate audiences into what Featherstone (1991) calls a 'learning mode to life', as the post-Fordist requirement for a multi-skilled, adaptive and 'flexible' workforce is internalised by individuals as a quest for knowledge about health and well-being. The popularity today of women's magazines that blend celebrity with psychology, such as Hachette Filipacchi's *Psychologies*, can be argued to reflect media audiences' growing interest in increasing their cultural capital through the consumption of narratives and information about mental distress. In the context of an individualised and 'psychologized' (Giddens, 1992) society in which subjects are concerned with the management of personal 'risk', magazine stories about the 'battles' and 'triumphs' of distressed celebrities can be seen as useful resources in the battle against stigmatisation. It might be added that women's magazines, like newspapers, offer a reasonable diversity of perspectives on the treatment of mental distress: while they often discuss mental distress in terms of illness, they also sometimes challenge the presuppositions of the medical model and the dangers of relying upon it; thus *Marie Claire* notes that the notion that 'depression is genetic' is a 'myth' (Berg, 2006: 207), while a *Glamour* feature entitled 'The UK's most popular anti-depressants' (2008) notes the many unpleasant side effects of these medications and recommends readers to try other therapies before turning to medication. Moreover, women's magazines sometimes hint at the role of economic exploitation and other forms of social oppression in the development of personal distress; thus a *Cosmopolitan* survey of attitudes towards 'stress' among 25–30 year-old women in September 2002 found that work pressures headed the list of potential 'stressors'.

Nonetheless, insofar as women's magazines do offer therapeutic resources and touch upon some of the social contexts of personal distress, these advances are vitiated by less progressive discursive elements. Women's magazines generate many contradictory messages about mental distress: they broach the social origins of distress in class and gender oppression, while framing the pursuit of mental health as an individual quest; they encourage 'retail therapy' as a solution to psychological unease, while also preaching contentment with one's lot as the key to mental health; they discuss the deleterious impact of magazines upon body image while proliferating images of thin models; and they frame potentially useful stories about female celebrity breakdowns in ways that reproduce conservative stereotypes of gender.

Going *Nuts*: Madness, irony and violence in men's magazines

The readership of lifestyle magazines has always been sharply divided along gender lines. Janice Winship (1987) argued in the 1980s that women's magazines constitute a discrete 'world' in which women can take refuge from patriarchal society. Men, Winship famously argued, do not require gender-specific general-interest magazines, since the world already belongs to them. Yet the rise of men's magazines since the 1980s, beginning with *Arena* and *GQ*, through to the 'lad mags' of the 1990s such as *Loaded* and, more recently, the cheaper weekly titles such as IPC's publication *Nuts* and Bauer's *Zoo*, has altered the landscape of magazine publishing since Winship wrote (although the survival of all of these titles is very much in question as circulations of men's magazines, at the time of writing, plummet in the face of economic recession and competition from online content providers).

Following the logic of Winship's argument, the rise of men's magazines might be taken as evidence that we now live in post-patriarchal times in which masculinist hegemony is no longer assumed, either by magazine publishers or readers. In the past 50 years there have certainly been major shifts in the way in which men are addressed by lifestyle media. It is true, as Bill Osgerby (2003) reminds us, that middle-class men have always been hailed as consumers by men's magazines (see also Register, 2001). Yet traditionally men in general have been more typically regarded as producers than consumers. In the present phase of capitalism, rates of profit in the print media sector are falling and media companies face increasing pressure to identify and exploit new markets – or at least new subsections of existing markets. In consequence, men, more than ever before, constitute an important marketing demographic. Yet while men's magazines increasingly address their readers as consumers, they do not embed mental distress in therapeutic and consumerist discourses to the same extent as women's magazines. While they may reproduce patriarchal stereotypes of femininity and liberal capitalist discourses of individualism, women's magazines at least keep psychological issues on their agenda: Calista's eating disorder or Britney's depression are presented as issues to inspire female solidarity and sympathy. Not only do men's magazines generally ignore mental distress issues altogether, but it is often magazines aimed primarily at *women* that contain the most sustained articles about *male* mental distress, reflecting the tendency for women to function as the health gatekeepers in family contexts. In fact, psychological issues feature only rarely in magazines for men and then in ways that reinforce traditional stereotypes of gender.

David Gauntlett (2002) argues that contemporary men's magazines contain a great deal of information about health, personal grooming and lifestyle, offering young men new scripts about masculinity; yet their mode of address and level of coverage of mental distress issues differ markedly from women's magazines. A key stylistic difference between men's and women's magazines lies in the former's heavy use of irony. This irony has been argued to have been vital to the success of magazines such as *Men's Health* since the 1990s, as they sought to introduce topics relating to health and psychology that might previously have been derived from women's magazines and seen as essentially female concerns (Crewe, 2003: 56–7). Rather as the soap opera *EastEnders* has attempted to break down the stereotype of the 'tough guy' with mental distress storylines involving Gary Hobbs and Phil Mitchell, *Men's Health* has attempted to smuggle a certain amount of information and advice about male mental and physical well-being into its features under the cover of irony.

Yet other discursive elements of men's magazines militate against the serious exploration of mental health issues. For one thing, men's magazines construct a hyper-masculine position for their readers to assume. This is particularly evident in the frequently violent tone of these publications. In women's magazines, as we have seen, mental distress is discussed in highly serious, lachrymose, even tragic terms. In men's magazines, by contrast, mental distress is either scorned as a token of weakness, or is rescripted as heroic aggression, as summarised in the popular expression 'mad for it'. Alongside the advice columns and advertisements for personal grooming products suitable for the 'new man', much content glorifies horrific injuries and physical violence. This is especially apparent in the relatively recent weekly 'lad mag' titles such as *Zoo* and *Nuts* (which contains features with titles such as 'Tiger Fights Croc'), although it is also a feature of more established and upmarket monthly titles, such as *Men's Health* (Stibbe, 2004). Discussions of psychological issues are often framed in ways that emphasise and validate unprovoked physical violence. An edition of *Zoo* (11–17 February 2005), for example, carries a feature on the 'Premiership's Top 20 Nutters', which includes a 'madness index' of some of Britain's most famous footballers. Another typical feature in the same issue ('Is 24-hour drinking *really* bad for you?') ironically glorifies heavy drinking – a well-known cofactor in the development of mental health problems, particularly among men. The playful excessiveness of such features invokes the Bakhtinian notion of the carnivalesque. There is in fact a Rabelesian, liberatory aspect to lad mags, whose focus on recreation and fun rather than work might be seen as a welcome relief from the staid, Blairite values of responsibility and discipline that have characterised (some would say stultified) British public life since the mid-1990s. Nonetheless, the tone of these publications seems to preclude serious engagement with men's social or psychological problems.

The Dionysian tenor of men's magazines is linked to the phenomenon of 'lad culture' that arose in the 1990s and was exemplified by the

BBC1 television situation comedy drama *Men Behaving Badly* and violent gangster narratives such as Guy Ritchie's 1998 film *Lock, Stock and Two Smoking Barrels* (Edwards, 2006: 41). Like these texts, men's magazines have been blamed for encouraging 'laddish' behaviours or habits that are ultimately deleterious to mental health:

> In June 1997, for example, both *Bella* magazine and the *Independent on Sunday* ran features on the increasing number of male anorexics, asking if 'the new wave of glossy magazines for men' had anything to do with it (*Independent on Sunday* 8 June 1997; *Bella* June 1997), and a report on Blur's Damon Albarn's apparent depression also made links to *Loaded*.
>
> (Jackson, Stevenson and Brooks, 2001: 41–2)

Whether men's magazines can be directly blamed for causing an increased disposition to mental distress is unclear; yet they certainly do not address psychological issues in a spirit of sympathy or solidarity.

Men's magazines typically discuss mental distress instrumentally in terms of 'losing it'. *Men's Health*, in December 2001, for example, ran a mental health quiz with the title 'Will You Lose Your Marbles?' Article titles in *Men's Health*, such as 'Joy provision' (a feature about antidepressant medications), 'Beat your addiction', 'Smash stress' and 'Instant relaxation' also instrumentalise the treatment of mental distress. As Jackson, Stevenson and Brooks (2001: 98) found in their interviews with readers of men's magazines, the mind is seen as a machine to be kept 'running along smoothly' and 'fixed' when broken. As in many film and television dramas, men are constructed as the masters, rather than the victims, of their own minds. Gauntlett (2002: 175–6) notes that the cover of the April 1999 edition of *FHM* magazine sports the headline 'Are You Going Mental?', taking this as evidence that men's magazines are 'riddled with anxiety'. It may be true that the frivolity of such headlines masks deep anxieties about masculine identity; what is clearer, however, is that the tone of such headlines is calculated to keep the discussion of mental distress at arm's length. Unlike women's magazines, which often feature first-person accounts of mental distress and which construct psychology as a distinctively feminine province, men's magazines present psychological problems as an external threat to be managed or kept at bay: madness and masculinity are never identified. Another distancing (not to mention stigmatising) strategy used in men's magazines is that of displacing experiences of distress onto others, as in the advice offered by the *Men's Health* web site in 2004 on surviving difficult family get-togethers: 'If your family get-togethers seem like a reality show with a cast of mental patients, try these suggestions for dealing with holiday nuts.' Men's magazines, then, tend to reject madness or to reify it as a technical breakdown to be 'dealt with'.

These criticisms are unlikely to convince those critics who emphasise the subversive irony of men's magazines. According to Gauntlett (2002), for example, the jocularity of men's magazines belies a degree of uneasy self-awareness that covertly undermines the apparent masculinism of the text and serves to underline the constructedness of masculinity. This generally positive view of men's magazines is broadly shared by Jackson, Stevenson and Brooks (2001). It is certainly true that 'lad mags' are steeped in postmodern irony and are therefore a highly knowing media form with subversive potential. In any particular instance, however, there seems to be no particular reason to assume that this ironic tone works subversively rather than as a rhetorical fig leaf covering the racism, homophobia and other problematic elements of the magazines' manifest content. Attempts to settle the question of what meanings audiences derive from these texts through empirical audience research must be treated with caution. The findings of Gauntlett's investigation into readers' responses to men's magazines are not as conclusive as they may seem, for example, since the questions he asks of readers seem to be distinctly leading ones. Gauntlett's question 'do these magazines help you to think of yourself as a particular kind of person?' (2002: 177), would seem to encourage respondents to reflect upon magazines as sources of identity construction rather than as sites of ideological manipulation. It therefore seems too quick to assume that the irony that characterises men's magazines functions progressively, enabling the expression of otherwise culturally inadmissible concerns with male well-being; it might equally well be seen an insidious mode of ideological regulation that authorises the articulation of sexist and other retrogressive discourses. In fact, as Žižek (1989: 28) reminds us, 'in contemporary societies, democratic or totalitarian, [...] cynical distance, laughter, irony, are, so to speak, part of the game. The ruling ideology is not meant to be taken seriously or literally.' Terry Eagleton (2007: 40), commenting on Žižek's point, adds: 'it is as though the ruling ideology has already accommodated the fact that we will be sceptical of it, and reorganised its discourses accordingly.'

While some medical and lifestyle magazines for men do sometimes carry informative stories about mental distress, their cavalier tone implies that ill-health in general, and mental distress in particular, is regarded as a token of weakness. Will Courtenay's (2000) work on masculinity in the US shows that masculine empowerment is very much dependent on not being perceived as weak or as suffering with psychological or emotional problems; in practical terms, this might translate into a number of health behaviours, such as avoidance of contact with doctors or indulgence in heavy drinking. For all their exuberance, men's magazines do little to challenge these behaviours and sometimes even encourage them. From an anti-stigma perspective, this is unfortunate, since men present far less commonly than women with mental health problems in primary care settings and suicides among young men far exceed those among young women in Western societies (Fortune et al., 2007). Indeed, the results of the Samaritans' 'Young Men Speak Out' survey published in 1999, at the height of concerns over 'lad culture', suggested that young men are more likely to 'smash something up' rather than talk about their problems and are overtaking women as victims of mental distress.

These cultural dispositions may be linked to the political and social transformations that have taken place in both Britain and the US over the past thirty years. In the neoliberal moment, the awareness of 'risk' has become heightened in advanced capitalist societies, generating a constant and pervasive low-level, background or 'ambient' sense of fear (Massumi, 1993; Lipovetsky, 2005; Bauman, 2006). Yet, as Godsi (2004: 188) argues, rising economic precariousness and the decline of heavy industry may affect the self-esteem of young men particularly harshly, since the erosion of full-time jobs in traditionally male industries such as coal-mining and ship-building has undermined many working-class men's former role as the familial 'breadwinners'. The feminist writer Ros Coward (1999) explains that men are particularly traumatised by redundancy because so much of their identity as men and as members of society comes from their job, rather than their roles as parents or husbands/partners (see also Suzik, 2001). This theory is supported by evidence that the suicide rate among young British males rose dramatically during the 1980s (Pilgrim and Rogers, 1993: 75) – the period in which Britain's traditional heavy industries entered sharp decline. In this context, it is plausible to argue, following Jackson, Stevenson and Brooks (2001: 146), that the hyper-masculinised scripts of men's magazines fulfil a psychological need for a sense of cultural rootedness, reproducing what Beck (1992) calls 'constructed certitude' and dispelling anxiety about the changing nature of masculine identity in a 'feminised' service sector economy. If this is the case, it is hardly surprising that mental distress is treated trivially in most magazines produced for men.

To find substantial treatments of mental distress in magazines aimed at men, one has to look at arts or music journalism. Here attitudes towards male mental distress are markedly different to those found in general magazines for men. Music journalists have long been fascinated by tortured male artists such as Brian Wilson, Keith Moon, Phil Spector, Syd Barrett, Paul Simon, Ian Curtis and Sting. Following the death of the rock musician Syd Barrett, Michael Hann (2006: 8) wrote in the *Guardian's G2* magazine:

> Sometimes I look at my CD and record shelves and wonder: am I a madness groupie? There are the Syd Barrett solo albums and the first Pink Floyd LP. There's a vast stack of Beach Boys and Brian Wilson obscurities, concentrating on Wilson's nervous-breakdown years. A small stack of 13th Floor Elevators recordings – their singer, Roky Erikson, lost touch with reality after spending time in a mental hospital in preference to serving jail time for drugs offences. There's an album by Daniel Johnson (schizophrenia), several by Sly Stone (drug-induced breakdowns) and plenty by Alex Chilton and Big Star (whose album *Sister Lovers* is mental collapse set to music).

The gender bias of Hann's *ad hoc* sample is remarkable; clearly, as the print media's treatment of Britney Spears attests, 'women do not enjoy the same mythologizing as their male counterparts, the gods, the kings, the shamans of rock' (Whiteley, 2006: 334). In an *Observer Magazine* feature, for example, Craig McLean (2006: 39) describes how the US singer–songwriter Fiona Apple was raped as a child, subsequently developing an eating disorder and self-harming; thus Apple became, as McLean puts it, 'the poster girl for over-sensitive youth'. Given the nature of the abuse suffered by Apple, McLean's implication that Apple is merely unduly sensitive strikes a rather dismissive note and is certainly discordant with the hagiographic tones usually reserved for male stars in the music press.

Indeed, in an analysis of the representation of women in (male-oriented) music magazines such as *Melody Maker* and *New Musical Express*, Helen Davies (2004: 172–3) argues that artistic credibility and mental instability go hand in hand for male rock artists, while female artists who discuss psychiatric issues are often ridiculed or ignored, even when the psychological problems under discussion are more likely to affect women than men:

> Men such as [Richey] Edwards, Kurt Cobain of Nirvana and Brett Anderson of Suede are praised for their exploration of the feminine and, particularly in the cases of Edwards and Cobain, are described

as emotional and tortured figures. Edwards was praised for his open discussion of his anorexia and self-mutilation, while the same topics were unpalatable when spoken of by female Riot Grrrls. If men can provide 'the feminine' then women are redundant.

The journalistic treatment of the troubled singer–songwriter Daniel Johnson illustrates how this mythologising is linked to notions of male creativity. In the *Guardian's Guide* magazine article about the singer, John Robinson (2005: 10) writes: 'when he was growing up in the 1960s and 1970s, there was no reason to suspect that Daniel Johnson was anything other than a particularly creative child', an observation that links Johnson's creativity to his mental disturbance. Print journalists' approbation for troubled male rock stars who appropriate 'feminine' therapeutic discourses – Syd Barrett, Keith Moon, Stuart Goddard, and more recently rock stars such as My Chemical Romance members Gerard and Mikey Way – recalls the gendered distribution of 'heroic' and 'tragic' images of madness in film television texts and reinforces the sexist definition of genius discussed in Chapter 3.

Conclusions

National print media treatments of mental distress in many ways mirror those to be found across the range of television formats and genres discussed in Chapter 4. Despite the rise in sympathetic newspaper coverage of mental distress, discriminations of social class continue to play a key role in determining how sufferers are treated. While the tabloid press often dubs 'ordinary people' (to use a well-worn media cliché) as 'nuts' and 'psychos', newspaper journalists seem to adopt a more sympathetic tone to describe professional and celebrity sufferers or ruling-class heroes such as Winston Churchill. Stories about female breakdowns, meanwhile, are often sensationalising and misogynistic. Such conclusions no doubt reflect the deep-rooted ideological and cultural distinctions of capitalism; yet the sensationalisation of mental distress may also be related to more immediate economic pressures. At the time of writing, the newspaper industry, at both the national and local level, is haemorrhaging readers and advertising revenue and entering financial freefall (Robinson, 2008). In such an economic climate, salacious stories and images of celebrity distress have an obvious appeal for reader-hungry editors.

Like newspapers, women's magazines contain practical advice and information about mental distress, offering advice on diet, relaxation and other techniques for combating psychological discomfort. Mental distress is clearly constructed as a topic of particular relevance and interest to women. Yet the proliferation of mental health advice in these magazines also seems to confirm the cultural assumption that women are psychiatrically impaired *by definition* (Chesler, 1972). As Lisa Appignanesi (2008: 6) puts it:

> A magazine like *Psychologies*, which looks at the softer side of psychic order and disorder, always carries a woman's face on its front cover, as if psychology, that whole business of understanding the (troubled) mind and relations, were uniquely a feminine undertaking.

This feminine gendering of madness in magazines is reinforced through the mode of melodrama. Just as newspapers filter female mental distress through fetishised, multiple images of tearful celebrities, so magazine stories of female distress are couched in a melodramatic register, even in magazines – such as *there there* – that profess to be guided by a medical, anti-stigma agenda.

Men's magazines, on the other hand, work by excluding or abjecting the 'other' (Benwell, 2003). Whereas some women's magazines – notably *Marie Claire* – contain testimonies and stories of distress of black and Asian sufferers, men's magazines project a very white world; categories of social difference rarely materialise in men's magazines and in lad mags racial and sexual difference is ridiculed. A *loaded* feature entitled 'The Hardest Gays in the Village' (2005), for example, superimposes silver handbags over photographs of several male homosexual celebrities, who, despite their supposed reputation for physical strength or violence, are ridiculed through sexual *double entendres* as well as racist remarks. As Bethan Benwell's (2003: 18) summarises:

> Ethnicity [...] is rarely addressed in a reflexive way in men's magazines, so the assumption remains, due to the near-invisibility of black celebrities, writers, readers, and positive or serious coverage of black culture more generally, that magazine masculinity is white in orientation. Work and fatherhood are rarely discussed and homosexuality is taboo.

The rejection, marginalisation and othering of mental distress in men's magazines can be seen as part of their ruthless expulsion of all non-hegemonic identities. The magazines' rejection of homosexuality can be seen as particularly problematic in view of the higher incidence of mental distress among homosexual men (Grant and Potenza, 2006: 374–5).

The absence of mental distress information in men's magazines helps to reinforce a culture of 'toughness' in which men's mental distress is not – indeed, must not be – taken seriously. As Jackson, Stevenson and Brooks (2001: 99) put it, 'the tough masculine body must keep at bay unconscious needs for feelings of emotion, care and Eros.' Besides posing a problem for male readers experiencing mental distress, the magazines' exaltation of 'toughness' may also perpetuate the unconscious tendency among medical practitioners to deliver less adequate healthcare to men than to women: Courtenay (2000: 1395) sums up a tradition of research which shows that men receive less contact time with doctors in their health visits than women and are provided with fewer and briefer medical explanations during medical encounters in primary care settings.

Insofar as men's magazines encourage reflection on questions of psychological well-being at all, they address their readers as active and even aggressive agents of their own mental health, rather than passive victims or sufferers. Historically, such gendered discrepancies in the cultural framing of distress are nothing new. Men and upper-class women in the nineteenth century, for instance, were often diagnosed with the relatively neutral condition neurasthenia, while lower-class women more commonly received the derogatory diagnosis of hysteria, which in turn implies a fundamental irrationality and lack of self-control (Showalter, 1987a). The evidence from contemporary men's and women's magazines suggests that this rational/hysterical dyad and an uneven attribution of personal agency to men and women continues to inform print media discourses of madness.

It may seem perverse or even contradictory to criticise the relative absence of mental health information from men's magazines, while simultaneously critiquing the hegemony of emotional regulation in women's publications. Yet the criticism here is not simply that women's magazines contain too much, and men's magazines too little information about mental distress; it is also a question of the nature of that information. Women's magazines are preoccupied with mental well-being from a narrowly individualistic perspective, while men's magazines adopt a dismissive, cavalier and instrumentalist attitude towards the topic. Both of these perspectives are therapeutically and ideologically problematic; taken together, they tend to reinforce the discursive dichotomy of active/dominant masculinity and passive/impaired femininity that we have observed in other forms of media.

I have suggested here that newspaper and magazine discussions of mental distress are typically circumscribed by individualism and usually disavow or minimise the social dimensions of personal suffering – a tendency particularly apparent in the consumerist framing of distress in women's magazines. The print media certainly do present a great deal of valuable and consoling information and advice, as well as broadly sympathetic stories about psychological suffering. It certainly cannot be said that the prevailing tone of print media coverage of mental distress today is unkindly – with the possible exception of men's magazines. Nonetheless, even when newspapers and magazines are at their most supportive and sympathetic, they reassert hegemonic presuppositions about class, race, gender, while obscuring the social causes of personal distress.

Conclusion: Media, Madness and Ideology

This book set out to explore how media images of mental distress intersect with discourses of class, gender and race. Exploring the ideological dimension of these images is vital today, as the task of interpreting and judging cultural images of mental distress is increasingly ceded to – and sometimes arrogated by – psychiatric professionals whose primary yet rather attenuated concern is with the enforcement of representational 'accuracy'. This situation might in turn be said to reflect the 'post-political' ethos of advanced capitalist societies, in which the ideological dimensions of social problems are minimised and public issues are increasingly packaged as technical problems to be discussed and resolved by experts (Žižek, 1999). Yet the analysis of media representations of mental distress must not simply be left to psychiatric professionals. Media images and discourses of madness are not merely more or less faithful reflections of psychiatric realities, but polysemous indices of social and political change. With this in mind, I shall briefly attempt to summarise my argument and to contextualise it in relation to some recent social changes and cultural theories.

I began this book by arguing for a reassessment of some of the central tenets of anti-stigma discourse. I argued, for example, that the assumption that the contemporary media mostly portrays people suffering with mental distress as violent or as criminals does not seem particularly convincing. I also suggested that previous studies of media representations of mental distress have insisted rather too rigidly on 'accuracy' as the sole criterion against which media texts are to be measured. It is not that questions of psychiatric accuracy are always and everywhere irrelevant. On the contrary, inaccuracy may be a particularly pressing consideration in certain non-Western media contexts, where sensationalising and fantastical explanations for mental distress are common. In West African films, for example, sorcery, witchcraft and charms feature prominently as explanations for mental disturbance, contributing to a frightening and misleading picture of madness and possibly discouraging sufferers from seeking psychiatric help in a culture in which traditional superstitions persist (Aina, 2004: 24). The medical model of madness – however flawed it may be – might be seen to constitute an advance over such potentially dangerous understandings of psychological distress.

Nor has this book advanced a wholly revisionist argument. While this book has, I hope, offered some fresh insights into the functioning of madness in media texts, it has also confirmed many of the findings of earlier, psychiatric critics of the media. Mental distress is often represented in stigmatising ways, particularly in 'comic' representations that – with no redeeming rationale or satirical purpose – encourage the mockery of mentally distressed people. Distress also continues to be seen as a token of infamy or sinfulness and is sometimes presented as being relatively easy to overcome. In film, especially, the exigencies of narrative form and the Hollywood impulse for a happy ending or a romantic resolution can tend towards the facile or premature foreclosure of the issues raised by mental distress narratives. Moreover, although violence towards others is not in itself problematic, some media texts, such as *Julien Donkey-Boy*, seem to treat the theme of violence to others exploitatively, while certain groups – particularly female soap opera characters – seem disproportionately prone to violent crimes of passion. In the light of all this, and despite whatever mitigating arguments have been presented here, the media's stigmatisation of those suffering with mental distress remains problematic.

However, I have also suggested that there is now a great deal of 'positive' and sympathetic treatment of mental distress in film, television and popular print media, a process whose first stirrings Wahl (1995: 132–63) perceived in the mid-1990s. While, as Wahl (1995) argues, the economic imperative to create sensational, crowd-pleasing entertainment is one important source of the misrepresentation of the mentally distressed as violent killers and social rejects, it seems that the requirement to entertain audiences and generate profits can be fulfilled equally satisfactorily by narratives of breakthrough, self-discovery and recovery. Today, films, television programmes, newspaper and magazine articles all frequently depict the lives and experiences of sufferers in broadly sympathetic terms. Analogously, there is evidence that public opinion is not entirely hostile towards people suffering from mental distress, even where media representations are stigmatising. The outcry against *The Sun*'s Frank Bruno slur indicates that public acceptance of offensive or stereotypical material cannot be automatically assumed. It also shows the efficacy of the growing anti-stigma culture that has developed over the past ten years in challenging hostile cultural representations of distress. Today, many media representations of distress are even quite radical. Fictional portrayals of mental distress sometimes use the trope of madness to dramatise inequalities of power in society, class and gender oppression, and the psychological consequences of warfare. Madness, it seems, has lost none of its traditional power to condense, figure forth and sometimes contest the depredations of social alienation and political disempowerment.

As I have suggested throughout this book, the discourse of madness in the media today is also a restless, reflexive, inter-textual and sometimes self-critical one. Mental distress is not only a common theme of television drama, for example, but is often a subject explicitly discussed by characters within television drama. Films such as *Julien Donkey-Boy*, meanwhile, recycle images and dialogue from previous movies about mental distress, while newspaper and magazine articles about distress often excoriate the mistreatment of the subject in other parts of the media. Another aspect of the new self-consciousness about madness in the media is the eclectic range of representations with which audiences are presented: images of psychiatric patients and decarcerated individuals living in the community jostle with stereotypes of madness drawn from preceding eras, from bestial madmen to mute hysterics. Media practitioners draw upon this stockpile of cultural images for a variety of purposes: some progressive, some retrogressive.

Indeed, while the media representation of madness has improved within certain parameters, it is impossible to offer a celebratory assessment of its development. The media's attempts at representational amelioration are negotiated within the context of advanced capitalism, which – while certainly no respecter of traditional ideologies – is nonetheless a system of structural oppression that operates through class, as well as gender and racial domination. While popular culture often valorises and destigmatises madness, some social groups fare better than others. In this sense, talk of 'positive' and 'negative' images of mental distress is sometimes unhelpful, as it elides social, economic and political determinations. As I have argued throughout this book, images of madness are not simply improving; sometimes hoary stereotypes are replaced by alternative images that are merely 'differently bad'.

For example, media representations of madness often uphold conservative ideologies of gender. While central to radical feminist sociology (Chesler, 1972; Ussher, 1991), the gendered nature of mental distress has not been a central concern of the recent psychiatric criticism of media images of madness; yet some clear conclusions emerge from the present study. While madness in boys and men is more often presented heroically or comically, female madness is presented far more ambiguously. Some media texts, such as the supernaturally themed television dramas *Medium* and *Afterlife*, valorise female madness as an alternative and even superior mode of knowledge. Indeed, the patriarchal construction of female madness is often subverted in contemporary cinema; a common narrative strategy involves morally vindicating the heroine by first asserting, then overturning the misogynistic stereotype of the 'crazy woman'. It is clear, however, that the most feted film dramas – and the ones that explore the psychology of mental distress most thoroughly and deeply – tend to be those produced by avant-garde male auteurs and which primarily feature male, rather than female sufferers. While contemporary auteurist treatments of male mental distress often attempt to reflect the inner, mental worlds of their heroes, female sufferers tend to be represented through the more corporeal dramaturgy of melodrama. Also, as argued above, films and soap operas often revive traditional stereotypes of tragic, helpless femininity, condensing what might be seen as a post-feminist backlash against aspirational femininity. While mental distress seems to function as a guarantee of authenticity in many films, celebrity chat shows and magazines – promising to reveal what celebrities are 'really like' or to expose the 'human truths' behind the public images of celebrated writers and artists – male individuals and characters are valorised by this process far more consistently than their female counterparts. These findings support Susan Bordo's (1993: 15) contention that the classical hierarchical oppositions of male/female, mind/body and active/passive continue to structure Western cultural representation, despite frequent calls from post-structuralists to deconstruct or 'move beyond' such binary sets.

More generally, while women spend increasing amounts of time on the management and discipline of their bodies (Bordo, 1993: 166), the management of *mental* health is also typically constructed as a properly feminine obligation. In films, for instance, female characters are often posited as the 'saviours' of disturbed men. Magazines, meanwhile, emphasise the importance to women of 'balanced living', self-care, self-discovery and positive thinking – discourses also dominant, incidentally, in pharmaceutical advertising (Gardner, 2007: 541). The demands of these discourses are increasingly insistent in a society in which the responsibility for psychic health falls more and more to individuals as well as mental health professionals.

It might seem contradictory to claim that film and television texts reinforce conservative gender stereotypes while noting that other media forms – most notably women's magazines – encourage the reflexive application of technologies of the self to the management of the psyche. Yet traditional stereotypes of female fragility and passivity are not necessarily unrelated to the more contemporary discourses of self-monitoring and the 'will to health'. These seemingly discrepant discourses might be argued to fulfil distinct functions in a class society in which social control involves the seduction of the wealthy and the repression of the poor (Bauman, 1992: 98). In crude terms, while wealthy women are enjoined to self-monitor their mental health and hailed as self-reflexive subjects, poor women are invited to accept their inferior status or abjection. From a more dialectical perspective, the seemingly opposed discourses of empowerment and passivity might be argued to work in tandem, demarcating the poles of female success and failure within neoliberalism in terms of self-actualisation and abjection. Soap narratives of out-of-control housewives or magazine images of broken-down female celebrities dramatise the risks of feminine self-construction: without constant psychological self-monitoring, there is always a danger that women may backslide into the 'natural', disordered, helpless state of femininity.

In contrast to the figuration of female madness as abjection, media representations of male mental distress are characterised by toughness, purposiveness or even aggression. In many films distressed men overcome psychic adversity by sheer strength of will. This is not to say that male fictional characters are never constructed as emotionally fragile; on the contrary, male characters in British soap operas and young adult dramas, for instance, are increasingly constructed as emotionally expressive, even tearful subjects. Yet in many cases this emotionality is recuperated into an instrumentalist discourse which sees the mind as a machine – a prominent discourse in men's magazines – and which casts men as the heroic agents of their own recovery. Although the flippancy, comedy and instrumentalism that characterise media treatments of male madness may seem preferable to the hysteria that surrounds female sufferers, they may be equally damaging, given how reluctant male sufferers typically are to seek help for psychological problems and the particular problems they can face in psychiatric settings. After all, as Pilgrim and Rogers (1993: 43) note in their criticism of Showalter's (1987a) account of women and psychiatry, '*men* are treated coercively by the psychiatric profession more than women.'

Some groups of sufferers are barely visible in the media. As the average age of people in most Western countries, such as the UK, continues to rise, many more older people are suffering from mental distress: according to the UK Inquiry into Mental Health and Well-Being in Later Life conducted in 2007, more than 3.5 million older people have mental health problems, although under-funding and age discrimination in mental health services prevent many of them from obtaining support or treatment. Yet the voices of mentally distressed older people are seldom heard in films, television or mass circulation magazines. This finding supports other research suggesting the media's general under-representation of the elderly (Charren and Sandler, 1983), who constitute a relatively unprofitable demographic as far as many media organisations are concerned. I have also argued that there are very few media representations of visible minority sufferers of mental distress in the British, or for that matter, the US media – a striking absence given the over-representation of black people in the mental health system. It is perhaps telling that the most radical British treatment of issues surrounding race and mental distress in recent years is arguably Joe Penhall's stage play *Blue/Orange* (2000), which dramatises a dispute between two white psychiatrists over whether to diagnose a black man as schizophrenic.

The reasons for the media's neglect of distress among black people are hard to fathom. Given that certain news media crime stories have sometimes invoked the stereotype of the monstrous black madman (Francis, 1993: 192; Neal, 1998), it is perhaps surprising not to find more references to black madness in, for example, horror film. Here, psychoanalytical arguments might come into play. If we accept Judith Halberstam's (1995: 4) argument that the racial other is the structuring absence of horror films – a figure of 'universal loathing who haunts the community' – then perhaps we could argue that the image of black monstrosity in fictional form might too directly invoke contemporary anxieties, requiring the audience's fears to be filtered through a more coded figure – often, in cinema, a 'white trash' redneck (Pinedo, 1997: 112). As we have seen, working-class characters in films are certainly frequently constructed as disturbed and violently unpredictable monsters.

Sympathetic, as well as hostile, treatments of black mental distress are also hard to come by in the media. Blackness has often been othered through the long-standing historical stereotype of the 'noble savage' who is by definition incapable of 'complex' mental illness (Francis, 1993: 179). To be diagnosed with psychological distress, a sufferer must have a degree of psychological depth that a patient being examined for signs of a physical ailment need not possess. Instead of simply reporting a pain or displaying a visible symptom, the depressed patient is most often recognised through the production of a narrative; hence, perhaps, the historical neglect of black distress by the white medical establishment that once – and arguably still – viewed black people as simple, insentient beings undeserving of psychiatric consideration (Fernando, 1991; Poussaint and Alexander, 2001). In her memoir of depression, Meri Nana-Ama Danquah (1998: 21) notes how difficult it is 'for black women to be seen as [...] emotionally complex', especially as black femininity is often perceived through the stereotype of the strong and resilient 'Mammy' (Turner, 1994).

Finally, and perhaps most crucially, representations of mental distress are shaped by distinctions of social class. Put simply, working-class sufferers attract more censure and/or derision than their middle-class counterparts across all the forms of media considered here. On television, talk shows and documentaries privilege middle-class dispositions and tend to derogate or spectacularise working-class suffering. The discourse of the 'mad genius', meanwhile, tends to surface most often in films, documentaries, talk shows, newspapers and magazine articles featuring celebrities or middle-class individuals. Some of these individuals, such as Alastair Campbell, have benefited from the public discussion of their problems, appearing regularly on talk shows and producing books and documentaries about their experiences; as Davi Johnson (2008: 44) notes, the difference represented by madness is increasingly 'not excluded but cultivated as a useful social and economic resource.' Yet the political divisiveness of figures such as Campbell and his precursor as a public depression sufferer, Winston Churchill, raises the question of the extent to which ruling-class politicians can or should represent or 'speak for' sufferers of mental distress. It certainly should not be assumed – as it routinely is among liberal anti-stigma campaigners – that the interventions of such individuals necessarily help to create a 'positive image' of mental distress. On the other hand, the representational advantages afforded by class and status can in any case be vitiated by misogyny and sexism, as many mentally distressed female celebrities, such as Britney Spears, have discovered.

Beyond the question of how sympathetically black, female or working-class sufferers are represented, however, lies the broader issue of how media images of madness intersect with the changing matrices of political control in the world today. As argued in Chapter 1, governments and corporate interests are working to expand both the boundaries of psychiatric diagnosis along with the market for pharmaceutical treatments. As Western nations transition between

Foucauldian 'disciplinary societies' characterised by physical enclosures (such as psychiatric institutions) to more 'fluid', Deleuzian 'societies of control', pharmaceutical regulation may be predicted to become increasingly central to the capitalist project of social domination. As we have seen, film and media representations often document the grim consequences of rejecting medication or of simply trying to escape from oppressive psychiatric control. While some film and media texts offer alternative perspectives on the treatment of mental distress, the medical paradigm of mental distress exerts an increasing influence on cinema, television and print media, as it does on many other areas of popular culture, such as literary biography (Zimmerman, 2007). This cultural emphasis on biopsychiatric understandings of madness supports Rose's (2007: 26) contention that capitalist subjects increasingly conceive of themselves as 'somatic individuals'. In the case of physical illness this can be, as Rose argues, empowering; but given the limitations of the medical model of madness, it seems likely to lead to an attenuated understanding of mental suffering.

Of course, individuals in advanced capitalist societies are hailed as emotional, as well as biological subjects. According to the social critic and therapist Susie Orbach, hitherto repressed Britons have become increasingly amenable to emotional expression, as supposedly evidenced by what the media presented as an outpouring of public grief following the death of Orbach's client, Princess Diana. Whether or not Orbach is correct, media texts today more and more embed mental distress within discourses of emotional management. From the tragic images of tearful celebrities in women's magazines to the emerging images of troubled young men in soap operas and young adult 'edutainment' dramas, madness is increasingly implicated within a therapeutic discourse that stresses the importance of 'open' communication and self-analysis.

While such reflexive competencies are usually seen straightforwardly as 'positive' from the perspective of liberal anti-stigma discourse, they can also be understood as reflecting the emergence of what Michael Hardt and Antonio Negri (2005: 108) call 'immaterial labour': the various forms of non-industrial labour that typify post-Fordist economies. Hardt and Negri distinguish two types of immaterial labour: intellectual/linguistic labour and affective labour. The latter category includes parental work and caring labour as well as service sector work. Globally, immaterial labour, Hardt and Negri argue, is qualitatively, if not quantitatively hegemonic, in that it now exerts its influence on other forms of labour: 'Just as in [the industrial] phase all forms of labor and society itself had to industrialise, today labor and society have to informationalize, become intelligent, become communicative, become affective' (Hardt and Negri, 2005: 109). More and more, personal emotions, communications and social relationships are directly transmuted into economic value. Hardt and Negri welcome this development, arguing that labour, having undergone the transition, in Marxist terms, between formal and real subsumption by capital, is in its new, socialised form, once again slipping the clutches of capitalist control, producing a 'creative commons'. Yet as Žižek (2008a: 359) points out, capital continues to play a central role in the organisation of production today, not least in bringing together the post-Fordist realm of affective/cognitive labour and the Fordist domain of material production (represented by the worlds mines, assembly lines and sweatshops), which are today often separated by state borders. The Marxist theory group Aufheben (2006) also raise numerous objections to Hardt and Negri's celebration of immaterial labour, including its suspicious affinity with the bourgeois enthusiasm for the 'information society', its flattening of class society into a community of producers and its elision of the harsh realities of work in sites of 'immaterial labour', such as call centres. Moreover, as Emma Dowling (2007) points out in her work on affective labour among restaurant workers, affect is not only the product of such labour, but also the form of its command. From a Marxist perspective, indeed, media messages about the centrality of communication and 'emotional honesty' to mental health, while removing the stigma that traditionally surrounded madness, can also be argued to constitute an emergent form of social control, creating subjects attuned to the new attitudinal and emotional requirements of an economy whose production is rooted in service sector industries and whose consumption is based on the generation of desires rather than needs. Moreover, the responsibility for undertaking affective labour is not equitably apportioned. Arlie Hochschild's (1983) study of the work of airline stewardesses suggests that the burden of what Hochschild calls 'emotional labour' falls primarily upon women. This state of affairs is reflected in media texts about distress; by posing mental health as a specifically female concern, women's magazines, for example, appear to legitimise the unequal division of emotional labour. In view of all this we should not, perhaps, uncritically celebrate a brave new world of 'affective labour'.

At the risk of theoretical over-determination, it can also be argued that the proliferation of sympathetic, therapeutic discourses around mental health invokes Michel Foucault's (2005: 239–64) conception of biopower. Biopower, according to Foucault, has its material origins in the industrialisation of the late eighteenth century. Contrasting with traditional modes of power based on the threat of death from a sovereign, biopower is concerned with the protection of life and with the monitoring and regulation of the population through, for example, censuses and the control of the mortality rate, as well as the regulation of health and well-being. The ascent of biopolitical modes of social control provides a framework in which to understand the state's intensifying monitoring and regulation of public health and the extension of the metaphor of 'health' into discourses of social policy. The former UK Prime Minister Tony Blair, for example, often talked about the need to create 'healthy communities' (Blair, 2002). In order to create such communities, the UK government increasingly supports programmes of psychological intervention in social life, such as the recommendation in 2006 that child psychologists funded by the government's Respect Task Force (described in the news media as 'super-nannies') should support the parents of young people who engage in anti-social behaviour. The official psychological regulation of capitalist subjects must be interiorised, however: Richard Layard, the Labour government's 'happiness guru', claims that the primary goal of public policy should be to make society happier, arguing that 'to become happier, we have to change our inner attitudes as much as our outward circumstances' (quoted in Furedi, 2006). In keeping with this agenda, as we have seen throughout this book, talk shows, documentaries and magazines typically construct mental well-being as a matter of personal, therapeutic adjustment through what Rose (1998) calls the 'psy' discourses of psychiatry, psychology and therapy.

The expansion of this 'culture of therapy' has been attacked from several ideological perspectives. The conservative critique of therapeutic culture has a long history (see Rieff, 1987; Lasch, 1991). Most recently, Christina Hoff Sommers and Sally Satel (2005) inveigh against a post-1960s 'therapism' that erodes the 'American' virtue of self-reliance. Interestingly, Sommers and Satel point to a body of evidence that suggests that emotional disclosure does not, in fact, help people to cope with traumatic experiences. They also usefully take aim at the instrumentalism, abstraction and self-absorption of the 'happiness industry', endorsing J. S. Mill's advice that 'the only chance is to treat not happiness, but some end external to it as the purpose of life.' On the other hand, some of their recommendations are highly problematic. For them, trauma is inevitable hazard of life that must be accepted but never 'helped'. This is a congenial enough conclusion from the perspective of capital's ruling class, as it seeks to roll back social welfare provision – including access to free psychiatric services – in the advanced capitalist countries. Furthermore, the psychic panacea touted by Sommers and Satel – 'self-reliance' – is hard to distinguish from the self-absorption they criticise, so that they seem to propose overcoming one form of individualism with another.

Another critic of therapism, Frank Furedi (2004), bemoans the encroachment of an infantilising therapeutic rhetoric and a sense of victimisation into every domain of human life, reducing first the desire, and eventually the possibility of individuals to determine their own destinies through self-reliance. The infantilising tendencies that Furedi detects in therapy culture are all too apparent in the case of a magazine title such as *there there*. Furedi's critique highlights the role of therapeutic discourse as an evasion of ideology in the post-political moment – a function clearly exploited by the many politicians who regularly appear on talk shows and documentaries to discuss their psychological suffering rather than their political ideas. But Furedi's opposition to therapism in the name of robust self-reliance does not take mental distress very seriously or offer much of a perspective on how it might be reduced through alternative social arrangements. Nor, like Sommers and Satel, does Furedi take account of how some social groups have greater access to, and exercise greater control over therapeutic resources than others.

Dana Cloud (1998) analyses the rise of therapeutic rhetoric since the 1960s from a broadly Marxist perspective. For Cloud, therapy culture has facilitated the personalisation of the political, constituting an individualistic and voluntaristic retreat from the radical political activism of the 1960s that is at best palliative or consolatory. Cloud explores the infiltration of therapeutic rhetoric into, for example, popular feminism, media coverage of Gulf War 'support groups', and New Age thinking. Of the critiques of therapy culture discussed here, Cloud's seems the most useful, since it alone traces the historical development of therapeutic discourse as a system of control within the disciplinary apparatus of advanced capitalism and shows how it forecloses the possibilities for radical, collective, social transformation that might prevent a great deal of psychological suffering in the first instance. Of course, as Cloud acknowledges, therapeutic rhetoric has its place: in the case of men's magazines, it could even be argued that a certain amount of therapeutic discourse would be preferable to none, or to the cavalier and dismissive attitude taken towards men's psychological problems in these publications. Cloud's critique, however, is not that therapeutic discourse is always useless, but that it hegemonises individualism. My own argument in this book provides ample support for this contention: there is a clear correspondence, for example, between the hegemonic individualism of 'therapy culture' and the meritocratic injunctions to self-actualisation implicit in many cinematic, televisual and print media treatments of mental distress.

Cloud's argument has several parallels with Wendy Brown's (1995) critique of what she terms 'wounded attachment'. Brown draws on the Nietzschian notion of *ressentiment* to explore how oppressed groups, particularly women, authorise their right to speak through appeals to experiences of pain and injury – a process in evidence in women's magazines and television talk shows. Yet while providing temporary comfort or relief from suffering, such a strategy, Brown argues, is ultimately individualistic and self-absorbing, since at some stage the injury itself needs to be dissolved. In short, to focus on one's injuries is to remain fixated on one's problems rather than overturning the system of power that generated them. Brown thus points to the appeal, but also to the limitations, of focusing on painful experiences for therapeutic purposes. From the perspective of Brown's argument, the utility of the therapeutic resources supplied in women's magazines, for example, is compromised not only by the magazines' individualist and consumerist tenor but also by their avoidance of structural critique.

While media representations of mental distress are often framed by medical and therapeutic discourses, they are also, of course, informed by larger political and ideological contexts. In particular, the emphasis on flexibility, meritocracy and individualism in contemporary media discourses of mental distress necessarily invokes the context of neoliberalism, a point appreciated by many critics. Jon Dovey (2000), for example, sees the rise of first-person media narratives of personal change as a distinctly neoliberal phenomenon. In her article on readers' letters to women's health magazines, Christy Newman (2007), meanwhile, notes that the independent, reflexive consideration of health issues fostered by readers' letters on health issues correlates with the ideal, flexible, 'deregulated' subject of neoliberalism. While this may be true, however, it is also important to consider that some subjects are positioned as more flexible than others: I have argued here, for instance, that while films and chat shows laud the psychological struggles of successful politicians and artists, contemporary talk shows typically ascribe working-class distress to a lack of responsibility and resourcefulness. Moreover, while the erosion of the welfare state undoubtedly condemns struggling individuals 'to lick their wounds and exorcize their fears in solitude and seclusion' (Bauman, 1999: 41), there are also certain problems with identifying neoliberalism, rather than capitalism itself, as the source of all social and psychological ills. For one thing, liberal/leftist critiques of neoliberalism often imply the preferability of some other, supposedly more clement form of capitalism, such as the social democratic Keynesianism which preceded the neoliberal turn of the 1980s. This seems to be the preference of Oliver James (2008), for example. Yet whatever the likelihood of a return to Keynesianism in the present conjuncture, I would argue, as a Marxist, for the supersession rather than the reform of capitalism; alienation and poverty are structural features of capitalism itself rather than the side-effects of any particular phase of its development.

Newman goes on to quote approvingly Mariana Valverde's (1998: 17) Foucauldian formulation that 'we are governed not against our freedom, but *through* our freedom'. But assuming that the 'freedom' referred to here is not purely notional or rhetorical, in what, precisely, is it presumed to consist? It can be argued that neoliberalism is carefully orchestrated by the state, representing not so much a brave new world of deterritorialised capital and labour as the latest form of state regulation. Indeed, the state and its repressive apparatuses are growing rather than shrinking: in the developed capitalist countries, massive standing armies remain on a permanent war footing, while national governments, as the continuing global economic crisis demonstrates, must increasingly intervene in the supposedly autonomous realm of the economy to prevent it from collapse. Even Foucault (1980: 216), while distancing himself from orthodox Marxism, makes it clear that resistance against capitalist processes of individuation also involves a struggle against the state:

> The political, ethical, social, philosophical problem of our days is not to try to liberate the individual from the state, and from the state's institutions, but to liberate us both from the state and from the type of individualization which is linked to the state. We have to promote new forms of subjectivity through the refusal of this kind of individuality which has been imposed on us for several centuries.

Valverde's idea that 'we are governed through our freedom' seems to presuppose that people in Western societies are as 'free' as neoliberal discourse asserts them to be – a position uncomfortably close to the suggestion often made in women's magazines that women are depressed despite being wealthy and liberated. As in the case of Slavoj Žižek's writings – which have been criticised for implying that the chief challenge for contemporary Western subjects is to overcome the oppressive tedium of a leisure-loving, democratic, permissive capitalism (Robinson and Tormey, 2006) – there is perhaps a danger here of underestimating the material sources of oppression in the Western world today, such as unemployment for many people and increasing working hours and decreasing salaries for others. To put the point bluntly, it seems likely that a great deal of the mental distress experienced by Westerners today is caused by too little, rather than too much freedom.

Media discourses of mental distress, I have argued throughout this book, encourage subjects to improve their mental health through consumerism, hard work and reflexive technologies of the self. The attainment of mental health or 'the pursuit of happiness' is increasingly seen as a quest to be undertaken by pre-social, atomised health consumers or a problem to be managed pharmaceutically. This hegemonic understanding of mental distress has been challenged by some of the most radical 'user groups', notably Mad Pride, who recommend 'linking up with those elements who wish to bring about a complete transformation of society' (Curtis et al., 2000: 7). Whether struggle around mental health can play a major role in any such radical social transformation is a moot point. Moreover, it is naively utopian to imagine that any amount of social reorganisation could eradicate mental distress from human society. Nonetheless, as I argued at the start of this book, social arrangements play a key role in the production of madness. While this is acknowledged in the more progressive media discussions and representations of distress, media texts too often elide the connections between personal distress and the chaotic social conditions of contemporary capitalist societies.

Bibliography

Abt, V. and M. Seesholtz (1999) 'The Shameless World Revisited', *Journal of Popular Film and Television*, 26(1), 42–9.

Ackroyd, P. (1982, June 22) 'The Dark Origins of Madness', *The Times*, p. 15.

Aina, O. F. (2004) 'Mental Illness and Cultural Issues in West African Films: Implications for Orthodox Psychiatric Practice', *Medical Humanities*, 30, 23–6.

Allen, R. (1985) *Speaking of Soap Operas*. Chapel Hill: University of North Carolina Press.

Allfree, C. (2008: March 19) 'Insanity: Is It a Girl Thing?', *Metro*, p. 40.

Amnesty International (2006) 'The Execution of Mentally Ill Offenders', http://web.amnesty.org (home page), accessed 6 February 2006.

Andrejevic, M. (2004) *Reality TV: The Work of being Watched*. Lanham, MD: Rowman and Littlefield.

Ang, I. (1985) *Watching Dallas: Soap Opera and the Melodramatic Imagination*, London and New York: Methuen.

Angermeyer, M. C. and H. Matschinger (1995) 'Violent Attacks on Public Figures by Persons Suffering from Psychiatric Disorders: Their Effect on the Social Distance towards the Mentally Ill', *European Archives of Psychiatry and Clinical Neuroscience*, 245, 159–64.

Appignanesi, L. (2008) *Mad, Bad and Sad: A History of Women and the Mind Doctors from 1800 to the Present*. London: Virago.

Appleton, J. (2001: April 19) 'Are You the One in Four?', *spiked*. http://www.spiked-online.com (home page), accessed 3 August 2004.

Archer, R. and D. Simmonds (1986) *A Star Is Torn*. London: Virago.

Arthurs, J. (2003) '*Sex and the City* and Consumer Culture: Remediating Postfeminist Drama', *Feminist Media Studies*, 3(1), 83–98.

Aufheben (2006) 'Keep On Smiling – Questions on Immaterial Labour', *Aufheben*, 14, http://libcom.org/library/aufheben, accessed 14 July 2008.

Axmaker, S. (2003) 'Cronenberg Explores a More Palpable Terror in *Spider*: Losing Control of Reality', *Seattle Post* online, http://seattlepi.nwsource.com (home page), accessed 24 July 2007.

Bailey, C. (1990–1991) 'A Cinema of Duty: The Films of Jennifer Hodge de Silva', *Cine-Action*, 23, 4–12.

Baker, N. (2008) *Human Smoke: The Beginnings of World War II, the End of Civilization*. New York: Simon and Schuster.

Banks, M. J. (2004) 'A Boy for All Planets: *Roswell, Smallville* and the Teen Male Melodrama' in G. Davis and K. Dickinson (eds.) *Teen TV: Genre, Consumption and Identity* (pp. 17–28). London: BFI.

Barker, M. (1989) *Comics, Ideology, Power and the Critics*. Manchester: Manchester University Press.

Barry, C. (2004: September 30) 'TV Review: *My Crazy Parents*', *Community Care*, p. 49.

Barthes, R. (1977) *Image, Music, Text*. London: Fontana.

Barthes, R. (1984) *Camera Lucida: Reflections on Photography*. London: Fontana.

Battersby, C. (1989) *Gender and Genius: Towards a Feminist Aesthetics*. London: Women's Press.

Bauman, Z. (1992) *Intimations of Postmodernity*. London: Routledge.

Bauman, Z. (1999) *In Search of Politics*. Stanford: Stanford University Press.

Bauman, Z. (2000) *Liquid Modernity*. Cambridge: Polity Press.

Bauman, Z. (2002) *Society Under Siege*. Cambridge: Polity Press.

Bauman, Z. (2006) *Liquid Fear*. Cambridge: Polity Press.

Beck, U. (1992) *Risk Society: Towards a New Modernity*. London: Sage Publications.

Becker, A. E., R. A. Burwell, D. B. Herzog, P. Hamburg and S. Gilman (2002) 'Eating Behaviours and Attitudes Following Prolonged Exposure to Television among Ethnic Fijian Adolescent Girls', *The British Journal of Psychiatry*, 180(6), 509–14.

Becker, H. S. (1963) *Outsiders: Studies in the Sociology of Deviance*. New York: The Free Press.

Bede (1968) *A History of the English Church and People*. L. Sherley-Price (ed.). London: Penguin.

Bell, E. (2008) 'From Bad Girl to Mad Girl: British Female Celebrity, Reality Products, and the Pathologization of Pop-Feminism', *Genders*, 48. http://www.genders.org (home page), accessed 15 December 2008.

Bentall, R. (2003) *Madness Explained: Psychosis and Human Nature*. London: Penguin.

Benwell, B. (2003) 'Masculinity and Men's Lifestyle Magazines' in B. Benwell (ed.) *Masculinity and Men's Lifestyle Magazines* (pp. 6–29). Oxford: Blackwell.

Berg, S. Z. (2006: November 1) 'What You Don't Know About Depression', *Marie Claire*, p. 207.

Beynon, J. (2002) *Masculinities and Culture*. Buckingham: Open University Press.

Bhabha, H. K. (1994) *The Location of Culture*. London: Routledge.

Bhungra, D. (2005) 'Mad Tales From Bollywood: The Impact of Social, Political and Economic Climate on the Portrayal of Mental Illness in Bollywood Films', *Acta Psychiatrica Scandinvica*, 112, 250–6.

Biddle, L., A. Brock, S. T. Brookes and D. Gunnell (2008) 'Suicide Rates in Young Men in England and Wales in the 21st Century: Time Trend Study', *British Medical Journal*, 336, 539–42.

Bisplinghoff, G. (1992) 'Mothers, Madness and Melodrama', *Jump Cut*, 37, 120–6.

Blair, T. (2002) 'New Labour and Community', *Renewal*, 10(2), 12–13.

Bloch, E. (1995) *The Principle of Hope*. 2 vols. Boston, MA: MIT Press.

Bloom, A. (1987) *The Closing of the American Mind*. New York: Simon and Schuster.

Board, B. J. and K. Fritzon (2005) 'Disordered Personalities at Work', *Psychology, Crime & Law*, 11(1), 17–32.

Bond, M. (2002: February 24) 'Nothing to Crowe Over', *Mail on Sunday*, pp. 66–7.

Bordo, S. (1993) *Unbearable Weight: Feminism, Western Culture and the Body*. Berkeley: University of California Press.

Bourdieu, P. (1984) *Distinction: A Social Critique of the Judgement of Taste*. Cambridge: Harvard University Press.

Bowers, L. (2000) *The Social Origins of Mental Illness*. London: Routledge.

Boyle, K. (1999) 'Screening Violence: A Feminist Critique of the Screen Violence Debate', http://www.skk.uit.no/WW99/papers/Boyle_Karen.pdf, accessed 20 December 2006.

Boyle, K. (2005) *Media and Violence: Gendering the Debates*. London: Sage Publications.

Boyle, M. (2002) *Schizophrenia: A Scientific Delusion?* London: Routledge.

Brampton, S. (2008) *Shoot the Damn Dog: A Memoir of Depression.* London: Bloomsbury.

Branigan, E. (1992) *Narrative Comprehension and Film.* London and New York: Routledge.

Breggin, P. R. (1994) *Toxic Psychiatry: Why Therapy, Empathy, and Love Must Replace the Drugs, Electroshock, and Biochemical Theories of the New Psychiatry.* New York: St Martin's Griffin.

Brenner, H. (1973) *Mental Illness and the Economy.* Cambridge: Harvard University Press.

Brooks, P. (1974) 'The Text of Muteness', *New Literary History*, 5(3), 549–64.

Brooks, P. (1976) *The Melodramatic Imagination: Balzac, Henry James, Melodrama and the Mode of Excess.* New Haven, CT: Yale University Press.

Brown, G. and T. Harris (1978) *The Social Origins of Depression.* London: Tavistock.

Brown, M. E. (1994) *Soap Opera and Women's Talk: The Pleasure of Resistance.* Thousand Oaks, CA: Sage Publications.

Brown, W. (1995) *States of Injury: Power and Freedom in Late Modernity.* Princeton: Princeton University Press.

Brown, W. (2006) *Regulating Aversion: Tolerance in the Age of Identity and Empire.* Princeton: Princeton University Press.

Brunsdon, C., C. Johnson, R. Moseley and H. Wheatley (2001) 'Factual Entertainment on British Television: The Midlands Television Research Group's "8–9 project"', *European Journal of Cultural Studies*, 4(1), 29–62.

Bunting, M. (2004) *Willing Slaves: How The Overwork Culture Is Ruling Our Lives.* London: HarperCollins.

Bunton, R. (1997) 'Popular Health, Advanced Liberalism, and *Good Housekeeping* Magazine' in A. Peterson and R. Bunton (eds.) *Foucault, Health and Medicine* (pp. 223–48). London: Routledge.

Burr, V. and T. Butt (2000) 'Psychological Distress and Postmodern Thought' in D. Fee (ed.) *Pathology and the Postmodern: Mental Illness as Discourse and Experience* (pp. 186–206). London: Sage Publications.

Busfield, J. (1996) *Men, Women and Madness: Understanding Gender and Mental Disorder.* Houndmills and London: Macmillan.

Byrne, P. (2001a) 'Psychiatric Stigma', *The British Journal of Psychiatry*, 178, 281–4.

Byrne, P. (2001b) 'The Butler(s) DID it – Dissociative Identity Disorder in Cinema', *Journal of Medical Ethics*, 27, 26–9.

Cadwalladr, C. (2008: September 7) 'When Reality Bites, It Leaves Deep Scars', *The Observer*, pp. 4–6.

Calcutt, A. (1998) *Arrested Development: Popular Culture and the Erosion of Adulthood.* London and Washington: Cassell.

Callinicos, N. (1989) *Against Postmodernism: A Marxist Critique.* Cambridge: Polity Press.

Cameron, D. (1995) *Verbal Hygiene.* London and New York: Routledge.

Campbell, E. A., S. J. Cope and J. D. Teasdale (1983) 'Social Factors and Affective Disorder: An Investigation of Brown and Harris's Model', *The British Journal of Psychiatry*, 143, 548–53.

Canadian Mental Health Association (2003). 'Stigma and Discrimination: Violence and Mental Illness', http://www.ontario.cmha.ca (home page), accessed 20 December 2006.

Caplan, P. J. (2001) 'Expert Decries Diagnosis for Pathologizing Women', *Journal of Addiction and Mental Health*, 4(5), 16.

Carr, S. (2008: February 10) 'We Can't All Check into the Priory', *The Observer*, p. 36.

Cassatta, M., T. D. Skill and S. O. Boadu (1979) 'In Sickness and In Health', *Journal of Communication*, Autumn, 73–80.

Castel, R. (1991) 'From Dangerousness to Risk' in G. Burchill, C. Gordon and P. Miller (eds.) *The Foucault Effect: Studies in Governmentality*. London: Harvester Wheatsheaf.

Centre for Economic Performance (2005) *Intergenerational Mobility in Europe and North America*. London: The London School of Economic and Political Science.

Centre for Economic Performance (2006) *The Depression Report: A New Deal for Depression and Anxiety Disorders*. London: The London School of Economic and Political Science.

Channel 4 (2006) *Shrink Rap* website, http://www.channel4.com (home page), accessed 9 October 2007.

Charren, P. and M. W. Sandler (1983) *Changing Channels: Living (sensibly) with Television*. Reading, MA: Addison-Wesley.

Chesler, P. (1972) *Women and Madness*. New York: Doubleday.

Chopra, A. K. and G. A. Doody (2007) 'Schizophrenia, an Illness and a Metaphor: Analysis of the Term "Schizophrenia" in the UK National Newspapers', *Journal of the Royal Society of Medicine*, 100(9), 423–6.

Churchwell, S. (2007: August 20) 'The Bourne Misogyny', *The Guardian*, p. 27.

Clara, A. (1995) 'The Image of the Psychiatrist in Motion Pictures', *Acta Psychiatrica Belgica*, 95, 7–15.

Clark, A. E. and A. J. Oswald (1994) 'Unhappiness and Unemployment', *The Economic Journal*, 104, 648–59.

Clark, T. (2002) 'Debate on Mental Illness and Violence was Oversimplified', *British Medical Journal*, 325, 1300.

Clarke, B. F. L. (1975) *Mental Disorder in Earlier Britain: Exploratory Studies*. Cardiff: University of Wales Press.

Cloud, D. (1998) *Control and Consolation in American Culture and Politics: Rhetorics of Therapy*. Thousand Oaks, CA: Sage Publications.

Clover, C. (1992) *Men, Women and Chainsaws: Gender in the Modern Horror Film*. London: BFI.

Cobb, S. (2008) 'Mother of the Year: Kathy Hilton, Lynne Spears, Dina Lohan and Bad Celebrity Motherhood', *Genders* 48, http://www.genders.org (home page), accessed 15 December 2008.

Cooper, D. (1978) *The Language of Madness*. Harmondsworth: Penguin.

Cooper, R. W. (1967: April 17) 'Strange Study of a Mental Delusion', *The Times*, p. 6.

Copjec, J. (1998) 'More! From Melodrama to Magnitude' in J. Bergstrom (ed.) *Endless Night: Cinema and Psychoanalysis: Parallel Histories* (pp. 249–72). Berkeley: University of California Press.

Corner, J. (2000) '"Influence": The Contested Core of Media Research', in J. Curran and M. Gurevitch (eds.) *Mass Media and Society*, 3rd edn. London: Arnold.

Corrigan, G. (2006) *Blood, Sweat and Arrogance: The Myths of Churchill's War*. London: Weidenfeld and Nicholson.

Courtenay, W. H. (2000) 'Constructions of Masculinity and Their Influence on Men's Well-being: A Theory of Gender and Health', *Social Science and Medicine*, 50, 1385–1401.

Coward, R. (1999) *Sacred Cows: Is Feminism Relevant to the New Millenium?* London: Harper Collins.

Cox, E. (2003) 'Hollywood Goes Mental', *The American Enterprise Online*. http://www.aei.org (home page), accessed 4 August 2007.

Crewe, B. (2003) *Representing Men: Cultural Production and Producers in the Men's Magazine Market*. Oxford: Berg.

Crichton, P. (2000: March 31) 'A Profound Duplicity of Life: Uses and Misuses of "Schizophrenia" in Popular Culture and Professional Diagnosis', *Times Literary Supplement*, p. 5.

Crisp, A. (2001) Review of J. Guimón, W. Fischer and N. Sartorius (eds.) (1999) *The Image of Madness: The Public Facing Mental Illness and Psychiatric Treatment*, *The British Journal of Psychiatry*, 178, 485–6.

Cross, S. (2004) 'Visualizing Madness: Mental Illness and Public Representation', *Television and New Media*, 5(3), 197–216.

Crossley, N. (2006) *Contesting Psychiatry: Social Movements in Mental Health*. Abingdon and New York: Routledge.

Curran, J. (ed.) (2000) *Media Organisations and Society*. London: Hodder.

Curtis, T., R. Dellar, E. Leslie and B. Watson (eds.) (2000) *Mad Pride: A Celebration of Mad Culture*. London: Spare Change Books.

Danquah, M. N.-A. (1998) *Willow Weep for Me: A Black Woman's Journey Through Depression*. New York: Ballantine.

Davies, H. (2004) 'The Great Rock and Roll Swindle: The Representation of Women in the British Rock Music Press' in C. Carter and L. Steiner (eds.) *Critical Readings in Media and Gender* (pp. 162–78). Maidenhead: Open University Press.

De Graaf, J., T. H. Naylor and D. Wann (2005) *Affluenza: The All-Consuming Epidemic*. San Francisco, CA: Berrett-Koehler Publishers.

Deleuze, G. and F. Guattari (1983) *Anti-Oedipus: Capitalism and Schizophrenia*. R. Hurley, M. Seem and H. R. Lane (eds.). Minneapolis: University of Minnesota Press.

Dent, G. (2004: June 18) 'Grace Dent's World of Lather', *The Guardian* (*The Guide*), pp. 13–14.

Department of Health (2006) *Our Health, Our Care, Our Say: A New Direction for Community Services*. London: The Stationary Office.

Deuze, M. (2005) 'Popular Journalism and Professional Ideology: Tabloid Reporters and Editors Speak Out', *Media, Culture and Society*, 27(6), 861–82.

Donnerstein, E., R. G. Slaby and L. Eron (1994) 'The Mass Media and Youth Aggression' in L. D. Eron, J. H. Gentry and P. Shlegel (eds.) *Reason to Hope: A Psychosocial Perspective on Violence and Youth* (pp. 219–50). Washington, DC: American Psychological Association.

Doob, P. B. R. (1974), *Nebuchadnezzar's Children*. New Haven: Yale University Press.

Double, D. B. (ed.) (2006) *Critical Psychiatry: The Limits of Madness*. Basingstoke: Palgrave Macmillan.

Dovey, J. (2000) *Freakshow: First Person and Factual Media*. London: Pluto.

Dowling, E. (2007) 'Producing the Dining Experience: Measure, Subjectivity and the Affective Worker', *Ephemera*', 7(1), 117–32.

Draper, R. (2007) *Dead Certain: The Presidency of George W. Bush*. New York: Free Press.

DuBrock, E. (1974) 'The "Marvellous" Madman of *Le Jeu de la Feuillée*', *Neophilologous*, 58, 180–6.

Duke, P., with G. Hochman (1999) *A Brilliant Madness: Living with Manic Depressive Illness*. New York: Bantam.

Dyer, G. (1982) *Advertising as Communication*. London: Methuen.

Dyer, R. (1997) *White*. London: Routledge.

Eagleton, T. (1996) *The Illusions of Postmodernism*. Oxford: Blackwell.

Eagleton, T. (2003) *After Theory*. New York: Basic Books.

Eagleton, T. (2007) *Ideology*. London and New York: Verso.

Ebert, R. (2005) *Roger Ebert's Movie Yearbook 2006*. Kansas, MO: Andrews McMeel Publishing.

Eco, U. (1979) *The Role of the Reader: Explorations in the Semiotics of Texts*. Bloomington: Indiana University Press.

Edwards, T. (2006) *Cultures of Masculinity*. London: Routledge.

Ehrenreich, B. and D. English (1978) *For Her Own Good: 150 Years of the Experts' Advice to Women*. New York: Anchor.

Elkin, I., M. T. Shea, J. T. Watkins, S. D. Imber, S. M. Sotsky, J. F. Collins, D. R. Glass, P. A. Pilkonis, W. R. Leber and J. P. Docherty (1989) 'National Institute of Mental Health Treatment of Depression Collaborative Research Program: General Effectiveness of Treatments', *Archives of General Psychiatry*, 46(11), 971–82.

Elliot, A. and C. C. Lemert (2005) *The New Individualism: The Emotional Costs of Globalization*. London: Routledge.

Elliot, L. and D. Atkinson (1998) *The Age of Insecurity*. London: Verso.

Ellis, J. (1982) *Visible Fictions*. London: Routledge and Kegan Paul.

Ellis, J. (2000) *Seeing Things: Television in the Age of Uncertainty*. London: I.B. Taurus.

Elms, E. (2003: March 1) 'I won't Allow Schizophrenia to Ruin My Life', *Marie Claire*, pp. 96–100.

Elsaesser, T. (2001) 'Postmodernism as Mourning Work', *Screen*, 42(2), 193–201.

Fairclough, N. (1995) *Critical Discourse Analysis: The Critical Study of Language*. London: Addison Wesley.

Fairclough, N. (2001) *Language and Power*. 2nd edn. London: Pearson.

Faludi, S. (1992) *Backlash: The Undeclared War Against American Women*. New York: Bantam.

Farina, A., J. D. Fisher, H. Getter and E. H. Fischer (1978) 'Some Consequences of Changing People's Views Regarding the Nature of Mental Illness', *Journal of Abnormal Psychology*, 87, 272–9.

Faris, R. and H. Dunham (1939) *Mental Disorders in Urban Areas*. Chicago: University of Chicago Press.

Featherstone, M. (1991) *Consumer Society and Postmodernism*. London: Sage Publications.

Fenton, N. (2000) 'The Problematics of Postmodernism for Feminist Media Studies', *Media, Culture and Society*, 22, 723–41.

Fenton, S. and A. Sadiq-Sangster (1996) 'Culture, Relativism and the Expression of Mental Distress: South Asian Women in Britain', *Sociology of Health and Illness*, 18(1), 66–85.

Ferguson, I. (2000) 'The Mental Health Users' Movement' in M. Lavalette and G. Mooney (eds.) *Class Struggle and Social Welfare* (pp. 228–49). London: Routledge.

Fernando, S. (1991) *Mental Health, Race and Culture*. Houndmills: Macmillan.

Fischoff, S., J. Antonio and D. Lewis (1998) 'Favorite Films and Film Genres as a Function of Race, Age and Gender', *Journal of Media Psychology*, 3(1), http://www.calstatela.edu/faculty/sfischo/media3.html, accessed 20 December 2008.

Fisher, J. D. and A. Farina (1979) 'Consequences of Beliefs about the Nature of Mental Disorders', *Journal of Abnormal Psychology*, 88: 320–7.

Fiske, J. and J. Hartley (1978) *Reading Television*. London: Methuen.

Fiske, J. (1987) *Television Culture*, London: Methuen.

Fiske, J. (1989) *Understanding Popular Culture*. London: Unwin Hyman.

Fitzpatrick, M. (2006a: February 6) 'A Sickening White Paper', *spiked*, http://www.spiked-online.com (home page), accessed 7 Jan 2007.

Fitzpatrick, M. (2006b: November 14) 'Get Off the Couch!', *spiked*, http://www.spiked-online.com (home page), accessed 12 March 2007.

Fleming, M. and R. Manvell (1985) *Images of Madness: The Portrayal of Insanity in the Feature Film*. Cranbury, N. J.: Associated University Press.

Fortune, S., A. Stewart, V. Yadav and K. Hawton (2007) 'Suicide in Adolescents: Using Life Charts to Understand the Suicidal Process', *Journal of Affective Disorders*, 100, 199–210.

Foti, A. (2004: October 5) 'Precarity and N/european Identity', *Mute*, http://www.metamute.org (home page), accessed 20 March 2006.

Foucault, M. (1980) *Power/Knowledge: Selected Interviews and Other Writings, 1972–77*. C. Gordon (ed.). Brighton: Harvester.

Foucault, M. (1983) 'The Subject and Power' in H. Dreyfus and P. Rabinow (eds.) *Michel Foucault: Beyond Structuralism and Hermeneutics* (pp. 208–26) 2nd edn. Chicago: University of Chicago Press.

Foucault, M. (1984) *History of Sexuality, Vol. 1*. R. Hurley (trans.). New York: Vintage Books.

Foucault, M. (1991) *Discipline and Punish*. London: Penguin.

Foucault, M. (2001) *Madness and Civilisation*. R. Howard (trans.). New York: Random House.

Foucault, M. (2005a) *History of Madness*. J. Khalfa and J. Murphy (trans.). London: Routledge.

Foucault, M. (2005b) *Society Must Be Defended: Lectures at the Collège de France, 1975–1976*. M. Bertani and A. Fontana (eds.), D. Macey (trans.). London: Penguin.

Frances, C., J. Pirkis, R. W. Blood, D. Dunt, P. Burgess, B. Morley, A. Stewart and P. Putnis (2004) 'The Portrayal of Mental Health and Illness in Australian Non-fiction Media', *Australian and New Zealand Journal of Psychiatry*, 38, 541–6.

Francis, E. (1993) 'Psychiatric Racism', in W. James and C. Harris (eds.) *Inside Babylon: The Caribbean Diaspora in Britain* (pp. 179–205). London: Verso.

Franks, B. (2006) *Rebel Alliances: The Means and Ends of Contemporary British Anarchisms*. Edinburgh: AK Press.

Friedman, R. A. (2006) 'Violence and Mental Illness – How Strong is the Link?', *New England Journal of Medicine*, 355, 2064–6.

Frith, M. (2004: April 16) 'Zulu Women Follow Western Trend for Eating Disorders; British Psychological Society Conference', *The Independent*, p. 19.

Fromm, E. (1963) *The Sane Society*. London: Routledge and Kegan Paul.

Fromm, E. (1989) *The Fear of Freedom*. London: Ark.

Fruth, L. and Padderud, A. (1985) 'Portrayals of Mental Illness in Daytime Television Serials', *Journalism Quarterly*, 62(2), 384–449.

Fuery, P. (2004) *Madness and Cinema: Psychoanalysis, Spectatorship and Culture*. Basingstoke and New York: Palgrave Macmillan.

Furedi, F. (2004) *Therapy Culture: Cultivating Vulnerability in an Uncertain Age*, London: Routledge.

Furedi, F. (2006: May 23) 'Why the "Politics of Happiness" Makes Me Mad', *spiked*, http://www.spiked-online.com (home page), accessed 1 October 2006.

Gabbard, G. O. and K. Gabbard (1999) *Psychiatry and the Cinema*. 2nd edn. Washington, D.C.: American Psychiatric Press.

Galbraith, J. K. (1958) *The Affluent Society*. Boston: Houghton Mifflin.

Galtung, J. and M. H. Ruge (1965) 'The Structure of Foreign News: The Presentation of the Congo, Cuba and Cyprus Crises in Four Norwegian Newspapers', *Journal of Peace Research*, 2, 64–91.

Gamson, J. (1998) *Freaks Talk Back: Tabloid Talk Shows and Sexual Non-conformity*. Chicago: Chicago University Press.

Gardner, C. and R. Young (1981) 'Science on TV: A Critique' in T. Bennett, S. Boyd-Bowman, C. Mercer and J. Woollacott (eds.) *Popular Television and Film: A Reader* (pp. 171–93). London: BFI.

Gardner, P. M. (2003) 'Distorted Packaging: Marketing Depression as Illness, Drugs as Cure', *Journal of Medical Humanities*, 24(1), 105–30.

Gardner, P. M. (2007) 'Re-Gendering Depression: Risk, Web Health Campaigns, and the Feminised Pharmaco-Subject', *Canadian Journal of Communication*, 32, 537–55.

Gauntlett, D. (2002) *Media, Gender and Identity*. London: Routledge.

Gee, A. (2007: July 30) 'Russian Dissident "Forcibly Detained in Mental Hospital"', *The Independent*, p. 19.

Giddens, A. (1991) *Modernity and Self-Identity: Self and Society in the Late Modern Age*. Cambridge: Polity Press.

Giddens, A. (1992) *The Transformation of Intimacy: Sexuality, Love and Eroticism in Modern Societies*. Cambridge: Polity Press.

Gilman, C. P. (1998) *The Yellow Wallpaper*, R. Shulman (ed.). Oxford: Oxford University Press.

Gilman, S. (1985) *Difference and Pathology: Stereotypes of Sexuality, Race and Madness*. Ithaca and London: Cornell University Press.

Gitlin, T. (1995) *The Twilight of Common Dreams*. New York: Henry Holt.

Glancey, J. (2003: April 19) 'Our Last Occupation: Gas, Chemicals, Bombs: Britain has Used Them All before in Iraq', *The Guardian*, p. 17.

Glass, J. (1993) *Shattered Selves: Multiple Personality in a Postmodern World*. Ithaca, NY: Cornell University Press.

'Glaxo Settles New York Drug Suit' (2004) BBC News online, http://news.bbc.co.uk (home page), accessed 17 October 2007.

Godsi, E. (2004) *Violence and Society: Making Sense of Madness and Badness*. Llangarron: PCCS Books.

Goffman, E. (1963) *Stigma: Notes on the Management of Spoiled Identity*. London: Penguin.

Good, B. J., Subandi and M.-J. DelVecchio Good (2007) 'The Subject of Mental Illness: Psychosis, Mad Violence and Subjectivity in Indonesia' in J. Biehl, B. J. Good and A. Kleinman (eds.) *Subjectivity: Ethnographic Investigations* (pp. 243–72). Berkeley: University of California Press.

Gosling, A. and T. Lemieux (2004) 'Labour Market Reforms and Changes in Wage Inequality in the United Kingdom and the United States' in D. Card, R. Blundell and R. B. Freeman (eds.) *Seeking a Premier Economy: The Economic Effects of British Economic Reforms, 1980–2000* (pp. 275–312). Chicago: University of Chicago Press.

Graham, T. B. (1967) *Medieval Minds: Mental Health in the Middle Ages*. London: George Allen and Unwin.

Gramsci, A. (1971 [1936]) *Selections from the Prison Notebooks*, Q. Hoare and G. N. Smith (trans.). New York: International.

Grant, J. E. and M. N. Potenza (eds.) (2006) *A Textbook of Men's Mental Health*. Washington, DC: American Psychiatric Publishing.

Gregory, A. (2008: August 28) 'Maniac Freed to Stab Dad 82 Times in Front of Kids', *The Mirror*, p. 18.

Greider, K. (2003) *The Big Fix: How the Pharmaceutical Industry Rips Off American Consumers*. New York: Public Affairs.

Grogan, S. (1999) *Body Image*. Routledge: London and New York.

Grow, J. M., J. S. Park and X. Han (2006) '"Your Life is Waiting!": Symbolic Meanings in Direct-to-Consumer Advertising', *Journal of Communication Inquiry*, 30(2), 163–88.

Gu, C.-J. (2006) 'Rethinking the Study of Gender and Mental Health', *Graduate Journal of Social Science*, 3(1), 1–26.

Habermas, J. (1987) *The Theory of Communicative Action, Vol. 2. Lifeworld and System: A Critique of Functionalist Reason*. Cambridge: Polity Press.

Haddon, M. (2004) *The Curious Incident of the Dog in the Night-time*. London: Vintage.

Hagan, P. (2005: June 19) 'First Drug to Tame Manic Depression', *Daily Mail*, p. 44.

Halberstam, J. (1995) *Skin Shows: Gothic Horror and the Technology of Monsters*. Durham, N.C.: Duke University Press.

Hall, C. (1997: December 13) 'Mentally Ill "Not a Threat to Strangers"', *Daily Telegraph*, p. 4.

Halliday, M. (1978) *Language as Social Semiotic: The Social Interpretation of Language and Meaning*. London: Edward Arnold.

Hann, M. (2006: June 12) 'The Lure of the Damaged', *The Guardian G2*, p. 8.

Harding, L. (2005: December 20) 'In the Grip of the Ankang', *The Guardian*, p. 16.

Hardt, M. and A. Negri (2000) *Empire*. Cambridge, Mass.: Harvard University Press.

Hardt, M. and A. Negri (2005) *Multitude: War and Democracy in the Age of Empire*. London: Penguin.

Harper, S. (2003) *Insanity, Individuals and Society in Late-Medieval English Literature: The Subject of Madness*. Lampeter and New York: Edwin Mellen Press.

Harper, S. (2005) 'Media, Madness and Misrepresentation: Critical Reflections on Anti-Stigma Discourse', *European Journal of Communication*, 20(4), 460–83.

Harper, S. (2006) 'Madly Famous: Narratives of Mental Illness in Celebrity Culture' in S. Holmes and S. Redmond (eds.) *Framing Celebrity: New Directions in Celebrity Culture* (pp. 311–27). London: Routledge.

Harrison, G. (2002) 'Ethnic Minorities and the Mental Health Act', *The British Journal of Psychiatry*, 180, 198–9.

Hatfield, J. (2008: November 23) 'A Heart That Hurts is a Heart That Works. I will Beat My Anorexia', *The Observer*, p. 30.

Hayot, E. (2008) 'Crying, Over You', *PrintCulture*, http://www.printculture.com (home page), accessed 30 June 2008.

Healy, D. (2004) *Let Them Eat Prozac: The Unhealthy Relationship between the Pharmaceutical Industry and Depression*. New York, NY: New York University Press.

Heaton, J. A. and N. L. Wilson (1995) *Tuning in Trouble: Talk TV's Destructive Impact on Mental Health*. San Francisco: Jossey-Bass.

Henderson, L. (1996) 'Selling Suffering: Mental Illness and Media Values' in G. Philo (ed.) *Media and Mental Distress* (pp. 18–36). London: Longman.

Henderson, L. (2007) *Social Issues in Television Fiction*. Edinburgh: Edinburgh University Press.

Hermes, J. (1995) *Reading Women's Magazines: An Analysis of Everyday Media Use*. Cambridge: Polity Press.

Hermes, J. (1999) 'Media Figures in Identity Construction' in P. Alasuutari (ed.) *Rethinking the Media Audience: The New Agenda* (pp. 69–85). London: Sage Publications.

Hewitt, J. P., M. R. Fraser and L. Berger (2000) 'Is It Me or Is It Prozac?' in D. Fee (ed.) *Pathology and the Postmodern: Mental Illness as Discourse and Experience* (pp. 163–85). London: Sage Publications.

Hillert, A., J. Sandmann and S. C. Ehmig (1999) 'The General Public's Cognitive and Emotional Perception of Mental Illnesses: An Alternative to Attitude-research' in J. Guimon, W. Fischer and N. Sartorius (eds.) *The Image of Madness: The Public Facing Mental Illness and Psychiatric Treatment* (pp. 56–71). Basel: Karger.

Hochschild, A. R. (1983) *The Managed Heart: Commercialization of Human Feeling*. Berkeley: University of California Press.

Holm, I., with S. Jacobi (2004) *Acting My Life: The Autobiography*. London: Bantam.

Holmes, S. (2005) '"Off-guard, Unkempt, Unready"?: Deconstructing Contemporary Celebrity in *Heat* Magazine', *Continuum: Journal of Media and Cultural Studies*, 19(1), 21–38.

Horwitz, A. V. (2002) *Creating Mental Illness*. Chicago, IL: University of Chicago Press.

Horwitz, A. V. and Wakefield, J. C. (2007) *The Loss of Sadness: How Psychiatry Transformed Normal Sorrow into Depressive Disorder*. Oxford: Oxford University Press.

'How Normal Are Your Moods?' (2008: May 1) *Glamour*, p. 52.

Hudson, C. G. (2005) 'Socioeconomic Status and Mental Illness: Tests of the Social Causation and Selection Hypotheses', *American Journal of Orthopsychiatry*, 75(1), 3–18.

Huffine, C. L. (1991) 'Social and Cultural Risk Factors for Youth Suicide' in L. Davidson and M. Linnoila (eds.) *Risk Factors for Youth Suicide* (pp. 40–54). New York: Hemisphere.

Hughes, R. (1993) *Culture of Complaint: The Fraying of America*. London: Harvill Press.

Hurt, N. E. (2007) 'Disciplining through Depression: An Analysis of Contemporary Discourse on Women and Depression', *Women's Studies in Communication*, http://www.accessmylibrary.com (home page), accessed 2 January 2008.

Illouz, E. (2003) *Oprah Winfrey and the Glamour of Misery: An Essay on Popular Culture*. New York: Columbia University Press.

'I'm so Stressed Out!' (2008: September 1) *Marie Claire*, p. 15.

Jackson, P., N. Stevenson and K. Brooks (eds.) (2001) *Making Sense of Men's Magazines*. London: Polity Press.

James, O. (1995) *Juvenile Violence in a Winner-Loser Culture: Socio-Economic and Familial Origins of the Rise of Violence Against the Person*. London: Free Association Books.

James, O. (1998) *Britain on the Couch: Treating a Low Serotonin Society*. London: Arrow.

James, O. (2007) *Affluenza*. London: Vermilion.

James, O. (2008) *The Selfish Capitalist*. London: Vermilion.

Jamison, K. R. (1996) *Touched with Fire: Manic-depressive Illness and the Artistic Temperament*. New York: Simon and Schuster.

Jaramillo, D. L. (2006) 'Pills Gone Wild: Medium Specificity and the Regulation of Prescription Drug Advertising on Television', *Television and New Media*, 7(3), 261–81.

Jermyn, D. (2003) 'Women with a Mission: Lynda La Plante, DCI Jane Tennison and the Reconfiguration of TV Crime Drama', *International Journal of Cultural Studies*, 6(1), 46–63.

Johnson, D. A. (2008) 'Managing Mr. Monk: Control and the Politics of Madness', *Critical Studies in Media Communication*, 25(1), 28–47.

Johnstone, N. (2004: October 26) 'Blue Notes: Television Programmes Dealing with Mental Illness are Sensationalist and Exploitative, as I found Out', *The Guardian G2*, p. 11.

Jorm, A. F. (2000) 'Mental Health Literacy: Public Knowledge and Beliefs about Mental Disorders', *The British Journal of Psychiatry*, 177, 396–401.

Jorm, A. F., Y. Nakane, H. Christensen, K. Yoshioka, K. M. Griffiths and Y. Wata (2005) 'Public Beliefs about Treatment and Outcome of Mental Disorders: A Comparison of Australia and Japan', *BMC Medicine*, 3, 12.

Kasser, T. (2003) *The High Price of Materialism*. Cambridge, MA: MIT Press.

Kessler, K. (2003) 'Bound Together: Lesbian Film That's Family Fun for Everyone', *Film Quarterly*, 56(4), 13–22.

Khorrami, S. (2002) 'Genius, Madness, and Masculinity: *A Beautiful Mind* Examined through a Men's Issue Model', *Men and Masculinities*, 5(1), 116–18.

King, D. (2003: October 9) 'Murderer Starts Life Sentence for Vampire Killing', *Edinburgh Evening News*, p. 4.

King, G. (2002) *Film Comedy*. London: Wallflower.

King, M., E. Coker, G. Leavey, A. Hoare and E. Johnson-Sabine (1994) 'The Incidence of Psychotic Illness in London: Comparisons of Ethnic Groups', *British Medical Journal*, 309, 1115–9.

Kirk, S. and H. Kutchins (1999) *Making Us Crazy*. London: Constable and Robinson.

Kirov, G. K., N. J. Birch, P. Steadman and R. G. Ramsey (1994) 'Plasma Magnesium Levels in a Population of Psychiatric Patients: Correlations with Symptoms', *Neuropsychobiology*, 30(2–3): 73–8.

Kneale, D. (1988: May 18) 'Titillating Channels', *Wall Street Journal*, pp. 1, 15.

Kozloff, S. (1992) 'Narrative Theory and Television' in R. C. Allen (ed.) *Channels of Discourse, Reassembled: Television and Contemporary Criticism* (pp. 42–75). Chapel Hill: University of North Carolina Press.

Krakowski, M., J. Jaeger and J. Volavka (1988) 'Violence and Psychopathology: A Longitudinal Study', *Comprehensive Psychiatry*, 29, 174–81.

Kramer, P. (1993) *Listening to Prozac*. New York: Penguin.

Kurtz, I. (2008: January 8) 'Dear Britney…Get a Grip!', *Daily Mail*, p. 36.

Laing, R. D. (1990) *The Divided Self*. London: Penguin.

Lane, C. (2007) *Shyness: How Normal Behavior Became a Sickness*. New Haven, CT: Yale University Press.

Lane, H. (2006: March 12) 'Voices in the Dark', *The Observer Magazine*, pp. 38–41.

Lasch, C. (1991) *Culture of Narcissism*. New York and London: Norton.

Lawrie, S. M. (1999) 'Stigmatization of Psychiatric Disorder', *Psychiatric Bulletin*, 23, 129–31.

Lawson, M. (2007: January 17) 'Why Baftas not Make Benefit Glorious UK film?', *The Guardian G2*, p. 28.

Layard, R. (2005) *Happiness: Lessons from a New Science*. London: Penguin.

Leventhal, A. M. and C. R. Martell (2005) *The Myth of Depression as Disease: Limitations and Alternatives to Drug Treatment*. Westport, CT: Praeger.

Levine, B. (2003) *Commonsense Rebellion: Taking Back Your Life from Drugs, Shrinks, Corporations and a World Gone Crazy*. New York and London: Continuum.

Lewis, B. (2006) 'Listening to Chekhov: Narrative Approaches to Depression', *Literature and Medicine*, 25(1), 46–71.

Lewis, D. O., J. H. Pincus, M. Feldman, L. Jackson and B. Bard (1988) 'Neuropsychiatric, Psychoeducational and Family Characteristics of 14 Juveniles Condemned to Death in the United States', *American Journal of Psychiatry*, 145, 584–9.

Link, B. G., H. Andrews and F. T. Cullen (1992) 'The Violent and Illegal Behaviour of Mental Patients Reconsidered', *American Sociological Review*, 57, 275–92.

Link, B. and A. Stueve (1994) 'Psychotic Symptoms and the Violent/Illegal Behaviour of Mental Patients Compared to Community Controls' in J. Monahan and H. J. Steadman (eds.) *Violence and Mental Disorder: Developments in Risk Assessment* (pp. 137–59). Chicago and London: University of Chicago Press.

Lipovetsky, G., with S. Charles (2005) *Hypermodern Times*. Cambridge: Polity Press.

Lishman, G. (2007: August 22) 'Our Mentally Ill Older People are Languishing at the Bottom of the List', *The Guardian (Society)*, p. 4.

Littler, J. (2003) 'Making Fame Ordinary: Intimacy, Reflexivity, and "Keeping it Real"', *Mediactive* 2, 8–25.

Livingstone, S. and P. Lunt (1994) *Talk on Television: Audience Participation and Public Debate*. London: Routledge.

Lloyd, J. and L. Johnson (2003) 'The Three Faces of Eve: The Post-war Housewife, Melodrama, and Home', *Feminist Media Studies*, 3(1), 7–25.

Lott, T. (2006: December 12) 'Losing the Plot', *The Guardian G2*, pp. 23–5.

Lunbeck, E. (1994) *The Psychiatric Persuasion: Knowledge, Gender and Power in Modern America*. Princeton: Princeton University Press.

Macdonald, M. (1995) *Representing Women*. New York: Hodder.

Malik, S. (1996) 'Beyond the "Cinema of Duty": The Pleasures of Hybridity: Black British Film of the 1980s and 1990s' in A. Higson (ed.) *Dissolving Views: Key Writings on British Cinema* (pp. 202–15). London: Cassell.

Maltby, J., L. Day, L. E. McCutcheon, R. Gillett, J. Houran and D. D. Ash (2004) 'Personality and Coping: A Context for Examining Celebrity Worship and Mental Health', *British Journal of Psychology*, 95, 411–28.

Marshall, P. D. (1997) *Celebrity and Power: Fame in Contemporary Culture*. Minneapolis; London: University of Minnesota Press.

Martin, E. (2007) *Bipolar Expeditions: Mania and Depression in American Culture*. Princeton: Princeton University Press.

Martin, L. (2008) *Woman on the Verge of a Nervous Breakdown: Life, Love and Talking it Through*. London: John Murray.

Marx, K. (1978) *Economic and Philosophic Manuscripts of 1844* in R. C. Tucker (ed.) *The Marx – Engels Reader* (pp. 66–125). New York: Norton.

Marx, K. (1999) *Marx on Suicide*. E. R. Plaut and K. Anderson (eds.) Evanston, Ill: Northwestern University Press.

Massumi, B. (ed.) (1993) *The Politics of Everyday Fear*. Minneapolis: University of Minnesota Press.

Massumi, B. (1996) 'The Autonomy of Affect' in P. Patton (ed.) *Deleuze: A Critical Reader* (pp. 217–39). Oxford: Blackwell.

McCallum, D. (1997) 'Mental Health, Criminality, and the Human Sciences' in A. Peterson and R. Bunton (eds.) *Foucault, Health and Medicine* (pp. 52–73). London: Routledge.

McGrath, P. (1990) *Spider*. London: Penguin.

McKee, A. (2003) *Textual Analysis: A Beginner's Guide*. London: Sage Publications.

McKeown, M. (1999: July 5) 'Sickness and Wealth: Experts Spell out Poverty and Mental Health Link', *The Mirror*, p. 14.

McKie, R. (2001: May 13) 'The Chair Man: Anthony Clare', *The Observer*, p. 27.

McLean, C. (2006: January 29) 'Second Bite', *The Observer Magazine*, pp. 36–40.

Mehta, S. and A. Farina (1997) 'Is being Sick Really Better? Effect of the Disease View of Mental Disorder on Stigma', *Journal of Social and Clinical Psychology*, 16(4), 405–19.

Men's Health (2004) 'Holiday Hell: Cope Better', http://www.menshealth.com (home page), accessed 5 December 2006.

'Mentally Ill Abused by the Young' (2001: March 12), BBC online, http://news.bbc.co.uk (home page), accessed 13 July 2007.

Merrill, R. (1987) *Sir Thomas Malory and the Cultural Crisis of the Later Middle Ages*. New York: Peter Lang.

Merritt, S. (2008) *The Devil Within: A Memoir of Depression*. London: Vermilion.

Meyrowitz, J. (1985) *No Sense of Place: The Impact of Electronic Media on Social Behavior*. New York: Oxford University Press.

Midelfort, H. C. E. (1980) 'Madness and Civilisation in Early Modern Europe: A Reappraisal of Michel Foucault' in B. C. Malament (ed.) *After the Reformation: Essays in Honour of J. H. Hexter* (pp. 247–65). Manchester: Manchester University Press.

Miller, P. (1986) 'Psychotherapy of Work and Unemployment' in P. Miller and N. Rose (eds.) *The Power of Psychiatry* (pp. 143–76). London: Polity.

Mitchell, K. (2004: June 1) 'Totally Frank', *The Observer Sport Monthly*, 52, pp. 18–25.

Moncrieff, J. and I. Kirsh (2005) 'Efficacy of Antidepressants in Adults', *British Medical Journal*, 331, 555–7.

Moncrieff, J., S. Hopker and P. Thomas (2005) 'Psychiatry and the Pharmaceutical Industry: Who Pays the Piper?', *Psychiatric Bulletin*, 29, 84–5.

Montgomery, M. (1986) *An Introduction to Language and Society*. London and New York: Routledge.

Moore, A. (2007: May 13) 'Eternal Sunshine', *The Observer Magazine*, 20–9.

Moores, S. (2005) *Media/Theory*. London and New York: Routledge.

Morgan, R. (1995) 'Pedro Almodóvar's *Tie Me Up! Tie Me Down!*: The Mechanics of Masculinity' in P. Kirkham and J. Thumin (eds.) *Me Jane: Masculinity, Movies and Women* (pp. 113–27). London: Lawrence and Wishart.

Morley, D. (1995) 'Acknowledging Consumption in Media Studies' in D. Miller (ed.) *Acknowledging Consumption: A Review of New Studies* (pp. 296–328). London: Routledge.

Morris, G. (2006) *Mental Health Issues and the Media: An Introduction for Health Professionals*. London: Routledge.

Mosher, L. R., R. Gosden and S. Beder (2004) 'Drug Companies and Schizophrenia: Unbridled Capitalism Meets Madness' in J. Read, L. R. Mosher and R. Bentall (eds.) *Models of Madness* (pp. 115–30). Hove: Brunner-Routledge.

Moynihan, R. and A. Cassels (2005) *Selling Sickness: How Drug Companies are Turning Us All into Patients*. Crows Nest, NSW: Allen and Unwin.

Nasar, S. (2002) *A Beautiful Mind*. London: Faber.

National Mental Health Association (2000) *Stigma Matters: Assessing the Media's Impact on Public Perception of Mental Illness*. Chicago: National Mental Health Association.

Neale, S. (1998) 'Embodying Black Madness, Embodying White Femininity: Populist (Re)Presentations and Public Policy – The Case of Christopher Clunis and Jayne Zito', *Sociological Research Online* 3(4), http://www.socres-online.org.uk/3/4/2.html, accessed 20 December 2008.

Neaman, J. (1975) *Suggestion of the Devil*. New York: Doubleday.

Negus, K. and M. Pickering (2004) *Creativity, Communication and Cultural Value*. London: Sage Publications.

Nelson, R. (1997) *TV Drama in Transition: Forms, Values and Cultural Change*. Houndmills: Macmillan.

Neumann, K. D. (2006: October 1) 'The Simple Secret to Happiness', *Cosmopolitan*, pp. 183–4.

'New Season, New You' (2001: October 1) *Glamour*, p. 50.

Newman, C. (2007) 'Reader Letters to Women's Health Magazines', *Feminist Media Studies*, 7(2), 155–70.

Niebuhr, R. (1941) *Moral Man and Immoral Society: A Study in Ethics and Politics*. New York: Charles Scribner's Sons.

Nunnally, J. C. (1961) *Popular Conceptions of Mental Health*. New York: Holt, Rhinehart and Winston.

O'Brien, C. (2007: May 23) 'Dog Gone', *The Times 2*, p. 4.

O'Hagan, S. (2005: February 13) 'That Way Sanity Lies', *The Observer Magazine*, pp. 12–16.

O'Hagan, S. (2007: December 9) 'Apocalypse then, Auteur Now', *The Observer Review*, pp. 10–11.

Osgerby, B. (2003) 'A Pedigree of the Consuming Male: Masculinity, Consumption, and the American "Leisure Class"' in B. Benwell (ed.) *Masculinity and Men's Lifestyle Magazines* (pp. 57–86). Oxford: Blackwell.

Outen, F. (2000: December 29) 'Mental Illness: All In Our Minds?', *spiked*, http://www.spiked-online.com (home page), accessed 3 August 2004.

Outen, F. (2001: April 5), 'Is Mental Illness Just "Different"?', *spiked*, http://www.spiked-online.com (home page), accessed 3 August 2004.

Packard, E. P. W. (1973 [1873]) *Modern Persecution; or Insane Asylums Unveiled*. New York: Arno Press.

Parfitt, T. (2005: 31 August) 'Uzbek Activist Held in Mental Hospital', *The Guardian*, p. 10.

Parkhouse, J. (1991) *Doctors' Careers: Aims and Experience of Medical Graduates*. London: Routledge.

Parkinson, D. (2006: March 11) 'Outcry at "Bad Taste" Sculpture of Winston', *The Express*, p. 13.

Patmore, A. (2006) *The Truth About Stress*. London: Atlantic Books.

Patterson, L. W. (1990) 'No Man His Reson Herde' in L. W. Patterson (ed.) *Literary Practice and Social Change in Britain, 1380–1530* (pp. 113–55). Berkeley: University of California Press.

Pearson, B. (2006: September 18) 'Get it under Control and Your Life can be Okay', *The Herald*, p. 8.

Perkins, T. E. (1979) 'Rethinking Stereotypes' in Barrett, M., P. Corrigan, A. Kuhn and V. Wolff (eds.) *Ideology and Cultural Production* (pp. 135–9). London: Croon Helm.

Perse, E. (2001) *Media Effects and Society*. London: Lawrence Erlbaum.

Peterson, D. (1982) *A Mad People's History of Madness*. Pittsburg, PA: University of Pittsburg Press.

Philips, D. (2000) 'Medicated Soap: The Woman Doctor in Television Medical Drama' in B. Carson and M. Llewellyn-Jones (eds.) *Frames and Fictions on Television: The Politics of Identity Within Drama* (pp. 50–61). Exeter: Intellect.

Philo, G. (1993) *Media Representations of Mental Health/Illness*. Glasgow: Glasgow University Media Group.

Philo, G. (ed.) (1996) *Media and Mental Distress*. London: Longman.

Philo, G. (1997) 'Changing Media Representations of Mental Health', *Psychiatric Bulletin*, 21, 171–2.

Philo, G. (ed.) (1999) *Message Received*. Harlow: Addison Wesley Longman.

Philo, G. and D. Miller (2000) *Market Killing: What the Free Market Does and What Social Scientists Can Do About It*. London: Longman.

Philo, G., L. Henderson and G. McLaughlin (1996) 'Media Content' in G. Philo (ed.) *Media and Mental Distress* (pp. 45–81). London: Longman.

Philo, G., L. Henderson and G. McLaughlin (1993) *Mass Media Representations of Mental Health and Illness: Content Study*. Glasgow Media Group: Health Education Board for Scotland.

Philo, G. and M. Berry (2004) *Bad News from Israel*. London: Pluto.

Pickering, M. (2001) *Stereotyping: The Politics of Representation*. Houndmills: Palgrave.

Pierce, A. (2007: September 8) 'We All so Want to Admire Kate McCann', *The Telegraph*, p. 26.

Pies, R. (2001) 'Psychiatry and the Media: The Vampire, The Fisher King, and the Zaddick', *Journal of Mundane Behavior*, 2.1.

Pilgrim, D. and A. Rogers (1993) *A Sociology of Mental Health and Illness*. Buckingham: Open University Press.

Pinedo, I. C. (1997) *Recreational Terror: Women and the Pleasures of Horror Film Viewing*. Albany, NY: SUNY Press.

Pirkis, J., R. W. Blood, C. Francis and K. McCallum (2006) 'On-Screen Portrayals of Mental Illness: Extent, Nature and Impacts', *Journal of Health Communication*, 11(5), 523–41.

Politkovskaya, A. (2004) *Putin's Russia*. London: Harvill Press.

Pollock, G. (1977) 'What's Wrong with Images of Women?', *Screen Education*, 24, Autumn.

Pollock, G. (1987) 'Feminism and Modernism' in R. Parker and G. Pollock (eds.) *Framing Feminism: Art and the Women's Movement 1970–1985* (pp. 79–122). London: Pandora/Routledge.

Porter, R. (1987) *Mind Forg'd Manacles: A History of Madness in England From the Restoration to the Regency*. Cambridge, MA: Harvard University Press.

Porter, R. (1990) 'Foucault's Great Confinement', *History of the Human Sciences*, 3, 47–54.

Poussaint, A. F. and A. Alexander (2001) *Lay My Burden Down: Unraveling Suicide and the Mental Health Crisis Among African Americans*. Boston, MA: Beacon Press.

Preston, P. (2008: January 7) 'Blame us all for Britney', *The Guardian*, p. 28.

Prins, H. (2005) 'Mental Disorder and Violent Crime: A Problematic Relationship', *Probation Journal: The Journal of Community and Criminal Justice*, 52(4), 333–57.

'Push Off!' (2006), http://www.itv.com (home page), accessed 13 September 2006.

Quinn, B. (2006: March 11) 'Outcry over This "insult" to Churchill', *The Daily Mail*, p. 33.

Rabinow, P. (1996) 'Artificiality and Enlightenment: From Sociobiology to Biosociality' in P. Rabinow (ed.) *Essays on the Anthropology of Reason* (pp. 91–111). Princeton: Princeton University Press.

Rasmussen, H. H., P. B. Mortensen and I. W. Jensen (1989) 'Depression and Magnesium Deficiency', *International Journal of Psychiatry in Medicine*, 19(1), 57–63.

Read, J. (2004) 'Does "Schizophrenia" Exist? Reliability and Validity' in J. Read, L. R. Mosher and R. Bentall (eds.) *Models of Madness* (pp. 43–56). Hove: Brunner-Routledge.

Read, J. and J. Masson (2004) 'Genetics, Eugenics and Mass Murder' in J. Read, L. R. Mosher and R. Bentall (eds.) *Models of Madness* (pp. 35–42). Hove: Brunner-Routledge.

Read, J., N. Haslam, L. Sayce and E. Davies (2006) 'Prejudice and Schizophrenia: A Review of the "Mental Illness is an Illness Like any Other" approach', *Acta Psychiatrica Scandinavica*, 114, 303–18.

Reardon, J. (2000: August 31) 'Mental Illness No Laughing Matter', *Wrexham Mail*, p. 1.

Rebeck, T. (2008: February 24) 'Why the Media Will Hound the Girls, but Leave the Boys Alone', *The Observer*, p. 32.

Register, W. (2001) 'Everyday Peter Pans: Work, Manhood and Consumption in Urban America, 1900–1930' in R. Horowitz (ed.) *Boys and their Toys* (pp. 199–228). New York: Routledge.

Reveley, A. (1997) 'Soap Tackles Stigma of Schizophrenia', *British Medical Journal*, 314, 1560.

Revill, J. (2008: February 24) 'How Depression Makes You Stronger', *The Observer*, p. 19.

Rieff, P. (1987) *The Triumph of the Therapeutic: Uses of Faith after Freud*. 2nd edn. Chicago: University of Chicago Press.

Ripa, Y. (1990) *Women and Madness: The Incarceration of Women in Nineteenth-Century France*. C. du Peloux Menage (trans.). London: Polity Press.

Roberts, Y. (2007: September 16) 'The Monster in the Mirror', *The Sunday Times Magazine*, pp. 24–33.

Robinson, A. and S. Tormey (2006) 'Žižek's Marx: "Sublime Object" or a "Plague of Fantasies"?', *Historical Materialism*, 14(3), 145–74.

Robinson, J. (2005: August 20) 'Personal Demons', *The Guardian: The Guide*, pp. 8–10.

Robinson, J. (2008: November 9) 'Newspapers Pushed Overboard in a Perfect Storm', *The Observer (Business)*, p. 8.

Rogers, A. and D. Pilgrim (2001) *Mental Health Policy in Britain*. Basingstoke: Palgrave.

Rogers, A. and D. Pilgrim (2003) *Mental Health and Inequality*. Basingstoke: Palgrave.

Rojek, C. (2001) *Celebrity*. London: Reaktion Books.

Rose, D. (1998) 'Television, Madness and Community Care', *Journal of Community and Applied Social Psychology*, 8(3), 213–28.

Rose, N. (2007) *The Politics of Life Itself: Biomedicine, Power and Subjectivity in the Twenty-first Century*. Princeton, NJ: Princeton University Press.

Rosen, A. and G. Walter (2000) 'Way Out of Tune: Lessons from *Shine* and Its Exposé', *Australian and New Zealand Journal of Psychiatry*, 34, 237–44.

Rowe, K. (1995a) 'Melodrama and Men in Post-Classical Romantic Comedy' in P. Kirkham and J. Thumim (eds.) *Me Jane: Masculinity, Movies and Women* (pp. 184–93). New York: St. Martin's.

Rowe, K. (1995b) *The Unruly Woman: Gender and the Genres of Laughter*. Austin: University of Texas Press.

'Roy Boulting Defends Mental Illness Film' (1968: December 4), *The Times*, p. 4.

Sagar A. and D. Socolar (2001) *Drug Industry Marketing Staff Soars while Research Staffing Stagnates*. Report. Boston, MA: Boston University School of Public Health, December 2001.

Salamon, K. L. G. (2000) 'No Borders in Business: The Managerial Discourse of Organisational Holism' in T. Bewes and J. Gilbert (eds.) *Cultural Capitalism: Politics after New Labour* (pp. 134–57). London: Lawrence and Wishart.

Sass, L. A. (1992) *Madness and Modernism: Insanity in the Light of Modern Art, Literature and Thought*. New York: Basic Books.

Sayid, R. and R. Smith (2002: November 20) 'No Pain, No Gain: The Geniuses Tormented by Ill Health', *The Mirror*, p. 6.

Schulze, B. and M. C. Angermeyer (2003) 'Subjective Experience of Stigma. A Focus Group Study of Schizophrenic Patients, Their Relatives and Mental Health Professionals', *Social Science and Medicine*, 56, 299–312.

Schumaker, J. F. (2001) *The Age of Insanity: Modernity and Mental Health.* Westport, CT: Praeger.

Scull, A. (1993) *The Most Solitary of Afflictions.* New Haven, Conn.; London: Yale University Press.

Scull, A. (2007) *Madhouse: A Tragic Tale of Megalomania and Modern Medicine.* New Haven, CT: Yale University Press.

Seale, C. (2002) *Media and Health.* London: Sage Publications.

Sedgwick, P. (1982) *Psycho Politics.* New York: Harper and Row.

Segal, L. (1990) *Slow Motion: Changing Masculinities, Changing Men.* London: Vintage.

Seiter, E., H. Borchers, G. Kreutzner and E. Warth (1989) *Remote Control: Television, Audiences and Cultural Power.* London: Routledge.

Sekula, A. (1984) 'Paparazzo Notes' in *Photography Against the Grain: Essay and Photo Works, 1973–1983* (pp. 23–31). Halifax: The Press of the Nova Scotia College of Art and Design.

Shain, R. and J. Phillips (1991) 'The Stigma of Mental Illness: Labeling and Stereotyping in the News' in L. Wilkins and P. Patterson (eds.) *Risky Business: Communicating Issues of Science, Risk, and Public Policy* (pp. 61–74). New York: Greenwood Press.

Shattuc, J. (1997) *The Talking Cure.* New York: Routledge.

Shaw, J. et al. (2006) 'Rates of Mental Disorder in People Convicted of Homicide', *The British Journal of Psychiatry*, 188, 143–7.

Shohat, E. and R. Stam (1994) *Unthinking Eurocentrism.* London: Routledge.

Showalter, E. (1987a) *The Female Malady: Women, Madness and English Culture, 1830–1980.* London: Virago.

Showalter, E. (1987b) 'Representing Ophelia: Women, Madness and the Responsibilities of Feminist Criticism' in P. Parker and G. Hartman (eds.) *Shakespeare and the Question of Theory* (pp. 77–94). London and New York: Methuen.

Showalter, E. (1997) *Hysteries: Hysterical Epidemics and Modern Culture.* New York: Columbia University Press.

Shuttleworth, S. (1993) '"Preaching to the Nerves": Psychological Disorder in Sensation Fiction' in M. Benjamin (ed.) *A Question of Identity: Women, Science and Literature* (pp. 192–222). New Brunswick, NJ: Rutgers University Press.

Sieff, E. M. (2003) 'Media Frames of Mental Illness: The Potential Impact of Negative Frames', *Journal of Mental Health*, 12(3), 259–69.

Signorielli, N. (1990) 'Television's Mean and Dangerous World: A Continuation of the Cultural Indicators Perspective' in N. Signorielli and M. Morgan (eds.) *Cultivation Analysis: New Directions in Media Effects Research* (pp. 85–106). Newbury Park, CA: Sage.

Signorielli, N. (1993) *Mass Media Images and Impact on Health.* Westport, CT: Greenwood Press.

Silverstein, K. (1999) 'Prozac.org', *Mother Jones* online, http://www.mother-jones.com (home page), accessed 17 October 2006.

Simmel, G. (1950) 'The Metropolis and Mental Life' in K. H. Wolff (ed. and trans.). *The Sociology of Georg Simmel* (pp. 409–24). New York: The Free Press.

Skeggs, B. (2004) *Class, Self, Culture.* London: Routledge.

Smail, D. (2005) *Power, Interest and Psychology.* Llangarron: PCCS Books.

Smith, C. J. (1999) 'Finding a Warm Place for Someone We Know', *Journal of Popular Film and Television*, 27(1), 40–6.

Smith, D. (2007: September 30) 'Therapy Experts Rap Kyle Show: Counsellors' Association Says it "Takes People Apart"', *The Observer*, p. 26.

Sommers, C. H. and S. Satel (2005) *One Nation Under Therapy: How the Helping Culture is Eroding Self-Reliance*. New York, NY: St Martin's Press.

Sontag, S. (1966) *Against Interpretation and Other Essays*. New York: Farrar, Strauss and Giroux.

Sontag, S. (1991) *Illness as Metaphor and AIDS and Its Metaphors*. London: Penguin.

Spender, D. (1998) *Man Made Language*, 2nd edn. London: Pandora.

Spitzack, C. (1993) 'The Spectacle of Anorexia Nervosa', *Text and Performance Quarterly*, 13, 1–20.

Stallybrass, P. and A. White (1986) *The Politics and Poetics of Transgression*. London: Methuen.

Starling, S. (2004) 'Depression: The Modern Condition?', *Healthy*, 31, pp. 117–8.

Stibbe, A. (2004) 'Health and the Social Construction of Masculinity in *Men's Health* Magazine', *Men and Masculinities*, 7(1), 31–51.

Strauss, B. (1998: March 22) 'Best Picture No Sure Thing; Don't Even Try to Predict How the Academy Vote will Go', *Los Angeles Daily News* online, http://www.thefreelibrary.com (home page), accessed 2 August 2007.

Summerscale, K. (2008) *The Suspicions of Mr Whicher, or The Murder at Road Hill House*. London: Bloomsbury.

Sumner, C. (1979) *Reading Ideologies: An investigation into the Marxist Theory of Ideology and Law*. London: Academic Press.

Suzik, J. R. (2001) 'Building Better Men: The CCC boy and the Changing Social Ideal of Manliness' in R. Horowitz (ed.) *Boys and their Toys* (pp. 111–38). New York: Routledge.

Swaab, P. (2007) *The Line of Beauty* [review], *Film Quarterly*, 60(3), 10–15.

Swanson, J. W., C. E. Holzer and V. K. Ganju (1990) 'Violence and Psychiatric Disorder in the Community: Evidence from the Epidemiologic Catchment Area Surveys', *Hospital and Community Psychiatry*, 41, 761–70.

Szasz, T. (1970) *Ideology and Insanity*. New York: Pelican.

Tallis, F. (2005) *Love Sick*. London: Arrow.

Taylor, C. (2001) *A Beautiful Mind* [review]. *Salon* online, http://archive.salon.com (home page), accessed 21 August 2007.

Teplin, L. (1985) 'The Criminality of the Mentally Ill: A Dangerous Misconception', *The American Journal of Psychiatry*, 142(5), 593–9.

'The Alahan Effect' (2004) http://www.itv.com (home page), accessed 30 October 2004.

'The Hardest Gays in the Village' (2005: March 1), *Loaded*, pp. 70–1.

'The UK's most Popular Anti-Depressants' (2008: January 1), *Glamour*, pp. 115–20.

Theodossiou, I. (1998) 'The Effects of Low Pay on Psychological Well-being: A Logistic Regression Approach', *Journal of Health Economics*, 17(1), 85–104.

there there (2004) Online editorial, http://www.theretheremedia.com (home page), accessed 13 December 2006.

Thompson, J. B. (1990) *Ideology in Modern Culture*. Oxford: Polity Press.

Thomson, P. (2005) '*Keane* Takes an Unflinching Look at Mental Illness', *American Cinematographer*, November, 94–6.

Thornton, K. (2000: June 1) 'Diary of an anorexic', *Marie Claire*, pp. 129–130.

Timimi, S. (2003) 'The Politics of Attention Deficit Disorder', *Healthmatters*, 52, 14–15.

Tomes, N. (1994) 'Feminist History of Psychiatry' in M. S. Micale and R. Porter (eds.) *Discovering the History of Psychiatry* (pp. 348–83). New York and Oxford: New York University Press.

Torrey, E. F. (1994) 'Violent Behaviour by Individuals with Serious Mental Illness', *Hospital and Community Psychiatry*, 45(7), 653–62.

Trend, D. (2007) *The Myth of Media Violence: A Critical Introduction*. Oxford: Blackwell.

Turner, G. (1986) *National Fictions: Literature, Film, and the Construction of Australian Narrative*. Sydney: Allen and Unwin.

Turner, G. (1993) *National Fictions: Literature, Film and the Construction of Australian Narrative*, 2nd edn. St Leonards, Australia: Allen and Unwin.

Turner, G. (2004) *Understanding Celebrity*. London: Sage Publications.

Turner, P. A. (1994) *Ceramic Uncles and Celluloid Mammies: Black Images and their Influence on Culture*. New York: Anchor Books.

Ussher, J. M. (1991) *Women's Madness: Misogyny or Mental Illness?* Hemel Hempstead: Harvester Wheatsheaf.

Valenstein, E. (1998) *Blaming the Brain: The Truth about Drugs and Mental Health*. New York: The Free Press.

Valverde, M. (1998) *Diseases of the Will: Alcohol and the Dilemmas of Freedom*. Cambridge: Cambridge University Press.

Wagg, S. (2000) '"With his Money, *I* Could Afford to be Depressed": Markets, Masculinity and Mental Distress in the English Football Press', *Football Studies*, 3(2), 67–87.

Wahl, O. (1995) *Media Madness*. New York: Rutgers University Press.

Wahl, O. (2003) 'Depictions of Mental Illness in Children's Media', *Journal of Mental Health*, 12(3), 249–58.

Wahl, O., A. Wood, P. Zaveri, A. Drapalski and B. Mann (2003) 'Mental Illness Depiction in Children's Film', *Journal of Community Psychology*, 31(6), 553–60.

Walsh, D. (2000) 'A Worried Face is Not Enough', World Socialist Website review of *Girl, Interrupted*, http://www.wsws.org (home page), accessed 30 June 2007.

Walsh, D. (2003) 'Sylvia Plath is Hardly Present', World Socialist Website review of *Sylvia*, http://www.wsws.org (home page), accessed 30 June 2007.

Walsh, E. and T. Fahy (2002) 'Mental Illness in Society: Contribution of Mental Illness is Low', *British Medical Journal*, 325, 507–8.

Warhol, R. (2003) *Having a Good Cry: Effeminate Feelings and Pop-Culture Forms*. Columbus: Ohio University Press.

Warmé, G. (2006) *Daggers of the Mind: Psychiatry and the Myth of Mental Disease*. Toronto: House of Anansi Press.

Warren, E. and A. Warren Tyagi (2003) *The Two-Income Trap: Why Middle-Class Mothers and Fathers Are Going Broke*. New York: Basic Books.

Welch, M. and T. Racine (1999) 'A Psycho for Every Generation', *Nursing Inquiry* 6, 216–9.

Werner, S., D. Malaspina and J. Rabinowitz (2007) 'Socioeconomic Status at Birth is Associated With Risk of Schizophrenia: Population-Based Multilevel Study', *Schizophrenia Bulletin*, 33(6), 1373–8.

Wessely, S. (1998) *Britain on the Couch: Treating a Low Serotonin Society* [review], *British Medical Journal*, 316, 83.

Whiteley, S. (2006) 'Celebrity: The killing Fields of Popular Music' in S. Holmes and S. Redmond (eds.) *Framing Celebrity: New Directions in Celebrity Culture* (pp. 329–42). London: Routledge.

Williams, R. (1990) *Television: Technology and Cultural Form*. London: Routledge.

Williams, R. (2007: October 29) 'Sheer Genius: From the Web to Homer Simpson', *The Guardian*, p. 13.

Williams, Z. (2009: January 1) 'Are We *Over* Celebrity Yet?', *Marie Claire*, pp. 27–30.

Williamson, J. (1986) *Consuming Passions: The Dynamics of Popular Culture*. London and New York: Marion Boyars.

Wilson, C. (1999) 'Constructing Mental Illness as Dangerous: A Pilot Study', *Australian and New Zealand Journal of Psychiatry*, 33, 240–7.

Wilson, C., R. Nairn, J. Coverdale and A. Panapa (2000) 'How Mental Illness is Portrayed in Children's Television', *The British Journal of Psychiatry*, 176, 440–3.

Wilson, S. (2005) 'Real People with Real Problems? Public Service Broadcasting, Commercialism and *Trisha*' in C. Johnson and R. Turnock (eds.) *ITV Cultures: Independent Television Over Fifty Years* (pp. 159–76). Maidenhead: Open University Press.

Wimsatt, W. K. and M. C. Beardsley (1954) 'The Intentional Fallacy' in W. K. Wimsatt (ed.), *The Verbal Icon* (pp. 3–18). Lexington, KY: University of Kentucky.

Winship, J. (1987) *Inside Women's Magazines*. London: Pandora.

Wolf, N. (1991) *The Beauty Myth*. London: Vintage.

Wollaston, S. (2006: September 20) Last Night's TV. *The Guardian*, p. 32.

World Health Organisation (2007) Depression. http://www.who.int/en/ (home page), accessed 7 December 2007.

Zimmerman, J. N. (2003) *People Like Ourselves: Portrayals of Mental Illness in the Movies*. Lanham, MD: Scarecrow Press.

Zimmerman, L. (2007) 'Against Depression: Final Knowledge in Styron, Mairs and Solomon', *Biography*, 30(4), 465–90.

Žižek, S. (1989) *The Sublime Object of Ideology*. London: Verso.

Žižek, S. (1997) 'The Big Other Doesn't Exist', *Journal of European Psychoanalysis*, http://www.lacan.com/zizekother.htm, accessed 3 December 2008.

Žižek, S. (1999) *The Ticklish Subject: The Absent Centre of Political Ontology*. London: Verso.

Žižek, S. (2008a) *In Defence of Lost Causes*. London: Verso.

Žižek, S. (2008b) *Violence*. London: Profile.

Index

PMDD, *see* Post-Menstrual Dysphoric
Disorder (PMDD)
Podheretz, N., 8
Poe, E. A., 76
Polanski, R., 65
Poliakoff, S., 112
political correctness, 22–4
Politkovskaya, A., 8
Pollock, 75, 76
Pollock, G., 54, 77
Pollock, J., 75
Poppy Shakespeare, 110, 113
Porter, G., 173
Porter, R., 5, 59
Post-Menstrual Dysphoric Disorder
(PMDD), 15
post-traumatic stress disorder
(PTSD), 88
Potenza, M. N., 184
Potter, D., 69, 147
Poussaint, A. F., 192
poverty, 12–13
Premonition, 86, 87
Preston, P., 152–3
Priest, P., 136–7
The Prince of Tides, 100
Prins, H., 10
print media, 27, 151–85
dominant ideology, 151
increased celebrity discourse in, 151
men's magazines, 175–82,
183–4, 196
arts journalism, 180–1
differences from women's, 176–7
gender differences, 181–2
instrumentalisation of mental
distress treatment, 178–9
lack of serious mental health
exploration, 177–8
lad culture, 177–8
masculine identity, 180
mental distress as token of
weakness, 179–80
music journalism, 180–1
rise of, 175–6
use of irony, 176–7, 179
newspapers, 152–62, 182
class differences, 156–7, 160–1
gender differences, 157

language used in, 153–7
medicalisation of madness,
161–2
political use of mental distress
stories, 158–9
reporting style, 154
stigmatisation as media
responsibility, 152–3
violence linked with madness,
153–4
women's magazines, 162–75, 182–3,
184–5
celebrities, 168–74
consumerism and mental health,
165–6
contradictory messages, 175
eating disorders, 166–8
gender differences, 172–3
individualisation, 162, 165
mental health policy, 174–5
race, 164
sensitive treatment of mental
health issues, 163–4
uncommitted reading, 162–3
progressive cinema, 54
In the Psychiatrist's Chair, 141
psychiatry, 5, 7, 11
concern with normality, 17
diagnostic labels, 24–5
in film, 99–101
industrial, 18
transcultural, 15
Psycho, 100
psychoanalysis, 18, 162
psycho-babble, 138
Psychologies, 165, 174–5
psychopathy, 85–6
psycho-pharmaceuticals, as coping
strategies, 13
psychosis, 85–6
PTSD, *see* post-traumatic stress
disorder (PTSD)
Punch-Drunk Love, 145
Puppy, 80
Putin, V., 8

Quills, 74, 100
Quinn, B., 160